THE
PSYCHOLOGICAL
EXAMINATION
A Guide for Clinicians

by
PAUL W. PRUYSER
The Menninger Foundation
Topeka, Kansas

INTERNATIONAL UNIVERSITIES PRESS, INC.

New York

Library of Congress Cataloging in Publication Data

Pruyser, Paul W
  The psychological examination.

  Bibliography: p.
  Includes index.
  1. Mental Illness—Diagnosis. 2. Personality
assessment. I. Title. [DNLM: 1. Mental-disorders
—Diagnosis. WM141 P971]
RC469.P75 616.8'9'075   78-70234
ISBN 0-8236-5605-5

To
Karl A. Menninger, M.D.
Teacher, Colleague, and Friend

Contents

Preface

This book is addressed to psychiatrists, neurologists, and clinical psychologists, particularly the candidates for these professions. It is conceived as a primer to familiarize the beginning clinician with basic psychological concepts, ordered in a cohesive framework tight enough to be comprehensible as a whole and eclectic enough to leave room for all kinds of clinical observations. It aims at clarity and orderliness of presentation, for it is conceived as a didactic work.

Clinical work is fascinating in part because of the endless variation of symptoms, behaviors, personalities, traits, motives, and values that the patients present and that emerge in the clinician himself when he is engaged in his professional work. These challenge his observational acumen, but their variety and details could easily overwhelm him if he had no ordering principles to systematize his observations and differentiate his inquisitiveness. The psychiatric landscape is lush and in places quite dense, if not dangerous, so that a topographical map, even a crude one, would stand the explorer in good stead.

Behind this book lies another book, Karl Menninger's *Manual for Psychiatric Case Study*,[1] which is the fruit of one psychiatrist's lifelong endeavor to bring diagnostic order to the chaotic manifold of clinical observations. It was my privilege to contribute to the second edition of the *Manual* as well as to the comprehensive psychiatric theory that undergirds it, formulated in Menninger's later work, *The Vital Balance*.[2] The latter is related to the former as a textbook is to a workbook. In the course of teaching psychiatric case study I have come to believe that another workbook or compendium is needed to deal specifically with that part of psychiatric examining that we have called the *psychological examination*. This new book is an expression of that belief as well as its *raison d'être*.

ix

Complicated as psychological examining is, it is by no means the whole or even the most significant aspect of diagnosing. Diagnosing requires much more: (1) taking the patient's history from a definite point of view, such as medical, psychiatric, neurological, biological, adaptational, social, etc.; (2) ordering other special examinations, laboratory tests, and observational studies, all of which are cross-sectional and thus specifically related to the dates of the diagnostic process rather than to the continuity of the patient's history; (3) knowledge of nosology and pathology in regard to any of the points of view taken. This book is therefore an insufficient guide to diagnosing, and should not be mistaken for a diagnostic manual, a textbook of psychopathology, or a classification system. It is intended to be only a vade mecum for professionals grounded in the medical, psychological, and other helping professions who have occasion to conduct close and systematic psychological examinations of their patients or clients.

The book stems from my years of teaching in the Menninger School of Psychiatry and my ongoing diagnostic work with a great variety of patients. The text has been read and criticized by the following colleagues, whom I now thank publicly for their work: Herbert C. Modlin, M.D., Senior Staff Psychiatrist, Professor of Forensic Psychiatry, and Director of the Foundation's Division of Forensic Psychiatry; Sydney Smith, Ph.D., Chief Clinical Psychologist and Director of the Foundation's Postdoctoral Training Program in Clinical Psychology; Samuel Bradshaw, M.D., faculty member of the Menninger School of Psychiatry, and Chief of Psychiatric Services, Topeka Veterans Administration Hospital; and John Fitzpatrick, Ph.D., Instructor in Psychohistory in the Menninger School of Psychiatry, and Fellow in the Foundation's Interdisciplinary Studies Program.

I also warmly thank Mrs. Kathleen Bryan, my secretary, for her enthusiastic work on the manuscript through several revisions.

Finally, the dedication page pays tribute to an esteemed mentor of modern American psychiatry who has influenced thousands of practicing clinicians and continues to inspire me.

Acknowledgments

To the following persons and publishers I wish to express my appreciation for permission to use copyrighted material:

Professor Charles E. Osgood and Oxford University Press for the use of figure 78a, page 314, from Charles E. Osgood: *Methods and Theory in Experimental Psychology.* New York: Oxford University Press, 1953.

Professor Byron L. Barrington and the *Journal of Clinical Psychology* for reprinting in full: Byron L. Barrington: A List of Words Descriptive of Affective Reactions. *Journal of Clinical Psychology,* 19 (2): 259-262, 1963.

Selections from Emily Dickinson's poems were taken from Thomas A. Johnson, editor, *The Complete Poems of Emily Dickinson,* Boston: Little, Brown and Company. Numbers 280, 536, 599 are reprinted by permission of the publishers and the Trustees of Amherst College from *The Poems of Emily Dickinson,* edited by Thomas H. Johnson, Cambridge, Massachusetts: The Belknap Press of Harvard University Press, Copyright (c) 1951, 1955 by the President and Fellows of Harvard College. Numbers 252, 341, 599 are reprinted by permission from Little, Brown and Company, from Thomas H. Johnson, editor, *The Complete Poems of Emily Dickinson,* Copyright 1929 by Martha Dickinson Bianchi, Copyright 1957 by Mary L. Hampson.

Chapter 1

A Perspectival View of Psychological Examining

No human endeavor is without philosophical bias. To the novelist, the most interesting view of reality is its unfolding as a plot. The artist approaches reality through the play of appearances and the intimations of concealed ideas that appearances make. The biologist finds in life the stimulus for his view of reality; the physicist dwells on forces and waves and particles. Sociologists are impressed by the reality of groups of people within which individuals have a somewhat ephemeral, transitional status. Psychologists, on the other hand, are impressed by the reality of distinct individuals who are embedded in processes of life, engage in plots, behave in social aggregates, and are enmeshed in physical forces and particles.

These philosophical biases and the disciplines that contain them are often thought of as having reached an accord by dividing the total reality, which nobody knows, into neat segments or compartments or territories, each presumed to "belong" to a particular discipline, profession, or other stylized human proclivity. In this way, one's area can be fenced in, the territory can be defended, and peace may be had. Innumerable attempts have been made to elaborate the territorial divisions by vivid models: the pyramidal model, which puts one "queen discipline" at the top and orders the subordinate disciplines hierarchically; the "layer cake" model, which puts

1

spiritual frostings on successive layers of mental, somatic, and materialistic cake discs; the diamond model, which holds each discipline to be a polished facet; the onion model, which regards most disciplines as peripheral peels enveloping some alleged core that is the "essence" or "really real"; not to mention the endless verbal variations on the theme of height and depth in which the most prestigious discipline is either the highest or the deepest.

Another attempt to bring peace has been made by assigning to each discipline a special substance, rather than a territory, with which it is preoccupied. Physicists deal with atoms, doctors with living (or dead) bodies, priests with souls, psychologists with psyches, sociologists with human masses, anthropologists with societies, potsherds, or skeletons. All kinds of discrete entities have been selected, or invented, to give each discipline its own substance or "things" on which it could legitimately concentrate without getting into trouble with other disciplines. These are proprietary rather than territorial strategies for interdisciplinary peace.

Reality, however, does not let itself be spatially divided or chopped up into bits. Moreover, some of the proposed substances, such as souls and psyches, prove to be quite insubstantial, even spurious and fictitious. Where does "soma" stop and "psyche" begin, where does "individual" give way to "group" and vice versa? What practicing physician can ignore the "mind," what psychiatrist can ignore the "nervous system," what psychoanalyst can ignore the "family"? What idealistic philosopher would intentionally try to walk through a tree to prove the ultimate ideality of all that is?

In this book, *psychology* is not taken as a spatial field or cake layer or facet or ownership of some substance. It is taken as a special perspective, next to other perspectives each of which attempts to make some sense of reality by highlighting it in a certain way, by throwing its particular searchlight on it, by approaching it with a distinct set of concepts and words, by applying a special craft or method of assessment to it, or by influencing it in some systematic and determined way. Behind this view of psychology and the other disciplines lies also a philosophy, no matter how embryonic. I believe that reality is one and indivisible, and that it is more like a process than a crystallized structure. I believe that human experience of reality, though often fragmentary and partial, has a built-in unitary thrust. I also believe that reality allows itself to be approached in many different perspectives, each of which, be it science, art, or craft, evolves proximately from the human mind and its diversification through culture, and ultimately from reality-as-a-whole itself, which includes the phenomenon of man.

In substituting a perspectival view for the more habitual spatial and substantive notions, we also become aware of the strong pull that space and substance categories continue to exert on our minds. Spatial thought is an entrenched habit that leads to territorial claims and border skirmishes between the disciplines. Interdisciplinary thinking, though today avowed as a noble goal, is always obstructed by the territorial imperative of spatial thought and the proprietary claim on special substances that each discipline tends to perpetuate. The perspectival view requires emancipation from these habits, especially in psychiatry, because that discipline is at once very specialized and very holistic. Seen from within the historical mainstream of medicine, psychiatry is a specialty that deals with "mind disorders," as cardiology deals with heart disorders and ophthalmology with eye disorders. But a little reflection shows that "mind" is not comparable in scope to heart and eye: It is not a part of the body like these organs—indeed, not a part of any conceivable whole. Psychiatrists themselves tend to look beyond some encapsulated "mind" to the human being as a whole, even to families and larger human groupings as a whole, in the belief that these entities are animated by motives, moved by emotions, articulated by perception and thought, guided by values and ideals, beset by conflicts, and in some way integrated by overarching gubernatorial processes that promote a fleeting dynamic equilibrium. Identified as psychiatry is with such holistic views, one could say that it is the only medical specialty that purports to deal not with any part but with the whole of the human being, aiding it to advantageous "wholesome" equilibria.

Let me draw a sketch (Figure 1) of the perspectival view in order to point to a few other pitfalls of thought and to clarify some practical issues. OR is observable reality: It is full of items, events, appearances, organisms, things, bodies, matter,

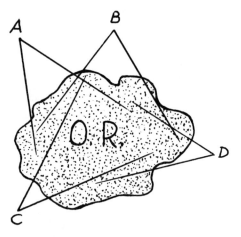

FIGURE 1. O. R. = Observable Reality. A, B, C, D = Various points of view or perspectives.

ideas, colors, tones, currents—in a word, "stuff." It presents itself to the child, as William James once said, as "one big blooming buzzing confusion."[3] It would be a chaotic manifold were it not for our capacity to approach it selectively and discerningly, following the mandates of our own mind, by zeroing in on it from a certain point of view, by placing it in perspective, by putting it in a light of our own choosing, by selecting our own focus. Each discipline is a special point of view, perspective, light beam, or focus, more or less systematized, guided by special rules, stylized by tradition, made more or less perfect by years of practice, made cohesive by a particular language game, body of knowledge, and social institutionalization.

These different perspectives do not divide reality into discrete bits. What we call a *datum*, which may be an event, a person, a thing, etc., can be shared by many different perspectives, each of which will "look at it" in its own way, play with it in its own language game, attach cause and effect linkages to it, and appreciate it as more or less relevant at the present time. Hence the various perspectives (disciplines) crisscross each other and often focus on the same "data." In fact, the word *data* is a tricky term, which we sloppily take to mean "being there, naturally," as if it were self-constituent. But *data* exist only for observers—one could say that they are created by a particular point of view that lifts them out of chaos.

For instance, what kind of datum is a mute five-year-old child? In the perspective of neurology this datum may be conceived as a case of aphasia. In psychiatric perspective, it may be a case of autism. The sociologist may appreciate it as an extreme case of cultural deprivation or parental neglect. Geneticists may approach it as a chromosomal mishap. The child's parents may see their mute boy as an unspeakable tragedy, maybe as punishment for ancestral wrongdoing. The theologian may take him as an example of human depravity, a result of the Fall of Man. Throughout these diverse perspectives, the boy is one. He is shared by many disciplines as a relevant datum, and it is entirely conceivable that the boy himself has an inkling of the relevance of these diverse perspectives *to him*.

When we deal with interventions, as we do in all the helping professions, the overlap of perspectives and the sharing of data may lead to referral and multidisciplinary cooperation. Let us imagine a man with a sore tooth. In our culture, he is sooner or later most likely to go to a dentist. He and his ailment are placed in the dental perspective, i.e., understood in terms of dental cause-and-effect relations and dealt with by dental skills. Despite certain dental interventions, the pain persists. The man becomes irritated: He starts nagging his wife, he becomes sour toward his children, and a spell of gruffness is cast over the family. His marriage deteriorates. Whether or not he and his wife seek marriage counseling, in the perspective of the psychology of family relations the sore tooth may now be approached as a precipitant or symbol of hidden family frictions, of jealousy between the spouses, or of inadequate role behavior. If the pain remains intractable, the dentist and other interested persons may refer the man to a neurologist, who may consider him and his ailment as an example of sensory nerve network pathology. When the pain causes absence from work, the case becomes an economic datum and his employers too may have to intervene in certain ways. As the man's predicament lingers on, he may begin to feel bitter and start swearing and abusing his friends—theologians may see all this as an instance of the problem of pain and suffering, and pastors may make home visits. Any one of the previously mentioned specialists may have made a psychiatric referral, or the patient himself may have voluntarily sought psychiatric help. Somewhere in the course of all these processes, the dentist may be needed again. All kinds of referral sequences are imaginable. There is no fixed series. There is no hierarchy. The list is determined by relevance, the accessibility of various helpers, the patient's own hunches, the advice of friends, the recommendations of the professionals already seen, financial resources, and a host of other considerations. Moreover, what appears in this narration as a hopping from one discipline to another need not require a long period of time. Nor is it necessary that one discipline leave off where the other begins. The various perspectives may be sought all at once—they may even be coordinated and synthesized by someone, for instance, a dedicated family doctor, with a broad vision and deep concern for this pain-haunted person.

Proceeding from such a perspectival perception of reality and the disciplines, any psychological examiner is potentially interested in anything about any person who comes to his attention. There is no theoretical limit to what he can assess. Distinctions between the patient's body, nervous system, mind, motives, friendships, possessions, and social position are not to be taken as proprietary boundaries marked with "no trespassing" signs. Anything of and about the patient can be seen as his internal and external environment, with much of both as his proprium, i.e., more or less intimately related to his self and valued by him as personal in some sense. While different professionals have technical grounds for distinguishing between psychological and neurological symptoms, between personal and family dynamics, between legal and moral responsibilities, and between the Oedipus complex and kinship structure, all these technical distinctions are experientially joined in the patient.

In recognition of this joining in the patient's experience of various perspectives, each with its particular frame of language and concepts, clinical psychology and psychiatry have become expressly holistic disciplines, deliberately attuned to the whole person, giving him the center of the stage in their evaluations. Maintaining this holistic view, despite technical attention to minute and sometimes very technical—i.e., discipline-based—details, is a clinical art that appears to be more highly developed and prized in some branches of medicine than in others, and more pronounced in clinical psychology than in, say, experimental sensory psychology. Short of such purposive holism, some clinicians and scientists specialize in an articulate coordination of two or more viewpoints, in recognition of the importance of observed interaction. This leads to quasi-holistic concerns expressed in compound designations such as neuropsychiatry, psychosomatic medicine, psychobiology, psychopharmacology, or psychosocial development.

What limits, if any, are set on the pursuits of a psychological examiner? If everything is potentially relevant and if there are no territorial boundaries, what does the psychological examiner take in and what does he leave out? What are his data? What are his crucial data? The pragmatic answer to these questions differs from the theoretical answer. The examiner is constrained by considerations of relevance, competence, skill, knowledge, time, money, and above all by the range of interventions at his disposal and their feasibility and side effects. Evaluations are made for a purpose: to bring about change in an untoward situation about which somebody has complained. And by the nature of the complaint, the change is to be in a

certain direction: toward betterment. All helping is me-
liorative—for somebody; in the first place for the patient,
but often for others as well: his family, his employers or em-
ployees, his community, with its mores, fears, and suspicions,
and in the largest sense his society, with its principles of order
and its standards of health, decency, and productivity.

All interventions affect an established equilibrium, or
rather a more or less integrated set of equilibria. Personal
equilibrium is embedded in family homeostasis, the family's
equilibrium is attuned to the equilibration patterns of
neighborhood, social and economic class, ethnic group, and
the state of the nation. All these units are adaptive to each
other, so that one can speak of an equilibrium of equilibria in
an endless series up and down the scale of larger and smaller
wholes. For better or for worse, but as an expression of commonly held values, the clinical focus tends to be on the individual person as the working unit. Thus clinical interventions
affect first and foremost personal processes, but the holistic
clinician is also aware, peripherally at least, and sometimes
focally, of the larger equilibrium patterns in which the person
is embedded. This awareness may codetermine the nature and
scope of his observations and his plans for the most effective
intervention.

Usually, the psychological examiner is from the outset
guided by the initial or presenting complaint, whether the patient's own or someone else's about the patient. This first signal provides a preliminary focus—it does not set limits. In the
course of the examination the focus may shift, and may be
expanded or narrowed, depending on the examiner's knowledge of cause-and-effect relations, the accumulated knowledge
of his profession, his skills and tools, and the contract between
himself and the patient or the latter's sources of referral.

But the examiner is also guided by a conceptual frame of
reference, by a system of descriptive and conceptual knowledge that he has acquired in the course of his professional
training and that has become his professional viewpoint. It has
both scope and depth. Using it, the examiner is able to make
certain observations, to spot data that others might overlook,

to see order in apparent chaos, to discover connections between seemingly unrelated phenomena, to find coherent patterns of functioning and dysfunctioning, to classify and compare his data. The aim of the following chapters is to present such a frame of reference and articulate its contours.

Chapter 2

Main Dimensions of the Psychological Viewpoint

By the nature of their work and by conscious intention, psychiatrists use two different evaluative frameworks at once. They take a history and they make examinations, which are not necessarily different acts. They are two different systems of ordering observations, into which are fed selections from the stream of data that emerges when the psychiatrist applies his main diagnostic tools: observation and interviewing. It is true that he may at times selectively focus his attention in interviewing on the past or on the here and now, or he may hold historical considerations in abeyance for a while in order to engage in direct observation of current behavior. But usually he converses purposively with his patient in a very complex network of signals exchanged between them, eliciting both historical and examinational data.

Humorously, but with didactic acumen, Karl Menninger used to clarify this point by drawing a sausage on the blackboard (see Figure 1). What is contained in the sausage's skin, A, is the patient's history—it is not accessible to direct observation. It is to be reconstructed from the patient's conveyed memories, from various informants, and from objective data such as school reports, previous medical charts, etc. What the patient in vivo presents is B, the place where the sausage is sliced, with the contents revealed for inspection and accessi-

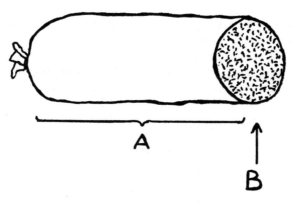

FIGURE 1

ble to examinations. One implication of this comparison is that in the final, written diagnostic report all statements about A are to be recorded in the past tense—"The patient was, had, felt, experienced, did, etc."—whereas all statements derived from B, the examinational data, are to be put in the present tense—"The patient perceives, feels, acts, wants, does, etc."—and preferably dated as to the time of observation. Any links between data from A and B, such as sameness or differences, continuities or discontinuities, stability or change, are to be constructed from comparisons between the historical and examinational data.

If a hospitalized patient acts jealously when younger patients seem to receive much attention from the aides or are allowed to gather around the nurse's office, and when that same patient says in an interview that "I used to get so frustrated at my mother's preference for my kid brother," we have a plausible case of dynamic continuity between past and present jealousy. Yet he may act differently in response to his frustration: In the past he may have thrown a tantrum, whereas today he may only mope, or hint at secret sexual liaisons between the nurses and the younger patients. In other cases the overt behavior may be the same: a flying phobia then and now, depressive states in the past and today.

Since this book deals with the process of examining, its

focus is on the sausage where it is sliced: the cross section of behavior today, which is open to direct scrutiny. In approaching this slice by observation, interviewing, testing, or experimentation, we are again reminded of the warning in Chapter 1: the slice cannot be subdivided into neat segments according to the disciplines, but the whole slice can be examined from different viewpoints (see Figures 2 and 3).

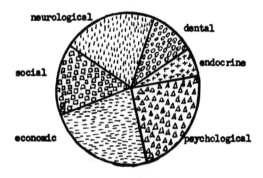

FIGURE 2. A territorial and substantive view of the disciplines.

The psychological perspective brings a system of descriptions and heuristic and explanatory concepts to bear on the examined cross section of behavior. Ideally, such a system should be applicable to a great variety of people exhibiting many different behaviors: It should therefore be comprehensive. It should also have depth, leading to differentiation of public and private processes, subjective and objective data, overt and covert acts, inner and outer worlds, motives and actions, perceptions and feelings. It should have some explanatory power and thereby pave the way for intelligent and purposive prescriptions. It should transcend both the narrowness of partisan schools of thought and the obviousness of common sense, so that it can be shared by the vast majority of psychiatric practitioners and their clinical coworkers. It should be able to gather up a great variety of pertinent clinical observations made by our forebears and scattered through reams of clinical literature, old and new.

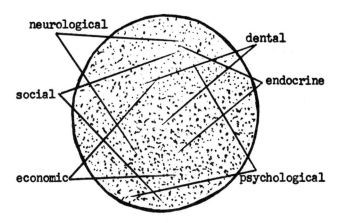

FIGURE 3. A perspectival view of the disciplines.

From the Reflex Arc to the Holistic Model

Perhaps the simplest and most entrenched system of psychological thought is based on the reflex-arc model (see Figure 4). It allows for a division of behavior into two large groupings, the essence of which is that any organism, whether low or high in the evolutionary scale, is equipped to respond motorically to incoming stimuli. This model underlies much historical work in psychiatry, neurology, learning psychology,

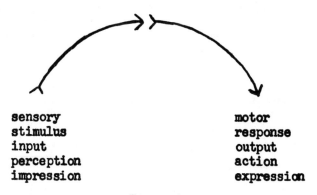

sensory	motor
stimulus	response
input	output
perception	action
impression	expression

FIGURE 4

behaviorism, and biology. It permeates the literature on aphasia, offering a useful classification of its manifestations. It is an inescapable model, patently attuned to some basic realities of the central nervous system and hence of the mind, however the latter is conceived. But it is simplistic.

Hence, in recognition of complex central processes and, particularly in human beings, of spontaneity of behavior, the simple synapse link became elaborated into a fuller and more articulated organismic model. The simple S-R scheme was rounded out to a complex $S \rightleftarrows O \rightleftarrows R$ model, in which both S and R were seen as functions of O. The organism is self-active, energized; it is a Self with structure, endowment, a history, influenced by many internal variables that codetermine what it will be responsive to in the outer world, and how this response will be modulated. In the organism's endowment one can differentiate some functions recognized equally by common sense, traditional psychology, and classical psychiatry, such as sensation and perception, feeling, judgment, willing, language and speech, and action. These we will call "part functions" (to be distinguished from "integrative functions" to be discussed later). They constitute the formal basis of Kraepelin's[4] system of clinical psychiatry, which describes syndromes as thought disorders and mood disorders. A wealth of clinical information in the neuropsychiatric literature is grouped under the headings of part processes: perceptual disorders, language disorders, memory disorders, disturbances of emotion (depression, elation), disorders of action and volition (aboulia, agraphia), and disorders of thinking (amentia and dementia, flight of ideas, loose associations).

Two new viewpoints were to enrich the S-O-R model further and make it clinically more useful: the psychoanalytic tradition and the adaptational psychiatry of Adolf Meyer,[5] each in time elaborated by many additions and refinements. Psychoanalysis made the O more articulated by drawing within it some "battle lines" derived from frequently observed internal conflict situations, by distinguishing between motivation (i.e., internal stimuli) and external stimulation, and by seeing mental processes as stratified in terms of conscious, preconscious, and unconscious qualities. The O can now be turned into the Freudian egg-shaped model (see Figure 5). Note that the stratification of consciousness is not the same for each of the four main internal structures: the proportions of conscious/preconscious/unconscious qualities vary considerably.

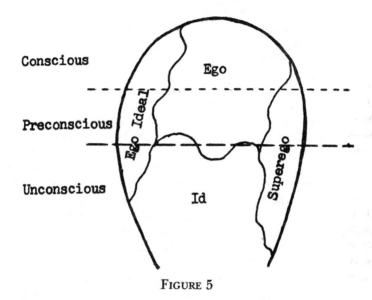

FIGURE 5

Letting motivation hinge on the clinical pre-eminence of drives, particularly sexual-erotic and aggressive-destructive impulses, psychoanalysis sees the organism as having a directional quality: It strives toward pleasure and satisfaction and it eschews pain and frustration. The egg-shaped model can be turned and provided with an arrowhead to indicate the organism's search (see Figure 6). Satisfaction is sought and secured through "objects." This word is used in a special sense, derived from Freud's "Three Essays on the Theory of Sexuality,"[6] which classifies as an "object" anything that satisfies the drives, in three major classes: (1) other people or parts and symbols of them; (2) the self or parts and symbols of it; (3) things, ideas, cultural pursuits, social institutions, and anything

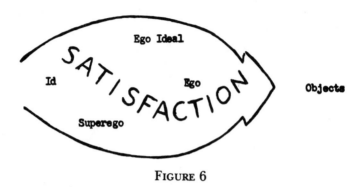

FIGURE 6

else that can be taken as a symbol of, or substitute for, human beings. In other words, the formal term "object" stands in this context for human or humanlike beings as the entities to which the person attaches himself in the search for satisfaction. In the original formulation, these objects were seen specifically as the objects of drives, as their satisfiers, but since drives and drive events, so prominent in early infancy, were thought to leave an impact on the slowly developing structures of the ego, superego, and ego ideal, these structures demand satisfaction also. Moreover, the superego and ego ideal are somewhat personlike anyway, derived as they are from processes of internalization and identification with significant persons during the early years of life.

The Adaptation Model

Meyer called attention to a few other dimensions worth systematizing. The organism is always embedded in an environment *to* whose nature and changes it *reacts with* the equipment it has received and the tendencies it has learned. Everything organismic is in some sense adaptational. Person and environment always interact, each bargaining, as it were, for advantageous positions. Instead of direct cause-and-effect relations between the two, the pattern of interaction often takes the form of precipitation and reaction: Upon the death of a loved one a person may become depressed. Is the depression caused by the death? And does someone's death always cause a depression in the bereft? Obviously not—it all depends on the equipment and the learned responses, on the meaning given to the event "death." Many external events occur without notable organismic response. Only some events precipitate a reaction, and among these is a special class that has great clinical significance: *stressful* events.

Thus many personal acts are in fact *reactions to stress.* Stress itself is an interactional phenomenon, for an event is perceived as stressful only by a distressed person who makes it so. One man's stress is another man's opportunity. Some people become depressed after receiving a promotion, and the common stresses of war oddly gratify some soldiers. These thoughts led Meyer to the development of the so-called Life Chart, on which the examiner lists, in chronological order, a life's major stressful events in one column (by somewhat loose, common-sense definitions of stress) and the patient's reactions in the next column, allowing for correlations between "events" and "response" attuned to idiosyncratic mixtures of stress and distress. In this vein, Meyer saw all psychiatric disorders as reactions and forms of adaptation, rather than as fixed diseases encapsulated in an isolated individual.

The Psychodynamic Model

We can now elaborate the previous diagram and turn it into a manageable conceptual model that can serve as a comprehensive guide for psychological examining (Figure 7). Embedded in a world where adaptation is the rule, the organism is bent on securing satisfaction by seeking out and attaching itself to objects. Its attachments are clinically significant for their emotional tones of love and hate, energized as the organism is by erotic and aggressive drives. These attachments and the satisfactions they bring not only locate the person in his environment but integrate him as an individual by enhancing his well-being, promoting his growth, protecting him against the ravages of time and destruction, and improving his chances for survival with a modicum of felt goodness and

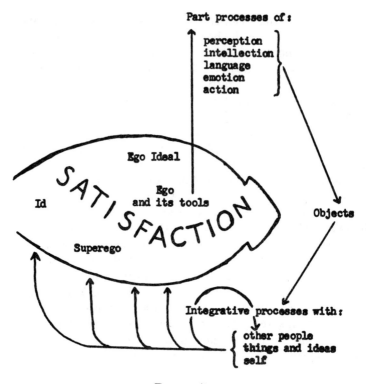

FIGURE 7

pleasure, possibly with the prospect of maximizing his poten-
tialities. Hence the term "integrative processes." These are
clearly of a holistic order, comprising a vast range of meanings, from biological necessities to humanistic values.

    To form, maintain, and nurture such attachments and to
deal with their vicissitudes, the person is equipped with special
tools or means. These are the part processes, listed in the diagram in terms of generally recognized, common human
functions about which a considerable amount of observational
and scientific knowledge has accrued. These functions are
typically not the ultimate goals of life, although each of them
can be valued and practiced as a proximate goal. Their de-

ployment is in the service of the person as a whole: They are the means of adaptation to bio-psycho-sociocultural realities. They require considerable learning and exercise to be serviceable, and, like everything learned or acquired, are vulnerable to mishaps, regressions, defects, and dysfunctions. Their good functioning is usually pleasure-laden in its own right, apart from the more ultimate pleasure of object relations that they help provide.

Therefore, the four arrows at the bottom of Figure 7 suggest a distribution of satisfactions. Each intrapsychic structure has its wants, so to speak, which must be gratified, each in its own style. The superego demands moral righteousness according to its rules and precepts; the ego ideal demands loyalty to its ideals and high aims; the ego demands gratification through competence. Obviously, then, the word "satisfaction" writ large on the diagram is no simple, primitively hedonistic term, but designates a scale of felt well-being with physical, cognitive, moral, religious, aesthetic, and many other dimensions.

Among the intrapsychic structures the ego is pre-eminent, for it is the most specialized and differentiated mental organ, requiring considerable time to develop. It is, to speak analogically, the executive, administrator, organizer, or synthesizer of the personality. It is a product of differentiation of labor and specialization of functioning, both phylogenetically and ontogenetically. Like the officers and apparatus on the bridge of a ship, the ego receives and decodes signals coming from within the person and from the outside, is capable of judicious responses as well as spontaneous action. It is doubly attuned: to the internal requirements of satisfaction and to the external requirements of reality testing and reality regard. The strategies of adaptation, the selective use of the tools of adaptation, the defenses against external and internal dangers, are devised *in* and *through* the ego. Note the careful choice of words: One cannot say that these are devised *by* the ego, for that would turn the ego into a manikin within the person, with complete control over the person's fate. The ego can never have complete autonomy, for it is only a specialized group of functions in the service of the survival and well-being of the person as a whole. Its administrative and regulative functional powers are only delegated to it by vote of the commonwealth that it is to serve. Indeed, the comparison of a person with a commonwealth or household makes great sense when we think of the many parties, internal and external, that clamor for satisfaction and whose potential conflicts must be arbitrated.

Much of the ego's specialized work can be described as *coping with stress,* particularly when a person becomes the subject of clinical attention. By definition, clinical work takes place in special life situations when a certain extremity of stress or distress has been reached. Clinical work is addressed to distress signals, to symptoms and signs, pain and agony, dissatisfaction and dysfunctioning. It is enlisted to assess disorder, in the hope that, through interventions, disorder may be replaced by order. Somehow, somewhere, something is felt to have gone wrong: Coping has gone awry. Maybe the coping tools are inadequate, maybe the tools have boomerang effects, maybe the person has not learned what tools to use for which job, maybe the job to be done must first be analyzed, maybe some very heavy tools have been overused with resulting great fatigue. These are all figures of speech, of course, but I find them appropriate to convey the sense of stress, distress, conflict, and extremity inherent in all clinical situations.

Chapter 3

Preliminary Use of Quasi-Quantitative Impressions

In ordinary life, not a day goes by without our making some snap judgment about someone else or ourselves in quantitative terms, or with an eye on the intensity of what we find noteworthy. "She is a very emotional character." "My son is quite an intellectual." "Grandma has slowed down a great deal in the last five years." "How can one manage such a hyperactive child in the classroom?" "He is one of those specialists who know more and more about less and less." "She's so hypercritical!" "My spirits are quite low today." "I wish he would concentrate on one thing instead of being scattered all over the place."

All these judgments involve a *more-or-less* dimension and amount to a quasi-quantitative evaluation. The standard of measurement may be poor and the judgment dubious, but that does not dissuade us from our evaluative mental set. Much in life appears to follow a rule or yardstick, a standard we have become accustomed to, an intensity we expect, a scale or measure, a typical degree, against which deviations stand out as exceptional, noteworthy phenomena that impress us precisely because they are deviant. As the above-cited phrases show, in our judgments we tend to focus selectively on a particular mental function, appraising it in a primitively quantitative framework.

Many clinical evaluations start with such observations and the judgments attached to them. Much medical work begins with registering impressions of *hyper* or *hypo* functioning of this or that organ or system, to be subsequently verified, if possible, by precise laboratory measurement. If precise measurement is not possible, we may seek consensual validation of our immediate impressions, because we believe that such impressions can be important clues for further observations and inferential knowledge.

Though there are limits to such a quasi-quantitative approach in psychiatry, it does provide clues and is used almost instinctively by most observers anyway, so that one might as well capitalize on it. Let us try it out on the part processes.

Perception. What observations convey the impression that a person perceives too much, is too intent on taking in perceptual stimuli, or is perceptually scanning his environment too intensely? There is, first of all, the hyperalert patient whose eyes and ears are on the watch, scrutinizing everything carefully for signs of danger. He cannot relax, for he cannot trust his environment. He must be vigilant, lest he be attacked or overpowered. He is anxiously scanning the examiner too, noting his movements, expression, tone of voice, wondering about his motives and intentions toward himself. There is the hyperactive child who is bound to respond instantaneously to every new or moving stimulus: Distracted by every sound and sight, he jumps from his chair to rush to the window when a bird flies by, or crouches under the table when he hears the examiner's shoes creak. There is the excited patient who promptly seizes on every person or thing, every word or phrase heard, every draft of air felt, in order to respond to it with a movement or thought or speech, sometimes getting to the point where he even asks to go to the isolation room for a simpler and quieter environment. There is the combat soldier overwhelmed by external and internal stimuli, traumatized by their intensity or suddenness. Unable to master them, he may have to relive the perceptual onslaught in his dreams, or in a supervised abreaction.

Clinical interviewers sometimes find their task made difficult by the confusional states that certain patients present. For instance, a patient may be so lacking in adequate stimulus barriers that he cannot avoid being captured by the hum of an air conditioner in the examining room, which to him is a specific stimulus overload that distracts him from attending to verbal interaction with the interviewer.

Too little perception is exemplified in accidental or experimental isolation, in which the amount or variety of stimulation is drastically reduced. Prolonged isolation can elicit hallucinations (the fata morgana of travelers lost in the desert) and provoke excessive imagery, which suggests the presence of self-righting mechanisms that compensate for perceptual deprivation. Apparently, perceptual input of optimal quantity and variety (exemplifying the reality principle) balances the spontaneous fantasy activity of the unconscious (operating under the pleasure principle). In inferior psychiatric hospitals the monotony of surroundings and schedules leads to the "rocking chair" syndrome, in which patients indulge in hallucinatory states or daydream uninterruptedly while rocking to and fro in their chairs. The absorbed patient turns his attention inward on his thoughts or fantasies, ignoring the sights and sounds and touch of the outer world. He perceives too little with his sensory organs, and when at last he begins to turn to the world again, his behavior is seen as the breaking of a vicious circle. A new cycle is set up, in which each perception of a person, thing, or event acts as a lure, drawing him out of his ruminations. The blind will compensate for their sensory loss by exercising the sense of touch. The deaf are prone to becoming suspicious. The perceptually handicapped child seeks self-stimulation through rocking movements or head banging.

Intellection. Lost in deep thought, the proverbial professor wanders aimlessly, becoming a target of derision. He is not really lost in thought, but lost to the world of action and social intercourse. In states of absorption and preoccupation the person shows diminished responsiveness to others, often with lack of affect. Intellectual diets can be too rich, leading to inhibition of action. Intellectualization cuts down on affect; indeed, as a defense it is directed against the experiencing of predominantly unpleasant affects that always lie in wait. The obsessional patient thinks and thinks and thinks, without resolution, going around in circles, eventually drained of energy. His thoughts are never finished. The depressed person is tied to his gloomy thoughts, endlessly reviewing his past, oblivious of life's ordinary tasks and opportunities, foregoing food, drink, and sleep.

Conversely, too little thought may give rise to impulsivity and restlessness, or, as a desperately handicapped ex-schoolteacher with Alzheimer's disease once said to me, "I just can't think of anything at all!" The result is a painful, dull emptiness. A thoughtless deed is an impulsive act, carried out without reflection or foresight. The repressive patient has too little memory: His recall is muffled by a blanket of repression. We find in some patients a paucity of thought, a failure to respond to intellectual challenges or tasks, and associative unproductiveness.

Language. Verbosity, logorrhea, incessant chattering, pressure of speech, are obvious manifestations of linguistic hyperactivity. Since words can both hide and express feelings, the reasons for these excesses can be quite diverse: In some patients verbosity is a form of intellectualization, in others it is an outpouring of pent-up affect or a compulsion to confess. Flight of ideas, as in manic states, tends to produce boisterous, loud, and uninterruptible streams of words, with quite an emotional charge.

Too little language activity accompanies guardedness, and the most radical suppression of speech can be witnessed in catatonic mutism. The latter condition is so striking that the observer, by automatic empathy or deliberate design, tends to become speechless himself, vis-à-vis such a patient. Reduced linguistic performance, with groping and qualitative alterations, characterizes many aphasic conditions. With guarded patients or with suspicious and negativistic persons, the interviewer or examiner is bound to feel as if he were "pulling teeth" in trying to elicit any communication from them. In childhood autism all common speech may be absent, the si-

lence being occasionally broken by grunts or nonsense sounds.
Emotion. Since feelings have so many variables (tone, depth,
intensity, etc.) by which they are evaluated, and since they can
easily be dissimulated, quantitative estimates of emotion çan
quickly become spurious. But the ease and demonstrativeness
with which they come to the surface and the proportion they
assume in overt behavior do form quasi-quantitative guide-
posts of clinical significance. The word "emotionality" is in
common parlance a shorthand term for quick affective arousal as well as for ease of display of feelings, or even for the
cultivation of feelingful states. Excessive emotionality is striking in states of manic excitement, in elation and euphoria, although in the latter two a quantitative judgment is already
mixed with a qualitative one. If excitement and elation are
cited as manifestations of hyperemotionality, one cannot rele-
gate depression straightaway to the opposite category of under-
emotionality, for it is a state of intense, abiding, and deep
affect, often with manifestations of tears, and sobbing. Both
elation and depression betray excessive emotionality, draining
energies away from other functions. So does shock, which
makes a person temporarily unresponsive and almost immobile. Hysterical overemotionalism partakes of dramatization: Its emphasis is on the display of feeling in the use of
overcharged words, exclamations, tragic gestures, laughing,
sobbing, and blasts of fury—all with a somewhat hollow ring
and out of proportion to the precipitating events.

A cleaner opposite of hyperemotionality is presented by
states of "flat affect," in which no smile, frown, excitement,
anger, grief, or sadness is elicited from the person, no matter
how powerful or emotional the stimulus. A humorous remark,
a sad story, the recall and narration of a painful episode in
the patient's life, the witnessing of a violent argument on the
ward—all are presented dryly, factually, or responded to
without animation or emotional tone of any kind. All feelings
are muffled, the face is without expression, the voice sounds
dull. Other patients may actually complain of boredom and
emptiness, knowing that something human is lacking in their
self-experience and overt behavior. They may feel lethargic,

act without zest or vigor, experiencing themselves as automatons pushed and moved by extraneous forces. The observer may find them bland, diffident, and hard to engage in anything, incapable of rapport.

Action. Taking the word "action" in the sense of motor activities, much of it is overt and easily perceived by an observer. Hyperactivity strikes the eye immediately: The manic patient rushes about in elation or furor; the hypomanic patient moves from person to person, accosting them for unwanted conversations or trying to enlist them for his plans; the hyperactive child cannot sit still in the classroom; the postencephalitic person flits about, attracted by every stimulus, or engages in aimless wandering. The anxious patient fidgets incessantly during an interview, or interrupts the conversation frequently in order to go to the bathroom; or he paces the floor, perhaps with tics, shoulder jerks, shiverings, and other ˙overflow phenomena of tension.

What striking contrasts these behaviors pose to the behavior of the patient who seeks to hole up in his bed during the day! Or to that of the catatonic patient who sits frozen in the same awkward or languid posture, unable to move or be moved. Hypoactivity is also the earmark of most depressed patients, who show psychomotor retardation in both central and autonomic nervous system functions: Their eating, digestion, and elimination processes are as slow as their overt movements. The general motor slowdown of aged persons in walking, talking, and working is even more pronounced in older patients with psychological or neurological disorders, and is striking in middle-aged patients with presenile dementias.

What is one to make of catatonic episodes in which a patient rigidly maintains one posture, stiff or flaccid, with no visible movement? Are they forms of hypoactivity? In one sense they are, of course: Stillness is the opposite of motion. But in another sense they may be manifestations of great tension between impulse and control, or between antagonistic impulses. Like two deer with their horns locked in battle, the still and frozen position is only a surface impression, which may give way at any time to a fierce, wild splash of destructive activity. Beneath the surface another kind of action goes on, much like the stewing of a "seething cauldron of forces."

The purpose of this chapter should not be mistaken. It is not to advocate quantification. It is not to subject everything to measurement. The aim is to show that we attach *more-or-less* judgments to our impressions of behavior, and that these judgments make some sense at their own impressionistic level. Many qualifications are needed when we go beyond impressions to explanations and inferences. Impressions play an important role in psychiatric diagnosis, and those that give rise to more-or-less judgments, no matter how intuitive, are the first sketchy lines we draw on our blank piece of paper that is destined to become a map of the person. They are signposts that give us a preliminary orientation about the wilderness we are visiting. To put it more scientifically, these quasi-quantitative observations and judgments turn into provisional hypotheses, to be tested and to serve as heuristic concepts goading us to further explorations.

Another purpose of this chapter is to make us, as observers, aware of our perceptual and conceptual habits, and to warn us against undue selectivities or blind spots. If one is at first glance impressed by a person's seeming motoric hyperactivity one must check back and forth between that person's other functions (perception, language, emotion, etc.) to assess them with the same quasi-quantitative yardstick in order to note correspondence, contrast, or some other relationship. Our descriptions have already intimated that no part process operates in isolation: To see each as a separate tool of the ego, as distinct from each other as a hammer, screwdriver, and saw in a carpenter's kit, is stretching the metaphor too far. The part processes coact and interact, and sometimes they function in a compensatory relationship. To point up this relation was the third purpose of this chapter. The motorically hyperactive person is often hypoactive in thinking; the intellectualizer often has much trouble in experiencing his own or anyone else's feelings; the emotionalist may be a poor perceiver. The fact that such observations are often grafted onto common sense does not make them psychiatrically useless—on the contrary, it points to the humanness of psychiatric observation.

In this context, the examiner's humanness also presents a danger. The standards of impressionistic more-or-less judgments are subject to cultural variation. A Scandinavian visiting the Mediterranean must calibrate his yardstick of emotional expressiveness, his estimates of moods and measure of verbosity. The decibels of the city are not those of the countryside. Normal activity levels in cramped apartments are different from those in wide open, rural spaces where children grow up with tractors and horses. At some funerals one is expected to keep a stiff upper lip; at others moaning and groaning are the things to do. Let the examiner therefore be aware of his own origins, his own ethnic background, his own class and caste affiliations, and make corrections for them in his quasi-quantitative estimates of other people.

Chapter 4

Assessing Part Processes: Perception

Etymologically, the word perception has something to do with *taking* and *receiving*, which hint at, respectively, an active and a passive form. In the passive connotation, our sense organs are bombarded by stimuli, wanted and unwanted, the latter sometimes to an unmanageable degree. If so, we may shut our eyes and stop our ears or seek a quieter place. We may escape into sleep or half-sleepy withdrawal in order to keep the sensory world at bay. Even so, sensations from our body may haunt us—we find no rest.

Fortunately, the sensory process itself comes to our aid through various adjustment and control mechanisms: It has built-in stimulus barriers, receptivity and conduction thresholds, screening devices, dampeners, focusing and tuning mechanisms, and propensities toward patterning. Much is screened out; many stimuli never reach our awareness with an appeal or demand. But despite these safeguards, one can be overwhelmed and suffer a kind of sensory shock. The booms and flashes of battle can become intolerable quite apart from being direct threats to one's life, pain may be so acute that one faints, the constant ear ringing in otitis media can elicit thoughts of suicide, and stroboscopic flicker may precipitate an epileptic attack.

The active connotation more often meant by the word "perception" implies alertness, and alludes to attention or the orderly deployment of energies. While sensation allegedly

29

deals with lights, tones, tastes, smells, vibrations, pains, and other physicalistically conceived qualities, perception is geared to things, forms, persons, situations, scenes, melodies, and other entities with complex qualities—as distinguished from mere light or noise or temperature. Perceiving puts us in contact with the world, the concrete world full of forms and things that beckon by presenting themselves, or that "shape up" in our paying attention to them.

So regarded, perception has a number of clinically important attributes.

1. It Has Inherent Organization

As Gestalt psychologists have pointed out, perception is subject to laws of *grouping.* In a row of dots, nearness and distance make us form visual groups whose components are seen as belonging together:

.. ..

The first two, the next three, one alone, then the next two. The perceptual process also imposes a figure-ground relation: the white space acts as a neutral void or background against which the dots stand out as figures. In the chaos of stars, we quickly see forms and configurations against the sky's blackness. It takes intellectual strain and analytical capacity to reverse figure and ground: Try to see the white spaces as figures on an inky ground. Chances are that you will end up seeing just another variant of the earlier perception by imagining a white card punctured with neatly spaced holes put as an overlay on a dark surface. These are not academic niceties: I once saw an elderly patient stooping down in a serious attempt to pick up rectangular patches of light that the sun, shining through the lattices of the window, cast on the floor. He saw these as things, perhaps as sheets of paper. Figure and ground relations had lost their stability for him.

The laws of the "good Gestalt" tend toward *closure:* They make us complete stimuli that are incomplete or fragmentary. It takes special alertness to see Figure 1 as simply a rounded

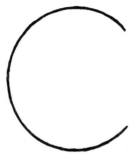

FIGURE 1

line. When we are reading, coming to it on the page of a book, we will take it as the letter C, or perhaps as a poorly printed O. If we are hungry, we may see it as the outline of a pie with one wedge served. In the field, it may appear as a coiled end of rope. Everything is perceived in *context* and in the guise of some definite form of something we know. As this example has also shown, we like to attach *meanings* to what we perceive, even when that takes some doing (see Figure 2). We like to know "what this is"—until we can take it for a soldier and his dog passing by an opening in a picket fence.[7] If meaning is not immediately apparent, which is one way of saying that our world seems chaotic, we will try to impose it by

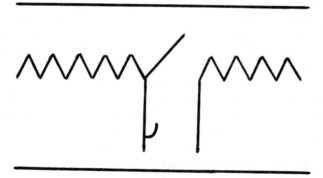

FIGURE 2

inferences and speculations, at the risk of distortion. In unfamiliar surroundings, we get intimations whose nature depends on whether we are anxious or suspicious, hopeful or gloomy. Lost in a forest on a stormy evening, we may see spooky figures in white sheets in a grove of birches. If this vision frightens us, we may see the spooks running after us; our own yelling augmented by the wind may scare us even further, and we end up in panic.

These considerations of perceptual organization entail an important question to the clinician himself: How structured or unstructured, how full or empty, how stable or ambiguous, how clear or unclear, how reassuring or frightening to the patient are your office, your hospital, your examining room, your instruments, your voice and manners, your evaluation procedures, your therapeutic techniques, your psychiatric words?

2. It Is Motivated

As the lost soul in the forest suggests, perception is not detached from wants and fears and wishes. Anxiety colors the way we perceive the world as well as what we focus on in that world. So do sadness and suspicion, hope and cheerful expectancy. Solley and Haigh[8] once showed that schoolchildren, asked to make daily drawings of Santa Claus beginning on December 1, drew ever larger Santa Claus figures as they approached December 25. The same went for the size of drawings of Easter eggs as they came nearer to Easter. Bruner and Goodman[9] found that to a poor child, a dime in his pocket feels nearly as large as a quarter; to a rich child, a quarter in his pocket approximates the size of a dime.

To the agoraphobic patient, the town square is full of people who stare or point their fingers at him. The hysterical girl sees snakes in the grass. The person who fears heights dares not take the elevator to the seventeenth floor, for already he has visions of a room with gaping holes in the outside wall; nevertheless, if he makes it he sees the window sills as paper-thin stage props and avoids leaning against them.

Held by a friend's hand, in a counterphobic flash of courage, he looks down through the window only to see a widening, monstrous pit, and feels himself already leaping.

Motivation is not confined to instinctual needs and drive derivatives. It also comprises interests and values. Perception is thus influenced by one's mental *set*. The artist will perceive a piece of driftwood differently from the camper who is collecting firewood on the beach. The person with low self-esteem is alert to the judgmental overtones in what he hears. The hypersensitive, suspicious soul will take a harmless remark as a slight. One patient I knew labeled the left half of each Rorschach card "evil" and the right half "good," seeing everywhere images of battle between cosmic forces. He happened to be a theologian suffering from many moral torments, embroiled in a stormy marriage.

Projective tests capitalize on the motivational dynamics of perception by providing ambiguous pictorial stimuli that allow much latitude for diverse perceptual interpretations. Their point is that strands of motivation come through directly in the perception itself: One "takes" the picture to be such and such *in* the act of perceiving, not by some kind of reasoning *after* some perception has been registered. The mechanism of *projection* is inherent in the perception, making the perception idiosyncratic. Projection also plays a dominant role in abnormal perceptions such as hallucinations, which will be described later in this chapter.

3. It Shapes the World and Creates Order

A good deal of classifying occurs in acts of perceiving. Touch responds to hard and soft, smooth and rough surfaces, and depending on preferences, the hand will almost automatically reach for the one and avoid the other. The world gets shaped into classes of pleasant and unpleasant, useful and useless, beautiful and ugly, desirable and undesirable things. The moment one enters a room, perceptual classification is at work: "That's furniture, there are rugs, over there books, and all around are art objects." This activity goes on without focal attention to any one particular object. But there are subtly different perceptual styles in this process. Some persons are struck by irreconcilable differences between chairs and tables; others quickly lump them together as furniture. Some people habitually *level* the differences between things, others characteristically *sharpen* the uniqueness of each thing.

Perceptual constancy normalizes the shapes of things for us by correcting variations in the retinal image. We will see the surface of a round table as a circle from whatever angle of vision, even when the retinal image is an oval or ellipse. The world's features must have enough stability and constancy, even in their immediate appearance, for us to be able to adapt ourselves to them. A purely phenomenal world is notoriously shaky. Lie on your back in the grass and stare upward at the blue sky without treetops in sight, and soon, in this contourless world, the blue will start twirling. Or sit in a train parked in the station while an adjacent train is slowly moving: One will feel his own train move. The phenomenal world is James's blooming confusion. Cézanne put aspects of that world on his canvases, which to the ordinary viewer show marked deviations in detail from the normative, intellectual, ordered way of seeing.

The museum visitor goes through the galleries with the "What is it?" question on his mind, if not on his lips. He wants to recognize something definite, namable, thinglike. In the course of growing up he has turned his perceptual world largely into a thing-world with stable, recognizable structures about which neither he nor others should ever be mistaken. Adaptation requires that the world be reliable and somewhat predictable.

It was not always so for that museum visitor. Early infancy presented him with sensory qualities and only vague forms. It took him about seven months to distinguish his mother's face from the faces of other people. As a toddler he saw the moon smile at him; for a few years he not only thought but actually *saw* that the moon traveled with him when he took an evening walk. Animistically, he endowed the moon, his toys, and the landscape with human feelings and intentions. Egocentrically, he assumed that everyone saw what he saw and heard what he heard and had the same magical influence on the course of events. A straight rod, stuck into the water to appear bent at the water's surface, became an altogether different thing—he could not yet perceive its constancy under various aspects. Going by his perceptual certainties, he thought that long and large things are always heavier than compact and small things. Only gradually did his world become a stable array of constant things and contexts, describable in the same words by many other perceivers.

This developmental sequence brings up the possibility of perceptual regression. In regressed states the world may take on a different character, depending on the depth of the regression and the mechanisms that brought it about. When we are anxious, the world may again take on an animistic mien: The cat becomes a witch's cat ready to jump on us. When we are sad, the tree limbs look droopy, the way our own arms and legs feel to us. Haunted by suspicions, one picks up a word out of context, hearing it as an accusation or malicious threat. Hypnotized by the group, participants in a séance hear the spirits rap, or feel the table rise. Is it just a bit of weird thinking when a patient reports that his insides are hollowed out, or may he actually feel a cavity in his trunk? Is he only literalizing the phrase "gnawing at the stomach" as if a beast were eating it away? How could that expression ever have emerged if there were no primitive sensory base for it in human experience?

Informed by this overview, the psychological examiner may have become curious about the perceptual functioning of his patient. The following clinical rubrics will guide his observations.

Alertness

Though there is a distinction between perception and attention, the function of attending, i.e., "turning one's mind or consciousness toward something," is typically gauged from the degree and modes in which one perceives the world, one's body, one's self, and the various relations between these. An alert person registers what is going on around him and inside him, via the perceptual process of vision, audition, touch, smell, and taste, and the kinesthetic, temperature, pressure, or pain sensations that emerge from his body. He is attuned, "in touch"—he directs his attention to something outside consciousness itself, much as a lighthouse throws its revolving beam on the landscape and the ocean, at each moment making something noticeable. Alertness itself may be likened to the candle power of the light: It can be weak or strong or of average *intensity*. Like a beam of light, attention has a *focus*, which can be narrow or broad, with sharp or fuzzy edges. The focus can be held steadily and for long periods of time (commonly attributed to power of *concentration*) or it can be wobbly and haphazard (in which case we speak of distractibility). The magnitude of focus helps define the number of things "lit up" at any time, describable as *span* of attention and *range* of its objects.

While I am typing this manuscript I am attending closely to the lines I have already typed; my mind is on the subject matter; my visual world is deliberately shrunk to a narrow field of notes on the desk, fingers on the keys, and white paper on the roller, and I am forcing my thoughts to follow a path. I concentrate, and by so doing I am warding off all kinds of possible intrusions on that narrow world—noises, phone calls, pictures on the wall, titles of books on my shelves. Concentration requires suppression, a conscious effort at relegating irrelevant or intrusive things to the periphery of awareness or beyond it. This aim presupposes, of course, that things I do not want to disturb my attention at this moment do not come storming at me on their own strong momentum. If I am greatly upset or deeply preoccupied with some worry I cannot keep my mind on my work: My efforts at suppression fail to keep the flotsam from the surface of my stream of consciousness.

Attention thus has much to do with energy and its deployment. Every act of attending is an investment of psychic energy in whatever is the object of attention: a thing, person, book, work to be done, a game to be played, a thought to be finished or crystallized. This act of attending presupposes that an energy pool is available from which the person can draw more or less at will—so-called free energy. In turn, attention hinges on (1) the person's endowment and the fluctuations of his vitality over periods of time, and (2) the degree to which his energies are marshaled for defensive purposes (e.g., to maintain repression, dissociation, counterphobic maneuvers), or are bound in long-range pursuits such as interests and predilections. From these considerations follows a clinical rule of thumb: The more energy is allocated for psychic defense, the less is available for investment in (or as the phrase goes, "paying" attention to) the external world with its various appeals and obligations, as well as the inner world with its mental opportunities. Preoccupations, brooding, compulsions, obsessions, and the maintenance of various other symptoms drain energies, preventing freedom in attention deployment.

A narrow attention span is therefore a clinical sign of defensiveness, but with interesting subdivisions. The hysterical patient spreads a blanket of inattention and forgetting over many things presented to his consciousness because of their capacity to arouse painful or forbidden fantasies. The very suspicious patient (as in paranoia) does pay much attention to the world but mostly to screen it for dangerous conspiracies and threats against him—his attention processes are like a radarscope constantly scanning the horizon. In his case, normal vigilance has become hypervigilance, with the result that he has little energy left for workmanlike tasks and the ordinary demands of living. The manipulative patient spends a lot of energy in plotting, in trying to triumph over others and expose their weaknesses, or on sadistic revenge—with the same result that he may fail in his schoolwork or be an inadequate worker who performs sloppily. All these conditions presuppose a normal energy flow at the biological sources of vitality.

In mood disorders and states of lethargy there may be, in addition to the syphoning off of energies in defense, a felt depletion at the vital source. In depression, the whole flow of energy seems to be reduced in all vital processes, including digestion, breathing, and sleep-and-wake rhythms, with one-sided attention to body processes (hypochondriasis) and absorption in sad thoughts and feelings. Alertness to the environment thus suffers greatly. In contrast, in elated moods and states of excitement patients report (and act to confirm) feeling an upsurge of energies so great that they fail to regulate their distribution by appropriate attention cathexis: They allow themselves to be aroused without proper screening by almost anything that comes along, flitting from one object or thought to another. Their span is wide and without durability. Their attention *wanders*.

The older neuropsychiatric literature (and some newer studies) held to a belief in the existence of primary attention disturbances. Kraepelin invented a test for detecting them—rapid serial arithmetical addition of thousands of digits, each column to be clocked by the examiner to make fluctuations of speed and accuracy recordable. On the Wechsler-Bellevue Intelligence Scale such attention disturbances tend to show up as odd success-failure sequences within each subtest that cannot be reduced to the objective degree of difficulty of the items or to the emotional charge of each question or task. These attention disturbances occur in *petit mal* and subclinical forms of epilepsy, where by definition levels of consciousness fluctuate.

While *concentration* requires a sharp focusing and an intense investing of attention, there is another state of alertness, which Freud once described as "evenly suspended attention."[10] Speaking of the psychoanalyst's attentive attunement to his patient, Freud noted that too strong an effort to concentrate makes the observer too selective, and likely to miss subtle clues. A state of evenly suspended attention is one of relaxation and great receptiveness, with little deliberate screening and free openness to the topic at hand, including its novelties and surprises. Freud's advocacy of this kind of attention in the psychoanalyst identifies a danger of effortful concentration, namely, that attention itself is dynamically affected by wishes and may cause blind spots as well as stereotypical, fixed ideas that interfere with adequate perception.

There is also *divided attention.* Some students do homework best with background music; some artists like to work on several projects at the same time, shifting back and forth between them as if to move them from the focus to the periphery of attention without relegating any of them to oblivion. While attention tends to be described as the outstanding feature of consciousness, the phenomena of divided and evenly suspended attention imply a correction of this view. Consciousness itself is stratified into distinguishable layers: the systems Conscious, Preconscious, and Unconscious, each with its own styles of registration, retention, and recall. Perception is similarly stratified into conscious, preconscious, and unconscious intake, recognition, and associative linkages.

Divided attention should not be equated with the ambiguous attention states of obsessional patients who suffer from intrusive thoughts that interfere with their endeavors to focus. Bombarded as they are by alternating, contrasting affects, these patients' gaze may wander from the left to the right side of Rorschach cards, spotting here a "nice," there an "ugly" detail. Their ears may scan the examiner's speech for "safe" and "unsafe" or "good" and "bad" phrases, with the result that their perceptual intake is reduced to a multiplicity of fragments in which a sense of the whole is lost.

Orientation

There is a somewhat trite psychiatric phrase, "The patient is oriented in all three spheres," which means that the person knows *where* he is, in what *time* he lives, and *who* he is. That phrase is a good example of the tendency to spatialize concepts. To locate oneself in space and to know one's whereabouts are, of course, appropriately spatial cognitions, but would knowledge of time or one's personhood be a "sphere"?

Orientation, as used clinically, refers to a person's awareness of the objectively existing situation he is in, especially with regard to such overriding dimensions of experience as space, time, and selfhood: *Where, when,* and *who* am I? Orientation is so fundamental to adaptation and such a basic condition of reality testing that only marked deviations from it will make us pause and think. Here is an example of a deviation. A man leaves his home at eight o'clock in the morning, to go to work somewhere in Topeka, where he lives. He kisses his wife goodbye and gets into his car. At ten o'clock he finds himself on a park bench in Manhattan, a town some 50 miles from Topeka, his car parked at the curb, wondering where he is, puzzled about himself, asking why he is in a park and how he got there. Somewhat in a daze, he searches his memory. He vaguely remembers having had breakfast at home, and he concludes that he must have gotten into his car, but his mind is a blank from then on. As he finds out that he is in Manhattan he becomes frightened when it dawns on him that he must have driven through crowded streets until he entered the highway, apparently obeying the traffic signals, for his car and his body are undamaged, and there is no policeman taking him to task. He goes through his wallet to see whether he spent any money, searching for clues to reconstruct the two-hour gap in his mind. He feels awkward, but as he slowly begins to feel sure of himself again, he cautiously drives home. The trip back is uneventful, which reassures him, and after sharing this weird episode with his wife he makes an appointment with his doctor.

This is a description of a *fugue state*. Disoriented about his existing reality situation, i.e., insufficiently aware of the space and time schemes in relation to his personal routines and duties, the man simply drove on after having started his car, oblivious to his tasks and the requirements of his life situation. Yet it is obvious, even to him after he has regained full consciousness, that he must have maintained an adequate, automatic alertness to the rules of the road and the handling of his car. In other words, he was in an altered state of consciousness, one in which many adaptive processes apparently continued and many perceptions were peripherally registered and responded to, but in which focal awareness of the three great schemes that govern life was absent. Had an alert policeman seen him sitting in a daze on the park bench and asked him for his name, he might not have been able to identify himself. The fact that the man was puzzled, sought to put together the pieces of the lost two hours, and was concerned enough to seek a doctor's appointment right away, speaks for the likelihood that this fugue state felt ego alien to him, an unwanted break in the flow of his consciousness, probably due to a brain dysfunction. His postictal behavior showed no sign of "la belle indifférence," that supreme form of afterrepression whereby hysterical patients seek to disown their symptoms and hold themselves unaccountable for the motives of their deviancy.

Confusion and disorientation are usually most noticeable when they occur in the spatial dimension: The patient wanders, looks around helplessly, appears to be lost. He may indeed lose his way from the ward to the dining room, not knowing what turns to make at corners, in hallways, and on paths—not only when he may be presumed to be unacquainted with the layout, but repeatedly, after a normal exposure period. Disorientation in time is more difficult to detect: It may appear in unpreparedness for mealtimes and neglect of prescribed schedules. Typically, some questioning is required about the time of day, day of the week, month of the year, etc., to find out whether the patient has his bearings in time. Some patients, such as those in regressed senile states, are confused about their age, thinking they are children.

Disorientation of personal identity as a function of inattention and confusion is to be distinguished from the delusional assumption of a false identity. The latter is part of a purposive, motivated, and defensive transformation of the self, for instance into a historical figure (Napoleon) or a magical figure (Jesus), or a member of the opposite sex, by means of which the person gains certain advantages in fantasy. Disorientation about one's person has a helpless, groping quality, often leading to a quest for help in re-establishing who one is and finding out one's name and address. For instance, in certain amnesic episodes a person walking the streets may suddenly find himself perplexed about who he is and where he lives, turning eventually to a police station for a search through his papers for clues. Though one may subsequently discover that the person had that morning suffered a severe setback or had a family quarrel that triggered the dissociated state (thus showing some motivation for the condition), his current *perplexity* over not knowing his name and who he is and his *groping* for clarification are the oustanding features of personal disorientation.

To round off this section and tie it in with earlier sections of this chapter, let me quote from the report of one patient's psychological examination:

> On admission, X's perceptions were very disorganized and he showed some confusion as to time, place, and person. He would temporarily misidentify himself as William Shakespeare or John Milton. He also experienced feelings of depersonalization and estrangement and changes in his body image, believing that he had died and was reborn, or that he was a pregnant girl about to deliver twins. Hyperalert and very distractible, he was frightened by loud noises. Mistrusting his visual perceptions, he had to touch objects in his field of vision to reassure himself that they were real. His visual perceptions were so distorted that he believed he saw men dancing in the terrazzo floor. Much of this has now subsided, although it is only tenuously suppressed.

Perceptual Defects

In addition to such clear-cut *sensory* loss as deafness, blindness, lack of pain sensation, smell, or taste, which impair basic forms of contact with the environment, there are *perceptual defects* that cannot be reduced to a failure of sensory organs and major neural tracts to the corresponding sensory areas of the brain. Leaving aside partial sensory losses and perceptual distortions due to faulty organ structure or functioning (such as diplopia, astigmatism, color blindness, scotomata, anosmia, anaesthesia, partial hearing losses, etc.) there remain certain disorders of perception that are apparently dependent on breakdowns in high-level processes of the central nervous system and complex psychological organization.

In the beginning of this chapter I mentioned a defect in stable visual figure-ground relations: a patient trying to pick up patches of light cast by the sun on the floor. The same patient could copy block and stick patterns only when a large, clear, desk surface to work on was available; the moment some other articles were lying on the desk (still leaving plenty space for him to work) he was utterly confused. He could not make sense out of simple black outline drawings on white paper— only when the pictorial bulk was suggested by filling in the surface between the contours could he recognize the image.

Other patients may show defects in Gestalt perception: Compact figures are seen as loosely arranged line fragments, which, though they can be accurately traced with the fingers, do not add up or round off into a recognizable pattern. Rorschach cards elicit no forms—only vague, amorphous impressions of white and black or dark and light grays.

The *agnosias*, though their name suggests cognitive dysfunctions involving thought and language-related processes, are typically distinguished into perceptual categories: visual, auditory, and tactile. This classification evolves in part from the way in which they are clinically detected: When one sees a man earnestly looking at a magazine picture, but holding it upside down, and if he fails to identify or adequately describe it when the examiner puts it right side up for him, one wonders about defects in that person's visual contact with and interpretation of the world, and his ability to recognize things, signs, and symbols visually presented. On checking, one may find that the patient cannot identify the content of small-size black-and-white pictures, but does recognize approximately life-size colored representations; that he can recognize geometrical shapes and forms, even in pictures, but not letters or numbers, let alone printed words or sentences. In other words, from the range of presences that make up our visual world, certain classes go unrecognized, particularly those of cultural, language-related origin such as signs and symbols.

Thus we speak of "word blindness" and "tone deafness," in recognition of the participation of perceptual processes in such defects, and because the agnosias are frequently restricted to a particular perceptual modality, such as vision, touch, or hearing, or pain sensations.

The fact that we automatically impose space coordinates such as left and right, above and below, near and distant (or in front of and in back of anything) on any scene, and that such ordering of space relations is fully caught up in our perceptions, give spatial disorders a logical place under the rubric of perception as well as under the rubric of action and motor behavior. Perhaps the purest examples of visual-space distortions involving no motor behavior whatever are *micropsia* and *macropsia*. In spells of micropsia an object the patient formerly visually located at a proper distance suddenly appears very small (while retaining its clarity), as if far removed from his eye; in macropsia, an object becomes very large (without getting blurred) as if it had moved in close to the eye. Both occur in temporal lobe disorders, as does the *déjà vu* experience. Though the latter is usually discussed as a paroxysmal disorder of memory, it really presents itself first as a perceptual paradox: Something currently in the field of vision (e.g., a stairway one climbs, a glimpse of a door passed by, a section of the pavement one stands on) assumes a momentary lucidity that elicits a double awareness—"I have seen this before, exactly so" and "I cannot have seen this before, just so"—both convictions being held with equal certainty and great immediacy during the perceptual act, and thus presenting the beholder with an unsolved puzzle that he is likely to remember and brood about for some time. In contrast, *feelings of familiarity and strangeness* tend to last much longer, are far less perceptual, and typically pertain to social scenes and the presence of persons to whom one stands in some affective relation, very different from the inanimate and impersonal perceptual fragments that are the most often reported content of *déjà vu* spells.

More action-demanding, but still perceptual, are *defects in space relations* in which, for instance, a person is unable to unfold his eyeglasses and put them correctly on his face with the lenses forward and the temples of the frame pointed toward him. I once saw a person struggle with this problem for some

time, and in trying to sort out the apraxic component affect-
ing his movements I found that he was unable, when I put the
opened glasses in various positions before him on the table, to
select the right position in relation to his body. Nor could he,
when I put a pencil alternately in front of and behind a block,
judge the dimensions of "in front" and "behind" and "on top"
and "below."

In such cases we cannot ignore the important role of the
body scheme as a stable frame of reference for all space relations. The body itself is phenomenologically divided into left
and right, front and back, upper and lower. These dimensions
of the body scheme are projected onto the world that faces us
in vision—witness the time it takes children to realize that the
left hand of a person facing him is diagonally opposite to his
own left hand. Like anything that is acquired or learned, this
bit of knowledge may get lost through an organic assault, and
we have a case of *left-right disturbance.* Or it may never be
established in the first place, as in schoolchildren with
strephosymbolia or *crossed cerebral dominance* who read a *d* for a *b*
or take 13 for 31, reading what we would call "backwards,"
from right to left. Or, on a clock without digits, the position of
the hands at a quarter to eleven is visually equal to a quarter
past one, if the body of the person is not endowed with a stable and reliable left-right scheme as a constant source of spatial orientation.

On moving to Kansas from elsewhere, I found that I had
to modify my customary left-right scheme, which had thus far
guided me in giving and asking directions, into a more
abstract scheme determined by compass positions. One goes
south on Main Street, turning west onto Thirteenth Street to
find the store one needs on the north side. One speaks of the
east and west sides of a house, not of the left and right sides.
In this scheme, one's body is no longer the point of orientation, but the wide, wide world as divided by the compass. This
useful abstraction seems to be within the grasp of millions of
people, so that the occasional person who fails to reach it
stands out as somehow defective. Some persons, otherwise intelligent and well-educated, cannot read maps and blueprints,

draw the layouts of their own houses, make road turns with certainty, or estimate correctly the distance between the curb and their car wheels. They suffer from a basic weakness in spatial organization. Others, having mastered the basic space scheme, may lose it as a result of damage to their parietal lobe.

Illusions and Hallucinations: Perceptual Distortions

The rule of thumb in distinguishing illusions and hallucinations is that in the former a perceptual stimulus is present but not veridically perceived, whereas in the latter the presence of a perceptual stimulus cannot be verified, although the patient insists that he sees or hears something without doubting its actuality or existence.

Many *illusions* are so widespread, and in that sense "normal," that they seem to be a function of our perceptual and cognitive apparatus. For instance, in Figure 3, the second line seems longer than the first, though the two are the same length; in Figure 4, the opposite-angled crosshatching ruins the physical parallellism of the two lines. When the moon is close to the horizon, it appears very large, much larger than it does when it is high in the sky. In illusions of inattention, one fails to see misprints in proofreading. In the constant background noise of air conditioners, one may hear little melody fragments or, if one is a parent, the crying of one's

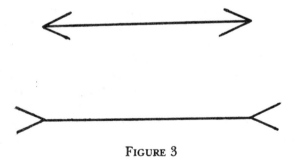

FIGURE 3

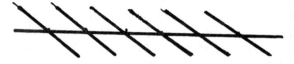

FIGURE 4

child. A fever makes us perceive faces in wall paper designs. Staring at a terrazzo floor, all kinds of figures fleetingly appear. In states of fear or fervent expectation we may grossly misperceive things: The shadow of a tree at dusk becomes a person or animal moving toward us; we seem to hear our telephone ringing when the trolley clangs in the street. In the early morning hours, we mistake last night's stale air for the smell of coffee brewing.

Between the relatively mild perceptual distortions of illusions and the grosser reality falsifications of hallucinations lie some benign intermediate phenomena, which bring out the role of projection. *Eidetic imagery* (Jaensch)[11] seems to be a gift some people have for projecting on a blank wall or sheet of paper all kinds of fantasy productions or remembered scenes, accompanied by the feeling that they visually scan or read these images, being able to focus at will on minute details that appear to them vividly present "out there." Mueller, the great sensory psychologist and physiologist, called attention to the figures we actually see with the eyes closed in the visual purple, sometimes mixed with positive or negative afterimages. Kandinski[12] described *pseudohallucinations* that consist of very vivid images, akin to dream images, but are projected outside and then seen as if they were visually real. Staudenmaier[13] studied pseudohallucinations that may occur in intense affect states, as when a man in love writes a letter to his girl friend with the strong feeling that she is present and near him at his desk—he may even stretch out his arm to embrace her. In all these cases the vividness and felt visual actuality of the projection do not adversely affect the person's judgment; in the end he remains aware of the irreality of these visions, despite their convincingly perceptual character.

True hallucinations presuppose at least a temporary severing of reality contact, and grossly inadequate reality testing. They imply a felt sense of the reality of what is perceived, to the point of responding to it in such action as fight, flight, anxiety attacks, talking back to the voices heard, or squeezing one's skin to eliminate the bugs one feels crawling there, as in delirium tremens.

Hallucinations are distinguished in terms of several variables, first along sensory lines: visual, auditory, olfactory, gustatory, kinesthetic, or, as is sometimes the case, multimodal. Another variable is the affective tone: pleasant or unpleasant, soothing or frightening. It is obviously important for the self-concept of the hallucinator whether he projects his own person into the visions seen or the voices heard; if he does, we have an autoscopic hallucination, in which the person is both subject and object and which presupposes a double awareness or a splitting of the self-image. Apart from analyzing the thematic content of hallucinations one can study their formal qualities, for instance, how close or distant to the perceiver the depicted objects are, how alien or familiar the dramatis personae appear, or how ego syntonic (i.e., embedded in and accepted as a natural part of the stream of consciousness) or ego alien (i.e., a disruptive, foreign-bodylike experience) the whole hallucinatory episode is felt to be by the person.

An instructive case of complex hallucinations (pieced together from several interviews) occurred paroxysmally in a 17-year-old boy with a long history of seizures, including "running fits":

At unpredictable moments things suddenly go dark before his eyes. Instead of perceiving the world before him, he now sees flashes of light which quickly turn into a formless red. These become red geometrical shapes such as circles and triangles in rotating motion. They next turn into a panoramic vision of a volcano from which red-hot lava pours out over the landscape. Now the patient sees himself in that landscape, threatened by lava about to engulf him. He runs for his life, hearing bangs (which he thinks come from the volcano), dashing over rocks in a mountain stream, in panic. He finds himself in a mountain stream becoming a maelstrom, panic increases, and he swims, grabbing wildly for logs in the turbulent water. Nearly exhausted, he smells a nasty odor as of something burning.

After this experience, the patient would have a focal motor seizure (in which I had a chance to observe him), making asymmetrical motions with his arms and legs as if he were indeed swimming. The case shows a progression of sensory modalities, from visual to auditory to olfactory. It also shows a progression of complexity, from lights to colored discs to a scenic landscape in wild motion, into which the patient now projects himself, also in motion. It is accompanied by vegetative reactions of fright and panic, which may be primordial rather than only a response to the awesome threat of the scene. According to the progression of mental symptoms, the brain discharge moves, with greater or lesser elaboration, from the occipital through the temporal lobe to the uncus, possibly also involving the limbic system and the island of Reil. Rare as such a case may be, it not only rolls nearly all important dimensions of hallucinations into one, it also shows in the integration of its almost narrative plot the ongoing synthetic activity of the ego, despite a grossly altered state of consciousness.

There is some argument about the relative commonness, hence seriousness as a pathology indicator, of *auditory versus visual hallucinations*. Some hold auditory hallucinations to be more common, but that belief may be due to the relative ease with which the patient affirmatively answers the question, "Do you hear voices?" Moreover, hearing voices may consist of only a few words, brief and uncomplicated, fairly easy to describe or share, since verbal exchange is so characteristic of human relations. In addition, a patient's lip movements when he subvocally talks back to his voices give away to an observer the secret of his hallucinating. Visions are often more difficult to describe and one may be loath to report them (in our culture) because of their erotic or religious qualities. The exception is when they are induced by drugs, in which case they may be reported as a frightening symptom—or, in psychedelic subcultures, even with pride. As a clinical rule, however, auditory hallucinations are held to be more common in schizophrenic conditions, whereas visual and tactile hallucinations are more frequently reported in toxic states, such as alcoholic delirium, and brain disorders.

The clinical relevance of hallucinations as symptoms hinges on their being taken by the patient as perceptual realities, so actual that they can elicit an observable behavioral response. That is why hallucinations are grouped as pathological perceptions. This definition is different from using the term "hallucinatory image" to signify a special bit of ideation or fantasy, as in hypnagogic or hypnopompic thought, in the imagery of dreams, or in the theoretical proposition that hallucinatory images (e.g., of the breast) are the stuff of thought spontaneously produced by a hungry infant when his mother is absent. In these cases, differences between the real and the fantasized objects are in some way maintained and behavioral responses are absent.

Nevertheless, sensory-deprivation phenomena alert us to an interesting psychodynamic balance. In accidental isolation (lost in the desert or in Arctic snow), in intentional isolation (imprisoned in extremely monotonous surroundings without human contact), as well as in experimental isolation (in tanks, with sensory intake, body movements, and kinesthetic feedback controlled), there is a marked tendency for the persons so deprived to start hallucinating or otherwise engage in drive-determined image formation. If the outer world does not provide stimulation of optimal intensity and variety, the self-system, guided by the ego, compensates by attuning itself to the id. Apparently, the primary process is always at work with great spontaneity but, in the adult waking state, is overtaken by the demands and opportunities of the external world, mediated by the senses, which stimulate the secondary process.

This homeostatic paradigm suggests the interaction of several factors in the production of hallucinations: Poor reality contact or active withdrawal from reality unleashes the primary process, enhancing the likelihood of hallucinations. Once hallucinations occur, their wish-fulfilling power and fascination with their content make the person increasingly self-absorbed, promoting further withdrawal from the external world. The disorientation that ensues promotes or increases depersonalization, which in turn stimulates further indulgence in primary-process activity. This chain reaction highlights the clinical importance of hallucinations as symptoms of serious mental disorder. The paradigm also suggests that hallucinations can be of purely functional origin, instead of or in addition to their being a symptom of faulty brain states. The clinical distinction between functional and organic hallucinations cannot be derived solely from their phenomenology; it requires a context of other examinational data. As a rule, however, organic hallucinations tend to be felt as ego alien by the subject.

Finally, there is some evidence that intersensory processes have an effect through neuronal interaction, which is of importance to psychiatric examiners. Hearing a loud noise may make a light or a color look brighter. This principle throws some light on manic and other excitement states by pointing to the accelerated, self-stimulating, more or less circular pattern of the patient's getting "keyed up" by himself. The same circular process seems to occur in psychedelic shows where loud music, beating rhythms, and glaring stroboscopic lights add up to press at the limits of stimulus tolerance. The reduction of stimuli is therefore a first step in breaking the vicious circle of excitement states.

A Phenomenological Consideration

At the end of this chapter we should pay attention to a lesson taught by phenomenologists. The phenomenological approach holds that understanding the patient is facilitated by knowing how the patient views his world, or more precisely, what picture of the world the patient constructs from the many impressions, whether realistic or distorted, that come his way. In each perceptual act, the perceiver is confronted with a self-presentation of a thing or situation or part of the world, and his corresponding percepts are somewhat like acts of faith: The perceiver takes the thing to be such and such or the situation to be thus and so. Though no one's world picture is solely built up from purely perceptual experiences, but is also shaped by intellectual, linguistic, emotional, and ideological factors, many of the latter processes are functionally inherent in the act of perceiving. For this reason, perceiving is given pre-eminent status by phenomenologists.

Though perceiving accurately is a condition for testing the common-sense denotations of reality, perceiving is apparently so idiosyncratic that different perceivers give reality different connotations. The subjective stratum of perceiving is evident from the ways in which momentary moods change the meanings of things and aesthetic judgments encroach on perception. One situation or stimulus pattern is pleasing to some and ugly to others: "Beauty is in the eye of the beholder." One object is frightening to some persons and neutral or pleasant to others; it is perceived as friendly or unfriendly, overpowering or manageable, familiar or foreign, trustworthy or threatening—not after long cogitation but in the immediacy of perceiving itself.

For these reasons phenomenologists believe that a precise and empathic assessment of a patient's world picture (or his "perceptual world") is a royal road to understanding the patient. Psychological examiners should heed this point.

Chapter 5

Assessing Part Processes: Cognition–Intelligence and Memory

It is a fact of development that the "blooming buzzing confusion" of infancy gradually gives way to order. Another developmental fact is that young children tend to act rather promptly on their impulses and the lure of anything that comes along in their world, whereas adults have the capacity to wait, postpone a gratification, and exercise caution in the face of enticements. They have learned to discern, consider, and reflect. It is as if growth interposes an increasing complexity of processes between stimulus (external and internal) and response. Activity confined to the reflex arc is simple, brief, and stereotyped, with rather fixed relations between stimulus and response; activity involving the whole brain is immensely complex, time-binding, and highly flexible.

Cognition in the broad sense, defined as *all* the processes of knowing, includes perception. In the narrower sense that we will use in this and the next chapter, acts of perception as such are excluded, but the processing of perceptions is considered, in the conviction that events and objects perceived are part of the "stuff" of thought, memory, judgment, and intellection. Cognition encompasses all the so-called "higher processes" traditionally associated with high-level central nervous system functions. These processes often involve abstraction, conceptualization, symbolization, and the forming of associative relations, comprising much of what is loosely called intelligence.

Paradoxically, cognitive processes seem to work in two opposite directions at once. By a principle of *reduction* they seem to simplify the chaotic manifold of immensely diverse sensory impressions, making it manageable; by a principle of *proliferation* they establish rich networks of associations, making for a complexity that adds many new dimensions to sensory reality, such as worlds of ideas, symbols, culture, and creative imagination. Both principles must act in the service of adaptation to the multidimensional world in which Homo sapiens makes his habitat—a world partially created by man himself. It follows that cognition can err in both directions. It may *fail to establish order in perceptual chaos*, leaving a person overwhelmed, as in the manic propensity to respond fragmentarily, indiscriminately, and seriatim to almost anything, and in the brain-damaged patient's enslavement to concrete sensory impressions; or it may *fail to maintain contact with the sensory world*, leaving a person at the mercy of imagination, as in paranoid delusions and the haphazard confabulations of patients with Korsakoff syndrome.

Intelligence

In ordinary conversation we make, with surprising frequency, evaluative comments about other people as "smart" or "stupid," "bright" or "dull." We apparently register clues by which to judge somebody's intelligence, in the conviction that this is an important, if not overriding, feature of personality that serves as a first-level criterion for classification. Lifetime workers in large factories keep some distance from the "smart guys" who obviously will put in only a few years of labor in order to pay their way through school, so as to gain access to "higher" work. In one fell swoop, all persons with intelligence quotients below 70 are legally considered mentally retarded. The ethics of this classification may be suspect, but the pervasiveness of intelligence judgments is an obvious fact.

Intelligence is an ambiguous term, referring both to processes of intellection and their accumulated outcome, i.e., the body of knowledge, the store of insights, the acquired cognitive skills, and their ever-ready generalization and application to new situations. Textbook definitions of intelligence vary greatly and are beset by problems of heredity, cultural influence, early learning, motivation, and whether it is a unitary trait or a composite, and if the latter, how much general ability is complemented by special knacks or talents.

The emphasis here is on the clinically useful dimensions of intelligence and what light they throw on psychopathology and symptoms. Clinicians have always known that conspicuous stupidity presents problems of adaptation or survival, and that a breakdown of intelligence factors may occur in grave illness, accident, or senility. The Ebers papyrus of 1500 B.C. described senile deterioration; Hippocrates knew of mental deficits after head injury; and ancient psychiatric nomenclature is full of words like "lethargy," "epilepsy," "fatuity," "amentia," "oblivion," "stultitia" and "feeble-mindedness" to indicate intellectual dysfunctioning of one sort or another. The neuropsychiatry of the second half of the nineteenth century devoted much attention to amentia, dementia, deterioration, imbecility, and idiocy, in the sweeping belief that mental disorder is brain disease. Impairment, decline, and defect were studied in great detail. Kraepelin meant by "dementia" a permanent and irreversible loss of intellectual capacity, and by "deterioration" a progressive loss of mental efficiency; the latter figured in his descriptions of dementia praecox. Indeed, the Belgian psychiatrist Morel[14] first noted, in 1852, before Kraepelin, the then strange occurrence of *precocious* deterioration of mental faculties in patients in the second decade of life.

Today, without dogmatic adherence to the belief that mental disorder is brain disease, we fare better with the purely descriptive, neutral word *deficit* to indicate one major clinical concern with assessments of intelligence. To clarify issues of psychopathology, the clinician evaluates various aspects of intelligence in order to know how they are affected, functionally or organically, by the patient's condition—and conversely, in order to infer the patient's psychopathology from the pattern of the manifest functions and dysfunctions of intelligence. The several aspects of intelligence and its dysfunctions or deficits merit successive discussion.

Indicators of Intelligence

Though some people look vacuous and others have a lively glint in the eye, facial expression and physical appearance are notoriously deceptive clues to intelligence, and understandably so, for intelligence is not a form or substance, but, as Stoddard[15] held, the ability to undertake various activities characterized by difficulty, complexity, abstractness, economy, adaptiveness, social value, and originality. Intelligence lies in the *quality of activities:* sureness of approach and speed in problem solving, ability to learn swiftly with maximum insight and minimal trial and error, capacity to retain what has been learned, to generalize from it with inventiveness, to substitute verbalization for motor action, and to think symbolically. The pragmatic arena for intelligence, then, consists in the variety of tasks that life and civilization impose and the rates of success or failure in accomplishing them, as well as the skill with which they are performed. Other things being equal, bright people are faster, more successful, more adaptive, more versatile, and more skillful at those tasks than dull people, and both groups are again different from the mass of average performers. Superior minds and people of genius are star performers, contrasted with dull-witted and stupid ones whose failures, awkwardness, and slowness are conspicuous.

Since it is the goal of formal intelligence tests to make crucial elements of life tasks operational and to take manageable samples of intellectual processes, finely graded from easy to difficult so as to allow measurement, we can get basic information about intelligence indicators from these tests. Typically, the following mental activities or processes are sampled:

a. *Ability to verbalize—vocabulary.* Along with size of vocabulary, the caliber of word usage is held to be an indicator of a person's native endowment as well as of his exposure to a stimulating cultural environment. Example: "What is mohair?"

b. *Soundness of judgment—comprehension.* This factor involves the marshaling of acquired knowledge of facts and situations, the grasping of relations between facts, the drawing of inferences, the ability to withstand impulsivity in favor of thoughtfulness. Example: "Why are people required to obtain a license to drive a car?" Or the interpretation of proverbs: "What is the meaning of 'a bird in the hand is worth two in the bush'?"

c. *Store of knowledge—information.* Education exposes a person to the worlds of culture and accumulated knowledge, innumerable bits of which he is to acquire and retain. Example: "What is a lunar module?"

d. *Concept formation and grasp of relations between concepts— similarities.* This factor involves the ability to abstract from concrete things and situations so as to arrive at higher-level thought categories, to distinguish essential from accidental features of anything, and to compare the essential qualities of two or more categories for possible likenesses. Example: "In what way are a glass of wine and a cigar alike?" Sometimes this task means fitting both class concepts (e.g., dinner drink and after-dinner enjoyment) into a superordinate class comprising a shared essence (e.g., both are drugs, toxins, luxuries, prestige items, etc.).

e. *Attention and concentration—in rote learning and in purposive problem solving.* How free is the person to deploy his energy to note, register, and momentarily retain stimuli so as to work with them on a set task? Examples are: to repeat series of digits of varying lengths spoken to the person (digit span); to say them backwards; to count backwards from twenty to one; to subtract seven from one hundred, and then again seriatim from the remainder (serial sevens). In the last two tasks the person must hold several items at once in consciousness plus the purposive task-set in order to do his computations. Even more concentration is required for solving arithmetical problems by mental computation. Example: "If six bananas cost forty cents, how many bananas can be bought for one dollar?" Moreover, arithmetic tasks demand ability to deal with a special symbol system: the world of numbers and their permutations, which can be selectively disturbed.

Note that all these tasks are verbal, requiring skill in language behavior and the ability to communicate through words. While sophisticated societies put a premium on verbal abilities, which give access to highly variegated symbol worlds, intelligence also comprises perceptual-motor skills and observational acumen. Hence, intelligence tests typically contain so-called *performance* tasks, sampling purposive finger movements, eye-hand coordination, visual alertness and structuring ability, pattern recognition, and writing or drawing skills, all graded for relative ease or difficulty (often age specific to assess children's development) and usually timed for speed of performance.

f. *Visual concentration and content analysis—picture completion.* Pictorial material is presented in which something is missing, or distorted, or in some sense wrong, or perhaps containing embedded subsidiary images, which the person is to point out. To spot the inconsistency, visual concentration is demanded, with knowledge of normative models, stability of figure-ground relations, and some analytical acumen about the relationships between parts and whole. Examples: picture of a child's face with one ear missing, picture of a dog chasing a rabbit while running in the wrong direction, picture of a hunter whose outlines coincide with the gnarled trunks of trees in a landscape.

g. *Reading meanings, with sequential planning and sense of plot, in a series of pictures—picture arrangement.* Given a scrambled series of pictures depicting stages of some ongoing activity or a story, e.g., a horse race in progress from start to finish, the person is to unscramble them and place them in correct order. This involves visual attention to details, recognition of an over-all theme, anticipation of sequence, and a feel for "what's happening"—good reality testing. Though the motor movements of the person are hardly relevant to this task, perceptual analysis and planning are demanded in the performance. The test is timed for speed, as is the picture completion test previously described.

h. *Visual-motor coordination in pattern analysis and pattern construction—block design.* This item is a tried and true standby of performance tests, in which the person is to copy with multicolored blocks a variety of geometrical patterns of two or more colors presented on cards. The two-dimensional pictorial models indicate only the outline and the patterned color-surfaces, which the subject is to analyze so as to reconstruct them with his three-dimensional, equal-sized blocks. He must abstract from two- to three-dimensionality and vice versa, and he must not be distracted by the upright sides of the blocks, which are in his visual field. Several dimensions of blocks and picture models can be varied, such as size or the overprinting of block edges on the cards. Speed of performance is measured, along with accuracy of designs.

i. *Solving jigsaw puzzles—object assembly.* Scattered, odd-shaped parts are put before the person without any hint at the nature of the whole that is to be achieved. The desired form is to be discovered by the person as he moves the scrambled parts, trying to fit some of their edges into a visually accurate joint. Eyes and hand move together or alternately, until the intended figure dawns on the subject's mind, sometimes in an "Aha" experience. Constructivist skill at acceptable rates of speed is also involved, as in the block design task, which makes these tests very difficult for people with apraxic deficits.

j. *Visual-motor coordination in printed copying of letter symbols—*

digit symbol. In presentation of the model, a digit (numerical symbol) is paired with a letter or letterlike symbol, in a series. The subject is to print (write) as fast as possible the correct letter symbol below each digit appearing in random order in a long list. He must look back and forth between the model pair and the cue number to find the right letter to print; and in completing the series as fast as he can, an element of learning and remembering is involved, as his eyes scan and his hand moves with the pencil in the act of printing.

These ten tasks, taken largely from the Wechsler-Bellevue Intelligence Scale and the Stanford-Binet Test of Intelligence, both of which are widely used in clinical practice and have a venerable history, represent samples of intellectual work. They are presented here to illustrate some proven indicators of intelligence, and to highlight some of the psychological functions that participate in it. Each task can be varied in several ways, and one can add several more examples to those mentioned. For instance, in young children, the age at which a bow can be tied in a shoelace, or beads of various shapes strung in a certain order on a piece of twine, or drawings made of geometrical shapes, or the number of body parts that appear in human figure drawings—all of these activities are developmental landmarks and samples of intelligence.

In addition to, or instead of, formal psychological testing for intelligence, the psychiatric examiner gets many clues to his patient's intellectual functioning in the course of his clinical interview, or when he takes the history. A potent and almost omnipresent direct indicator is the patient's vocabulary and what his word usage alludes to in terms of thought processes, range of information and interests, the level of learning he appears to have acquired, the scope of his contact with the world of culture, his ease in dealing with symbolic realms, and the discipline he maintains in his reasoning. The clinical interview also allows the examiner to insert short tasks, such as having the patient interpret a proverb, solve some arithmetic problem, or find a similarity between two or more things. The patient can be asked to write or draw something, to copy some figures, or, as neurologists are wont to request, to construct some pattern from matchsticks. A host of little tasks and experiments can be invented on the spot, if the examiner knows what psychological function he wishes to assess.

Not to be overlooked are the indirect or inferential clues to intelligence: the degree of schooling obtained and the grades achieved over the years, and the patient's work record. Most jobs (and hobbies or recreational activities) demand certain skills of a verbal and/or performance type, and the patient's job successes or failures thus throw much light on the level or type of intelligence he has manifested in the past. Some estimate can also be gained from asking the patient how he solved difficult life problems in the past: How did he react to a move from the country to the city and what did he observe during the process of adaptation? What did he do when he looked for employment on graduating from school? How does he manage his financial affairs? How did he choose his vocation, profession, or academic career? What books does he read, what TV shows does he watch, what plays has he seen, how does he travel on his vacation?—not only to know of his interests but to detect something about his intellectual level and pursuits.

Intelligence Levels and Patterns

Intelligence quotients are *compound* measures, products of intricate computations, derived from number values assigned to successes on tasks graded for difficulty. As such they are artifacts of science, not raw mental data and certainly not mythical entities. IQs are also highly *condensed* measures, products of an averaging process of many scores obtained on a range of diverse tasks. Other things being equal, the wider the range of tasks, the more reliable is the IQ. Many things contribute to successes and failures on tasks averaged out in the IQ: disposition or native endowment (including special talents or lacks), exposure to a stimulating environment, motivational states, enduring personality traits, as well as momentary or transient conditions such an anxiety, preoccupation, depression, fatigue, or bouts of madness. These diverse contributions mean that the IQ is not likely to be static over long periods of time, despite the fact that in normal persons, it has considerable stability and in children a respectable degree of predictability. But it is vulnerable to psychopathological and neurological conditions as well as to situations of cultural deprivation, especially in childhood, and it is precisely this vulnerability that makes intelligence testing clinically significant.

Usually, the clinician is spared from embroilment in the scientific and ideological controversies about the IQ (mostly on the nature-nurture question) since his concern is not typically with an allegedly absolute IQ in any person. The clinician's interest is in the IQ's fluctuations over time, for instance, as a means of ascertaining the existence or exacerbation of deficits, or so as to assess the impact of derangement, inhibitions, or faulty reality contact on a patient's intellectual functioning. In addition, he may wish to have only a rough estimate of the person's intelligence level (not the precise IQ), for instance, to arrive at a diagnosis of mental retardation (and its degree of severity), or to judge suitability for a demanding, verbally oriented, and intellectually taxing psychotherapy. Knowledge of intelligence levels and patterns is of course also needed for psychiatric advice about vocational choice, study plans, or job placement, and for organizing a suitable therapeutic milieu during hospitalization.

The IQ is a function of the intelligence test used, not only in terms of the different varieties of intelligence samples that characterize each test, but also in terms of the statistical treatment of scores, the ratios of mental age to chronological age, and the standard deviations from the mean. Basically, however, intelligence is regarded in all tests as a biopsychological variable that in large populations follows the normal Gaussian distribution curve (see Figure 1). Qualitative groupings of intelligence levels, translated from IQ ranges, are mapped as dispersions from the mean.

In sampling sizable populations that include persons with

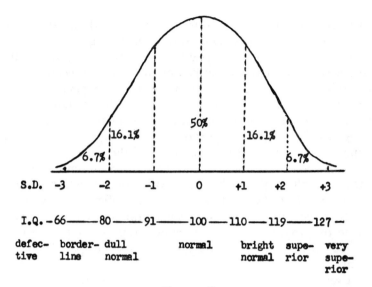

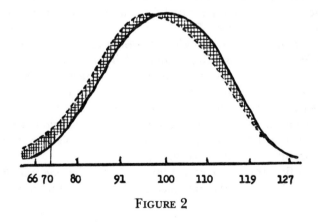

FIGURE 1

pathological conditions, it appears, however, that the distribution curve of IQs is somewhat skewed toward the left, in the direction of lower IQs (see Figure 2). This skewing teaches an important point. It illustrates the sad fact that a good many people function below their own norm or potential, due to a great variety of conditions ranging from cultural deprivation

FIGURE 2

through neurotic inhibitions, illnesses, and accidents to psychotic disturbances and severe neurological disorders. Many people are handicapped, but there are cardinal differences in the reasons and causes of those handicaps. Some defective and quite a few borderline defective persons are so by virtue of the statistically expected distribution of intelligence itself: These are normal biological variants of intelligence, in equal proportion to the ˙superior and very superior persons at the upper end of the scale. The cross-hatched section of Figure 2 would then represent an increment over the expected biological variation, for which specific causes need to be postulated. These deficits are *acquired,* whether they are functional or structural, temporary or static, stable or progressive. The increment represents people who can be considered ill, handicapped, or in some special way deviant.

Even those regarded by measurement as mentally retarded (often legally defined as persons with an IQ below 70) form two different groups: Some are handicapped by their native intellectual dullness, making them ill-adapted to a complex society that puts a premium on verbal abilities and school learning, whereas others are victims of neurological, psychological, or social mishaps, i.e., of acquired deficits.

We have stressed that the IQ is both a compound and a condensed measure. The IQ summarizes in numerical language a *pattern* of intellectual functioning, which in test language is called *scatter.* The essence of scatter is presented in Figure 3, taken from the Wechsler-Bellevue Intelligence Scale. The first column lists the samples of intelligence taken, which are much like the series of intelligence indicators listed above (pp. 56–60), and are known as *subtests.* On each subtest the subject's successes and failures are given a raw score, which is converted into a weighted score with values ranging from 1 to 17, allowing the drawing of a *scattergram* by placing marks in the appropriate number columns.

The first thing a scattergram teaches is that *the same IQ* (or IQ range) can be the product of very different patterns of

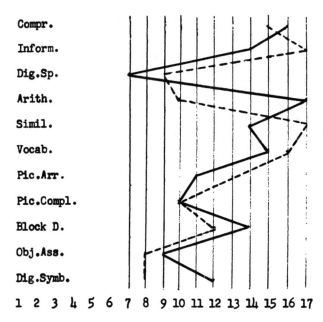

FIGURE 3. Person A (————): Verbal IQ 130; Performance IQ 107; Total IQ 121. Person B (— — —): Verbal IQ 127; Performance IQ 114; Total IQ 122.

intellectual functioning, because the IQ is computed by an averaging process. The figure contains the scatters obtained from two persons with doctoral degrees, with IQs of 121 and 122; both psychiatrically normal, one excelling in speed (on arithmetic, block design, and digit symbol), but bored by the (for him) nonchallenging task of digit span; the other much slower and more cautious, but with a talent for precise and shrewd verbal reasoning and astute thought processes (comprehension, information similarities, vocabulary). The scatters teach, second, that, especially at the higher intelligence levels, *the scores are not bound to be the same for all tasks presented:* What comes through is an individual pattern of relative strengths and weaknesses.

Third, *the vulnerability of intellectual functioning to psychopathological conditions produces diagnostic scattergrams.* Figures 4 and 5 illustrate how, in a few psychiatric cases, the pathological condition impinges selectively on the patient's intellectual processes. Premorbidly, the patients represent different levels of intelligence and different degrees of formal schooling.

Figure 4 is the scattergram of a young woman with a college education, suffering from severe depression with suicidal ruminations. The vocabulary score, information, and object assembly, as well as her educational achievement, suggest intelligence in the bright normal range—yet the IQ registered at

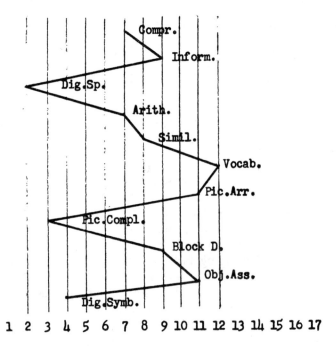

FIGURE 4. Test scatter of a patient with severe depression. Verbal IQ 95; Performance IQ 72; Total IQ 88.

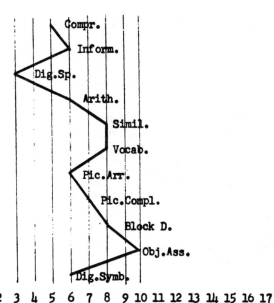

FIGURE 5. Test scatter of a patient with temporal lobe syndrome. Verbal IQ 80; Performance IQ 89; Total IQ 84.

this time is only 88. She suffers from inattention due to morbid preoccupation, finds it hard to concentrate on objective tasks, feels and acts lethargically, and is slowed down, gaining no points for speed of performance on any task. Scores vary greatly, ranging from a low of 2 to a high of 12.

Figure 5 is of a 34-year-old patient with a high-school education, whose higher subtest scores and work history suggest intelligence in the upper normal to bright normal range. The actual full-scale IQ is only 84, with a nine-point difference between the verbal IQ of 80 and the performance IQ of 89. Nearly all verbal scores are significantly depressed—much below her already lowered performance scores. Even the vocabulary level is below expectation. Word-finding difficulties and other verbal memory deficit as well as marked fluctuation in attention pervaded her test responses. In the context of

clinical seizures of diverse types, a temporal lobe syndrome
was diagnosed.

Intellectual Deficit

One can learn from the foregoing illustrations that the
clinician's concern, unlike, say, that of a school administrator
or a job placement agency, is largely with the detection and
accurate description of any patient's intellectual *deficits,* using
the patient as his own norm or standard of comparison. "Deficit" is here used as a purely descriptive term, the dimensions
of which must be analyzed before it can be interpreted
etiologically.

There are several ways of using the patient as his own
standard. One way is to compare the patient's present intellectual functioning with his previous functioning, e.g., during an earlier phase of illness or during his premorbid years.
For practical reasons such longitudinal assessment can often
be made only inferentially, from school reports, work records,
observations by relatives, or the patient's testimony that he is
"slipping" in some way, "much better" now, or "has always
been very poor in mathematics." The other way is cross-
sectional: The examiner evaluates how the various aspects of
the patient's intellectual functioning at the present time stack
up against one another. There are two basic methods for this
evaluation. One derives from the fact that some intellectual
functions are more refractory to psychopathological en-
croachment than others: For instance, vocabulary tends to remain rather stable even in serious anxiety states, depressions,
and character disorders (but not in the aphasias, of course).
Hence poor reasoning, slow thinking, faulty perception, difficulties in concentration, or bad eye-hand coordination may
flagrantly deviate from the patient's good word usage, thereby
providing evidence of inner inconsistency in marshaling his
intellectual resources. The other method derives from the fact
that certain mental abilities of importance for intelligence are
selectively vulnerable to brain disorders, leading to more or

less circumscribed losses that stand out against the patient's intact functions, or, especially in adults with some past achievements to their credit, against their previous intellectual accomplishments. For instance, a parietal lobe disturbance may disorganize all the patient's space relations, a temporal lobe syndrome may create word-finding difficulties and memory loss, a lesion at the angular gyrus may produce a Gerstmann[16, 17] syndrome (left-right disturbance, finger anomia, constructional apraxia, agraphia, acalculia, and, often, hemianopia).

From this short discussion, several dimensions of deficit emerge. Descriptively, deficit may be *general or specific*. General deficits imply a widespread inadequacy of intellectual functioning in which a good many, if not most, intellectual tasks are adversely affected. Serious disorganization of psychotic proportions with grossly inadequate reality testing tends to leave many traces on intellectual performance; so do senility, the presenile dementias, and the majority of cases of mental retardation. Specific deficit is seen in anxiety states, which encroach especially on attention and concentration; in psychopathic personalities suffering from impulsivity, which affects their reasoning and planning abilities but leaves perceptual-motor functions intact, if not excellent in regard to speed; and in the aphasias, apraxias, and agnosias, which are by definition circumscribed losses.

A second descriptive dimension of deficit is its *acute or chronic* character, a distinction that obviously implies something about its duration. How long has the patient functioned intellectually below par as against his own baseline? Finer features of this dimension address the question whether the deficit found is, longitudinally speaking, relatively *stable* (and for how long), or whether it shows a noticeable increment, e.g., as a progressive deterioration, and at what rate; or, conversely, whether there is a noticeable betterment over time.

A third dimension of deficit reckons with the patient's development. Is the deficit *native or acquired?* Again only descriptively, was the patient always slow in mentation, did he take his developmental hurdles at a retarded rate, was he

earmarked as handicapped from the beginning of life
(whether his condition was explained as pre-, peri-, or post-
natal), or was there somewhere a discernable turning point at
which things seemed to go downhill (personality change in
adolescence; menopausal depression; a head injury; febrile
convulsions in childhood)? Or was there an insidious process,
spanning perhaps as much as a decade, in which an over-all
worsening was noted (suspiciousness developing into paranoia
during the middle years; the exacerbation of moodiness into
pronounced mood swings; fluctuating, spotty, somatic complaints summating in evidence of multiple sclerosis)?

The fourth dimension leaves description for a rough
etiological classification. Deficit can be *functional or organic*
(structural). These terms are charged with theoretical assumptions, the gist of which is that functional deficits are held to be
reversible since they are largely determined by emotional and
motivational factors, whereas organic deficits are held to be
largely irreversible since they derive from structural brain
changes or grossly abnormal physiochemical nervous processes. "Structure" is a broad concept that does not apply solely
to the body and the nervous system; it can also apply to personality, for instance, to the enduring traits that make up
character (which in turn may be rooted in genetic anlagen,
hormone balances, body morphology, and other constitutional
factors, as well as in early childhood experiences that shaped
the personality into a definite pattern or type.) In this sense,
there may also be structural-characterological deficits of intelligence, for instance, poor verbal ability (and all associated
skills such as reading and writing, with subsequent aversion to
literary culture, an early dropping out from the educational
system, but perhaps with marked mechanical aptitude), or
awkwardness on all perceptual-motor tasks with pronounced
trends to flights of fantasy.

Etiological inferences about intellectual deficit must take all
descriptive dimensions into account, particularly the longitudinal ones. Assigning etiology requires knowledge of syndromes of psychiatry as well as of neurology and their bor-
derlands, and demands a holistic kind of reasoning. For in-

stance, the lethargy of the depressed patient (Figure 4) was clinically so conspicuous and stood in such marked contrast to her history that the current intellectual deficits could be seen as due to temporary intrusions of her acute depression on her stream of thought, reversible if her mood could be elevated and her interest redirected to the outer world. The registered deficits of the temporal lobe syndrome patient (Figure 5) tally with her subjective experience of an insidious decline of her mental capacities, largely independent of her motivational states and felt as ego alien. Moreover, the score pattern and the observation of dysphasic and verbal memory problems happen to form a known psychological correlate of a neurological syndrome, evoking the likelihood of a brain-induced deficit. In such a case, it is important to know whether there is progressive decline, and if so, what its rate is, in order to draw further inferences about the nature of the assumed brain lesion.

Memory

Among the cognitive faculties of man, memory holds a strategic place. It is the basis of all learning. Communal mnemonic techniques (poetic narration, writing, art, etc.) are the basis of culture. A whole school of psychiatric thought, psychoanalysis, started from observations about the failures of memory. Repression, that basic psychic defense mechanism, is the attempt to exclude something from memory. Interest in amnesias is shared by psychiatry and neurology alike. Memory was among the first mental processes studied by experimental psychology; it was also the cornerstone of Plato's philosophy. The improvement of memory has been sought assiduously by many would-be savants, past and present; failures of memory have been known for ages as the symptoms of many forms of incipient mental disorder. Hence the frequency of memory questions in any psychiatric examination, from the rather poor, if not trite, "What did you have for breakfast this morning?" to "What is your first childhood memory?"

Consider the following letter written by a psychatric patient, an elderly man recently hospitalized:

Dear Sister:

I am still in the Hospital yet, but I am feeling a little better.

I am getting the best of care from the people and can say I receive the best of treatment from the people of the Hospital and I have corporation from the cast which is very coporated and cast are very corropated in every way.

I hope you and Bunny are in good health and are getting along fine.

I have the best of corporation from the cast.

I hope you and Bunny are in the best of health and can enjoy Xmas to the best of your feelings and also can enjoy the "New Year" to the best of your ability.

I have a great for the cast here in the institution as they are very co-operation in all ways.

I hope you and Bunny are in good health and are happy and enjoying the best of life.

I have made a lot of friends while here. Everyone is so coapporative and Kind.

I hope you and Bunny are in the best of health.

I have been here for a few days and everyone is so co-operative and good.

Be good and I write you lates, be good and I will write you again soon. Hoping you and Bunny the best of health and a very great Christmas, as I think I will enjoy the one here in the ward.

Love to you and Bunny and a Merry Xmas.

Love to Both

What, really, is *perseveration*—the official psychiatric word that describes this letter? Why would a person, seeing in front of him what he has just written, repeat the same ideas over and over again? Are these ideas so important to him that they constitute a preoccupation, or is his mind so unproductive of ideas that he has to make do with the few notions he has? Is his mind so empty that seeing the line he has just written provides the only cue for content—which then turns into the "same old" content? Does his mind echo itself—response being taken as stimulus in endless cycles? Does his hand move mechanically over the paper—imitating previous strokes and slants—thoughtlessly? Is the patient crazy—denying the tragic reality of his hospitalization and turning it into the fantasy of one great Christmas party?

Comparison with another case might give clues. A patient coming out of brain surgery was wheeled on a stretcher back to the ward just as I entered it. When I said "Good morning!" to the other patients, the voice under the bed sheet started: "MORNING, MORNing, MORning, MOrning, Morning, morning, morning . . .," mechanically repeating the phrase, parrotlike, about fifteen times, diminuendo until it was barely audible. A perfect case of echolalia, this: a reflexlike repetition of some phonemes, not intended to be communicative or meaning-laden, just an echoic response to sound.

Our letter writer was not like a parrot. He wished to communicate, with concern and feeling, and he wanted to give information. But he suffered from severe memory loss, not only for recent but for remote events, on account of which his mind lacked the associative richness and versatility that make for diversity. He felt quite empty of mind, able to *register* what went on around him but unable to *retain* it or later to *reproduce* it at will. An amiable fellow of quiet temperament and pleasant disposition, he was not particularly defensive about his condition either, taking everything in his stride. His very *dearth of ideas* may have saved him from overengaging in fantasy, as delusional patients might do, or from filling his memory gaps with scrambled, inventive elaborations, as patients with Korsakoff syndrome might do.

The case shows that memory is a complex process—actually only a name for a number of quite diverse processes. It contains at least the following basic "three Rs":

registration	*retention*	*recall*
intake	storing	recognition
experiencing	traces	recollection
alertness	synaptic connec-	retrieval
attention	tions	
	engrams	

Since the adequacy of memory can be assessed only in terms of recall (voluntary, spontaneous, or under artificial conditions such as hypnosis), clinical knowledge about registration and retention is bound to be only inferential. For recall to be possible surely registration must be normal, with adequate attention to the data to be remembered. And proper engram formation and associative linkages must occur for recollection to ensue. Disorders of attention and concentration doom the memory process, or at least handicap it; retention defects, however caused, interfere with retrieval possibilities.

Furthermore, the three-R series is vastly complicated by the stratified nature of consciousness. While alertness implies a conscious attending to something, many things are attended to marginally, through preconscious or unconscious registrations that also leave their traces. Intentional as the selectiveness of consciousness may seem to be, the unconscious has its own selectiveness, which allows us to note certain things whose registration and retention will be evidenced later, when a recollection occurs. This point is demonstrated, for instance, in the *Pötzl*[18] *effect:* After looking intently at complex pictures, subliminally presented by a tachistoscope, subjects reproduced in their dreams over several successive nights significant details of the pictures, of which they were unaware while viewing them, and which they could not recall immediately after looking at them. Only retrospective analysis showed how much had been taken in and retained beyond the span of conscious awareness and voluntary recall.

This order of observations lies at the heart of hypnosis, where the ratio of conscious to unconscious processes is changed in such a way that people on the one hand engage in complex acts of which they remain afterwards oblivious, if so instructed, while on the other hand "forgotten" memories may be recalled that had thus far remained unavailable to ordinary consciousness. The word *forgotten* is put in quotation marks to throw doubt, retrospectively, on its genuineness. How can we speak of forgetting when certain memories, not hitherto available, can nevertheless be retrieved under special conditions? Is recall a function of a particular state of consciousness and of the motivational states impinging on it?

It is indeed. And that is why a special word had to be invented to set such forgetting apart from the forgetting that follows from poor registration or faulty retention and the mind's normal organic "wear and tear" effects, at one time considered to be a neuronal trace decay. That word is *repression*, suggesting a dynamic process in which some force (or mental "reason") is pushing away from awareness some bit of experience that has its own force (or "meaning") for lingering in the mind. Repression is to be understood as an active neuronal inhibition. The wear and tear of memory follows *Ribot's*[19] *famous law:* With advancing age and the normal decline of mental faculties, *recent* memories fade out first, then the more *remote* memories as well. Patients with memory loss for recent events may have considerable mental traffic with childhood experiences, still knowing the names of their first-grade teacher and the children they played with—until these begin to fade out too, gradually. Repression, on the contrary, is a selective process directed against painful, shameful, irritating, or stressful memory fragments (and their associated ideas or feelings) whose recurrence in consciousness would upset the accustomed homeostasis. Like flotsam in a river, such memories would despoil the clarity of the stream, unless they are decomposed and absorbed. Repression implies the possibility of unrepression, thus proving that it is a functional process. Repression is not, however, merely a *post hoc* attempt to expel from awareness or thought something that has already been taken in. Repression is also a warding-off maneuver at the gate of awareness: It can affect registration by narrowing consciousness, by selective screening, or even by a general obnubilation of perception, thus preventing registration. It can be spread like a blanket or a veil before the mind's eye and over the mind's content.

This fact is demonstrated by the different qualities of amnesias. A man drives home from work and at six o'clock, a few blocks from his home, has a serious car accident producing a concussion that "knocks him out." He comes to at eight o'clock, lying in a hospital bed, first recognizing his anxious wife. Nurse, doctor, and wife ask what happened, and the patient recalls being hit by an oncoming car on narrow Grove

Street—he can still feel the fear that overcame him when the other car swerved in his direction. Then things went blank—he is now lying in bed, bandaged, with some pain, but, thank God, no loss of limb. Soon he'll be better. All's well that ends well. Thus the doctor notes a *simple amnesia,* covering the period from six to eight o'clock on Tuesday evening. Next evening, the doctor returns for a visit and again asks about the accident. He now finds that the patient no longer remembers the scene of the accident, and indeed cannot even recall leaving work to go home. He can no longer recollect what he did at work that afternoon—the last thing he is sure of is eating lunch in the cafeteria with some friends. The amnesia has spread backwards in time to encompass a longer period: from a simple amnesia it has become a *retrograde amnesia.* Maybe it will spread further back—next week the patient may have to face the fact that all of that gruesome Tuesday is a complete blank in his mind, irretrievably lost. It may also happen that the amnesia spreads forward in time: On Thursday the patient may no longer remember that his wife was at his bedside when he came to at eight o'clock on Tuesday. All of Tuesday night may be lost to retrieval: Life began again on Wednesday morning with breakfast, despite the perfect clarity of his consciousness at eight the previous evening. The simple amnesia has become an *anterograde amnesia.*

Do not such *post hoc* elaborations of an unconscious episode suggest a dynamic process resembling a purposive eviction of memories from the stream of thought? What is "mind" and what is "brain" in such complicated affairs? How does psychological purpose stack up against neurological fate? Though there is no final answer to these questions, since so little is known about neuronal integration, there is a clinical rule of thumb to distinguish two plausibilities. If the patient is distressed by his progressive forgetting and "racks his brain" to put the pieces together, the ego-alien quality of his memory loss suggests a neurological cause, although even in this case mind cannot be separated from brain. But if he is unperturbed by it, taking it all with a "belle indifférence" or even with some glee or misplaced pride, the scales seem tipped to-

ward an explanation in terms of motivated forgetting, or repression (which surely is also a neuronal event). Empirical
proof would lie in any successful attempt to reverse the amnesia, from a sodium amytal interview to the occurrence of
traumatic fragments of the accident in the patient's dreams—if
he could recall them the next morning! In fact, it may be
found that only the retro- and anterograde elaborations of the
originally simple amnesia are reversible.

Further evidence of repression as a memory dynamism is
found in the phenomenon of multiple personality. Using
Stevenson's Dr. Jekyll and Mr. Hyde as an example, when the
person assumes the Jekyll personality he is amnesic about
anything pertaining to Hyde, and vice versa. A partial, selective amnesia keeps each of the assumed personalities pure and
the basic person intact, at least to the extent that the latter is
trying to maintain the feeling that he is only *one* at a time.
The partial amnesia serves, by selective inattention and selective repression, to keep up a semblance of personality organization.

Nearly all the foregoing syndromes and symptoms constitute memory deficit or dysfunction, whether of organic or
functional origin. More difficult to comprehend are the
paramnesias, which are in essence temporary, often paroxysmal, disruptions of consciousness entailing conviction of recognition that the subject himself considers impossible or false.
The French term *fausse reconnaissance* emphasizes the falseness
of such recognitions. Paradigmatic is the *déjà vu* experience,
which Emily Dickinson has described so vividly:

A thought went up my mind today
That I have had before
But did not finish, some way back,
I could not fix the year

Nor where it went, nor why it came
The second time to me,
Nor definitely what it was
Have I the art to say

But somewhere in my soul I know
I've met the thing before,
It just reminded me, 'twas all,
And came my way no more.[20]

The experience is paradoxical: Something is perceived (Dickinson says "thought") with the startling conviction that it is
strikingly familiar in all details, yet the person finds it impossible to come up with a true recollection that matches it. It
leaves a nagging feeling of unfittingness; in fact, the person is
bound to judge that he cannot have had exactly the same perception before. In other words, something in the stream of
thought is given the attribute of familiarity, but unconvinc-
ingly, without empirical evidence, and the person's memory is
not coming to his aid in tracing or locating it. Conversely, in
the experience of *jamais vu* something patently familiar is perceived with a startling conviction of newness and a feeling of
"this is the first time," equally paradoxical because the person
knows that he has seen it before. Such psychic events cannot
be classified simply as hyper- or hypomnemonic processes:
They seem unique combinations of fragments of both. The
same is true for their analogues: *déjà raconté, déjà pensée, déjà
entendu,* Jackson's reminiscences, etc. The recollection (*déjà . . .*)
or the failure of recognition (*jamais . . .*) is illusory. That is why
the paramnesias may be misnamed as disorders of memory; it
seems more likely that they are dysfunctions of image formation, time sense, or the unity of consciousness.

Freud[21] saw the paramnesias as products of repression, or
rather as manifestations of attempted but incomplete repression. This understanding is clearer in those longer-lasting
states described as *feelings of familiarity or unfamiliarity,* often
mentioned as early precursors of schizophrenic conditions.
For instance, a person is at a party, with friends or relatives he
knows well, only to be gradually overcome by the feeling that
these people are strangers and that he is in a strange place; or
conversely, he is indeed in strange company but develops the
feeling that he knows these people well, perhaps even their
innermost thoughts. In these states something happens to the
rapport between the person and those around him, creating

unexpected feelings of distance or closeness, with changes in the person's sense of identity vis-à-vis his objects. Aspects of object relations and the sense of belonging become repressed, maybe denied or split off from the self-concept, and these mechanisms now seem to operate at the point of registration, not retention or recall.

Can memory function in an exaggerated way? The term *hypermnesia* suggests so. If the term is taken to designate an unusually good memory, it may pertain to special talents such as a photographic memory, a keen memory for melodic lines, or an excellent retention of names. But if the term means that a person's thoughts are beset by vivid memories that haunt him or forcefully intrude on his mental activities, we have a disturbing interference phenomenon. Traumatic experiences may preoccupy the waking mind or populate one's dreams; past misdeeds may take the limelight in the inner world of a depressed patient; anxiety-laden memories may linger unduly and interfere with work to be done, and when a person feels seriously wronged he may devote himself to revengeful thoughts and spinning elaborate plots. Emily Dickinson saw the activity of memory functions in remorse:

Remorse is memory awake,
Her parties all astir,
A presence of departed acts
At window and at door. . . .[22]

Any preoccupation with the past suggests that memory processes can evolve into highly charged, more or less isolated tension systems seeking discharge. In people with a strong goal-orientation, interrupted tasks linger on in memory like quasi drives until closure can be reached—the *Zeigarnik*[23] *effect.* Jung[24] spoke of "complexes," nuclei of associations with magnetic power to attract new threads of experience, which implies something like a hypermnesia for ideas with a high valence.

Obsessions and fixed ideas may be sustained by hypermnemonic tendencies, but they are more typically regarded as thought pathologies, which are taken up in the next chapter.

Chapter 6

Assessing Part Processes: Cognition— Thought and Thought Organization

When Köhler[25] experimented with apes on Tenerife, engaging them in problem solving, he always started with a perceptual situation. A hungry monkey is in a cage with bars through which he can stick his arms. Outside the bars, just beyond arm's length, lie some bananas; somewhere in the cage lies a stick. Will the monkey, eager to get the bananas, discover the stick and use it as a means to his end? It all depends. When the stick lies in front of him, between himself standing before the bars and the bananas outside, he may soon grab it and push the fruit toward him; if it lies behind him or in a remote corner of the cage it takes much longer, and more intelligence, for the monkey eventually to regard it as a potential tool and use it. First the animal must detach himself momentarily from the visual lure of the bananas, turning his back on them, yet remembering them and his purpose of getting them, making a detour to see and get the stick, and return with his stick-lengthened arm to the lure. He must *back off from the perceptual field,* delay his gratification, and suspend his impulse so as to restructure the situation operationally. The monkey's discovery, his "Aha" experience of finding something that can serve as a means to his end, goes hand in hand with his restructuring the given field of perceptual data, establishing between the objects dynamic relations of his own making, serving his goals. Similarly, when one shows children a straight metal rod and then sticks it halfway under water, the visual impression strikes the naïve observer either as two rods lined up at an angle of less than 180° or as one rod sharply bent at the water level. The child's task is to bring all these sense data together, take account of their transformations, and come up with the thought that a straight stick stuck into water appears bent but physically remains straight. In a word, *thinking stands in a relation of some tension to perceiving:* It consists of a restructuring of perceptual data, of imposing an original human structure on perceptual data, or of establishing relations between perceptual data, serving the thinker's own special purposes.

Though there is some margin of freedom for the individual to restructure his perceptual field whimsically or even haphazardly, human purposes are sufficiently shared to impose certain canons on thinking. As members of a culture engaging in common tasks and wanting to communicate with one another, we demand that thinking be consistent, logical, clear, purposive, fruitful, expressible, and have references to the observable world, a tradition of thought, and a language system, following widely accepted rules. One tinkers with these rules only at the risk of being pronounced mad or stupid, more rarely eccentric, and very occasionally original or creative. Though thinking may seem an exquisitely private affair from one angle, it is consensual and public from another angle, if only because so much of it is done within the framework and with the tools of one nation's language.

A very important benefit of thinking is that it is more *economical* than action. It serves economy of living, allowing us to experiment with our world without drastically intervening in it. Bain[26] held that thinking is a restrained speaking and acting; Watson[27] defined thinking as implicit speech; and Freud[28] saw thinking as provisional experimentation with action, using only small quantities of energy. Interposed as it is between percept or impulse and action, thinking *delays* motor

response, *refines and adapts* it through anticipation and experimental trial runs, or *substitutes* for it.

The "world of thought" is not a replica of the sensory
world; it is both less and more than it. Particularly through
concept formation and abstraction, thought reduces the chaotic manifold of the sensory world to a more manageable scale
and fixes its flux; but through fantasy and image formation it
also elaborates the sensory world or supplements it with entirely new entities such as ideas, which have no sensory reality.
Both possibilities affect the consensual validation of thought
because they imply that reality testing is not a simple affair of
checking one's thoughts with the data of the sensory world.
One also has to check one's thoughts with the thoughts of
others, with cultural traditions, with the "world of thought"
(i.e., ideas, including fictions) handed down through the gen-
erations, and with the kind of ideation that prevails in one's
community. For there are all kinds of thought that meet with
some group's approval: scientific thought, political thought,
poetic or romantic thought, practical or utilitarian thought,
creative thought, philosophical thought, cosmic thought, pure
thought, and that most indefinable yet down-to-earth kind of
thinking called "common sense."

Despite these subtleties, there are some useful psychiatric
benchmarks for judging the normality or pathology of a person's thought processes or thought content. Patent madness or
craziness come across clearly in deranged thinking, which
leads neither the professional psychiatrist nor the ordinary
citizen astray. Summing up centuries of psychiatric discernment, topped off by Freud's[29] distinction between the primary
process governed by pleasure seeking and the secondary process governed by reality testing, and Bleuler's[30] descriptions of
autistic thought, McKellar[31] envisions a scale:

    R:A   A:R

R————————————————————————————————A

R-thinking (for reality-oriented thought) and A-thinking (for
autistic thought) are by definition distinct, but empirically

occur in certain ratios, because most thinking is stratified in conscious and unconscious layers or patterns acting concomitantly. Most thinking is somewhere on the continuum between R and A, in ratios that have various degrees of approximation to R/A or A/R. R and R/A thought honors the obvious features of reality, such as that one cannot walk through a hard wall, that 2 and 2 are 4, that Joe Doe is not Buddha or Hitler, that apples are not oranges, that one must make money to live in an industrial society, that checks cannot be drawn on empty bank accounts, and that Judge Schreber[32] cannot have been God's wife as he claimed to be. To deny these truths is folly; to assert their contraries is wishful thinking or engagement in fantasy—proof that one has lost contact with reality. R and R/A thinking have public references and can be consensually validated; they can be expressed in the words of a communal language, and the meaning of any word used by two speakers has a degree of stability and sameness that makes verbal exchange possible. The words retain their common meaning, despite the fact that they may have idiosyncratic surplus meaning or connotations unique to the individual speaker or listener.

Not so with autistic thought. Its origins and many of its referents are private and idiosyncratic to the person generating it. Guided by the pleasure principle, it seeks satisfaction of the thinker's own wishes or gives vent to his emotions in disregard of any objective frame of reference. We are all autistic in our dreams, but when dreams are enacted openly as if they were actualities of the waking state, and when dream thoughts are offered as items of serious discourse with others, the thought process is derailed and communication comes to naught. Autistic thought is private, unverifiable, outside the canons of reason, and presents puzzles in communication. It disobeys the principle of noncontradiction (A ≠ B), the rules of logic, and the discipline of language. When the nurse says, "Give me a hand," and the patient replies, "No, I can't spare it," words and meanings are distorted, and intentions grossly misjudged. When a patient gets panicky at thirty-three minutes past six because he thinks that the two hands of the wall clock above his head will become an arrow meant to pierce him, he may have many private associations that subjectively justify the threat, but he overlooks the simple, innocuous nature of clock hands.

Concept Formation and Its Derangements

To clarify once more the tension between phenomenal perception and conceptual thought, let us assume that young chicks are trained to look for their food grains only in triangular trays of the form shown in Figure 1A. When that habit has been established, the experimenter wants to study its generalization potential, and introduces two alternative trays (Figure 1B and C). He finds that generalization is much quicker from A to C than from A to B. Why? The answer is that A and C are *impressionistically* more alike than A and B. A rational thinker, however, will establish entirely different relations among the three figures: He groups A and B in one *conceptual order*, the class of triangles, relegating C to the different class of trapezoids. In other words, conceptual thought imposes on the perceptual world a new order that follows the dictates of reasoning, not impressions. Immediate impressions

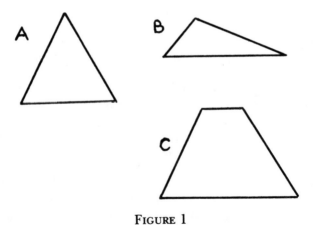

FIGURE 1

notwithstanding, the world is now organized according to a classification system that serves the purposes of man and is commensurate with the way his mind works. For the human mind, impressions are only the starting point of thought, not the "stuff" of it.

Conceptual thought hinges on the capacity to establish *identity* between various stimulus configurations, e.g., by regarding them as appearances or forms of the same thing: the phases of the moon offer three different appearances (Figure 2), but only one concept—moon. Even the "absent

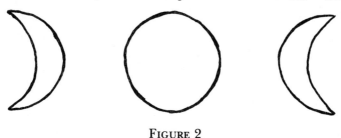

FIGURE 2

moon" is conceptually taken as a presence! This principle of conceptual thought also has some bearing on a person's self-concept: Can he keep the various aspects of his personality together in the conviction that they are all appearances of *one* self, or does he find some aspects so different or discordant that he puts them in different classes, through dissociation from his stream of consciousness, memory, and vital feelings, and ending up in a multiple personality syndrome?

Another requirement of conceptual thought is the capacity to establish *equivalence:* Such obviously different things as a table, a chair, a desk, and a wall mirror are regarded as *belonging to the class of furniture.* Clearly, such a grouping is not established on the basis of physical forms or visual impressions, but on grounds of use, the spatial clusters they form in houses, the ease in living they offer, the stores in which they can be bought, the craftsmen who make them, etc.

Equivalence judgments may be seriously impaired in various pathological conditions. In some states of brain damage the world is a cornucopia of particular, discrete items: this particular apple in front of me on my table, that pear hanging outside on the tree limb. All things are doomed to remain concrete items—the patient cannot arrive at the class concept: fruit. In such *concretism,* the patient's language also tends to be specific: He speaks of *the* or *this* apple and not typically of *an* apple, and he is likely to be even more specific by adding its sensory qualities: the *red* apple, this *small* apple, etc.

In schizophrenic thought, equivalence judgments tend to be wild or spurious. "In what way are praise and punishment alike?" "Both begin with the letter 'P'." "In what way are a fly and a tree alike?" "That would be feet. A fly has feet, and you can measure how many feet a tree is." That such derangements are not direct results of poor intelligence is illustrated by the very bright but also very paranoid patient who, when asked, "What is an apple?", answered, "You eat it—our first love—and our mother Eve." The simple fruit, the metaphorical "apple of the eye," and the legendary cause of man's fall from Paradise were all rolled into one, the patient neatly ticking off very different orders of representation and different levels of abstraction.

Both identity and equivalence judgments involve the capacity for *abstraction.* To abstract, one has to disengage oneself from anything's immediate and total impression in order to select from it one or more attributes that are important to one's purposes. Thought has various levels of abstraction; these result in groupings of greater or lesser *span,* or classes. The zoological and botanical classification system of phylum, class, order, family, genus, species, and variety is an arrangement from very large to ever smaller groups at descending levels of abstraction.

Hence we can illustrate the abstraction process by the figure of a ladder standing upright on the ground of sensory reality: In the accompanying sketch (Figure 3), SR is the unassorted amalgam of items, things, animals, people, machines, trees, houses, etc., presented to our senses. The room in which I sit offers a desk, a desk chair, several easy chairs, some tables, and a hundred other things. At the SR level, un-

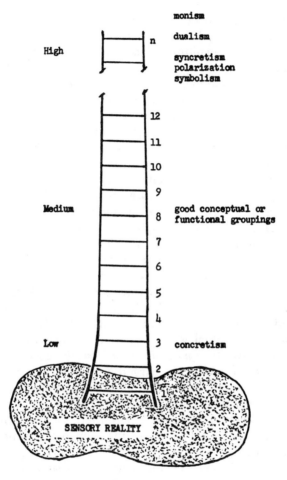

FIGURE 3

abstracted, these are all separate things. When I recognize desk, chairs, and tables as "furniture" I go, as it were, two or three rungs up the abstraction ladder, removing myself from the concreteness of each item and selecting instead some common attributes that make them furniture: things to sit on or to sit at for the work I am doing. Some of my easy chairs, however, look so homey that they could well stand in my living room. In a finicky, hairsplitting mood, I might consider that I have two kinds of furniture in my office: office furniture and home furniture. That distinction brings me down again to, say, the second rung of my abstraction ladder. "Furniture" is now subdivided into two "lower" classes, each of which is smaller (with less span) than the "higher" category. The lower classes of concepts with smaller spans are fairly close to the observable items; the higher classes of concepts are further removed from concrete, sensory reality. Or, as one might say: the less abstraction, the more specific; the more abstraction, the less specific (and sometimes the more abstruse). Abstraction is in part a process of *reduction*.

For clinical assessment of thought processes, abstraction levels matter greatly. In some syndromes the abstraction capacity is grossly deficient: Certain forms of brain damage doom a patient to dwell concretistically at, or very close to, the ground level of sensory reality with its discrete, individual items. In syndromes of a hyperideational kind the patient prefers to dwell at very high levels of abstraction, and thinks in terms of colossal abstractions of great cosmic moment to him: He makes conceptual groupings of the order *man or woman, good or evil, the All, unity, divine or demonic, world disaster,* or *rebirth,* each of which is charged with affect and meaning. Much of what we call adequate reality testing and good thought organization boils down to operating at medium abstraction levels. That is the range where the common classes are, widely recognized as useful for human life, representing everyday needs, communicable constructs, and shared formulations of the differences and similarities that count, all with some degree of verifiability.

It is obvious that philosophical and religious thought tends to deal with very encompassing concepts at very high levels of abstraction, such as being or nonbeing, origin and destiny, Platonic ideas, the nature of man, Nirvana, creation. Some scientific constructs, such as the atom, curved space, or the periodic table, are also pitched at very high abstraction levels. These are not pathological abstractions: The philosopher, theologian, or scientist is aware of their purpose, symbolic status, or heuristic intent, and he can articulate these concepts.

Not so for the spurious, glib, or empty abstractions used by thought-disordered patients to solve their life conflicts or shoulder the tasks that reality may impose. A patient's conviction that "all-power is in the air . . . everything is infinite" may be a lofty thought, but it is one that is likely to interfere with his work as an automechanic and be positively dangerous when he draws too many checks on his meager bank account. If preoccupation with evil leads to the thought that everything is contaminated, no food is to be ingested and no doorknob is to be touched: everything is approached with exhausting warding-off rituals. A certain patient is presented with a heap of diverse small articles of all kinds, from which a cardboard disk is selected with the instruction to put with that disk everything that belongs with it. Soon he has put everything with the disk, passing over some very obvious and commonsensical groupings, and says, "If you figure that this [the disk] is the sun, all of this stuff would go with it, for the sun is over everything in the world." Obvious, useful, and culturally shared distinctions are here skipped in favor of an upward flight on the abstraction ladder, near that highest rung where "everything belongs" because we are now at the level of the All. The abstraction is spurious, useless, fatuous. It is an example of *syncretism:* everything is declared to be alike in some respect because in the meantime everything has been stripped of its outstanding features. It bespeaks a turning away from that order of reality where the discernible and useful distinctions are, where animals and furniture and men and machines are not one homogeneous blur, but discrete orders to be approached by different adaptive responses.

To the question "Why are shoes made of leather?", one paranoid patient with an extensive delusional system answered, in a split second and with a poker face, "For the wealth of the soul." That is no stupid, intellectually impotent response; on the contrary, it implies a capacity for word play (sole/soul) and for shifting from one realm of discourse (economics; cost range) to another (wealth as luxurious good to the spirit). Here is a penchant for *symbolic* thought, which happens to be out of place in the task setting of intelligence testing aimed at eliciting good judgment. Another patient reports that he ate rocks, cigaret butts, soap, a comb, and worms, adding "They mixed in my stomach and thus mixed the peoples of the earth. There came an end to all wars and I forestalled the destruction of the world." Here is an odd mixture of the symbolic (the ingested things standing for people) and the concrete (the patient's chewing and digesting them literally made the mix)—two extremes on the abstraction ladder are chosen to the utter neglect of the sensible middle ranges. Note also that the intended explanation takes the form of a narration, with a plot, as in myth.

On the very high rungs of the greatest abstractions, there is opportunity for transforming the philosophical dualisms of all time into fierce mythical or symbolic battles. These convey pronounced *ambivalence*, and transpose the patient's inner conflicts to cosmic dramas. Wars between good and evil, the imminent collapse of the world with the magical thought that its fate hinges on the patient's own ultimate thought, the idea of a cosmic transformation that will give birth to sexual neuters or change men into women and vice versa—these themes belong to delusional systems that habituate the patient to the use of *momentous polarizations* at symbolic levels of thought: He splits all things into left and right, clean and dirty, male and female, carnal and spiritual, good and bad, safe and dangerous, laden with cataclysmic apprehension. Ordinary distinctions and groupings are swallowed up into these large pairs of opposites.

Neglect of common, adaptive groupings also leads to *bizarre* forms of reasoning, apart from the derangements of abstraction in concretism, syncretism, and hypersymbolism. Conceptual thought requires an adequate transition from one conceptual group to another, with good linkages that are adapted to the purpose of the train of thought. Good thought has a goal: to solve a problem, to make a discovery, to guide action, to receive or convey information, etc. *Disturbances in the train of thought* are chain reasoning, flight of ideas, and certain forms of confabulation.

In *chain reasoning,* the person hops from one item of thought (or perception) to another, without a preconceived overarching scheme that gives each item its logical place. He bows rather haphazardly in the direction of reason by *forging* some link between *a* and *b, b* and *c, c* and *d,* etc., with the risk that these links are confabulated. Working on a sorting test, a patient picked out a rectangular white file card, a green paper square, a red cardboard circle, and a cardboard matchbook with the picture of a car on it, with the following "explanation" for this grouping: "This [white card] is the color of my town. It's the football field, with the bleachers running this way—I imagine the folks sitting there are squares [all square pieces of paper]. Mr. Cherry drives a green [green square] Oldsmobile [picture on matchbook] and Red Dougherty [red circle] is with them." Another patient, using different items, made seriatim the following grouping: "You'd connect the *ball* to the rubber *cigar* because they are rubber; and the *cigar* to the *cigaret* because they are smoking; and the *cigaret* to the *hammer* because they are both the same long shape, and the *hammer* to the rest because they are all metal."

Flight of ideas is illustrated in a patient's response to Card IX of the Rorschach test: "That's the world itself, with the USA and Russia kind of bickering back and forth [left and right side of whole card]: Statues on top are of Eisenhower and Malenkov with guns. Underneath [in pink areas] a sleeping soldier from each side who died; and the fertile world [green areas] is underneath all of it. It seems the world is kind of split between them and both have a good hold on it." And here is a spontaneous speech fragment of a hypomanic patient: "I worked with Burns for two years, and got burnt. What a hothead he was! Gosh, I am shivering—can't we close some windows here? [Moves to window.] Look at those two sitting in that car—a long-haired fellow and a short-haired girl—You'd think she is going to be on top! [Sings.] I'm sitting on top of the world."

In *Korsakoff's syndrome* (which is by no means confined to alcoholic psychosis despite frequent references in the literature to that effect) the patient's poor memory for recent

events (and immediate recall of stories) makes him fill in the
gaps between the few recalled fragments with fantasy
material—or so his productions will appear to the examiner at
first blush. A closer look may show that the bits of fantasy are
not fictitious, but derive by association from the lost items,
substituting for them in a garbled sequence. On these grounds
it has been proposed that the Korsakoff syndrome is essentially a disturbance of time sense, forcing the patient to invent
a reasonable-sounding sequence for the scattered thought
fragments that come to his mind. If this hypothesis is correct,
it would be a telling example of a disturbance in the *train* of
thought.

Fabulation in all its forms, normal as well as pathological, is
a unique device for creating order in the chaotic manifold of
percepts and thoughts. Unlike concept formation (rational,
syncretistic, concretistic, or functional) and symbolic thought,
which impose a cross-sectional order or a rational cause-and-
effect sequence on things, fabulation imposes order by a principle of unfolding. It narrates an arrangement of events in
time, in which some "truth" evolves from deeds of human or
cosmic actors by means of a plot. In this sense it is related to
myths, legends, sagas, fairy tales, and other mythopoetic literary forms. Its plot character makes it, however, a favorable
thought pattern for private delusional schemes.

Precision and Imprecision of Thought

It is with thinking somewhat as it is with living rooms:
Some rooms are always neat and tidy, with everything in its
exact place; other rooms give the impression of a rich wilderness, overgrown and dense as a jungle. This simile illustrates
the old dictum that if thinking is deep and rich, it is seldom
clear; and if it is clear, it is seldom deep. Apparently, then,
thinking has two basic stylistic options, which also means that
it can go awry in two opposite directions.

In one direction, the *boundaries of a thought can be narrowly
drawn* and tightly guarded. Overprecision is the earmark of
the thought of obsessive-compulsive neurotic persons. For in-

stance, the thought "What time is it?" may first evoke not a casual glance, but an intent look at the wrist watch, then a check on the wrist watch's accuracy by comparison with the office clock or a radio signal, then a formulation in minutes or fragments of minutes, then perhaps some thoughts about the speed of time's passing, which makes any formulation outdated the moment it is pronounced, then a reflection about different time zones on earth, with a glance at the sun, followed by new despair about the deviations within time zones, which cause the sun to stand unevenly between the western and eastern edges of the zone. Asking for an ash tray, the finicky thinker will hesitate to accept a bowl or saucer; when thinking of women, he will exclude girls, and he can hardly regard a child's hammer a tool, for to him it is only a toy, incommensurate with the "real thing." The master classifier keeps the boundaries of his concepts finickily clean and clear, allowing no fuzzy edges. Hence his sentence structure: It abounds in qualifying phrases, a clause leads to a subclause that slightly modifies the clause just stated, in an endless series of two steps forward and one step back.

In the other direction, the *separate thought can be too accommodating to other thoughts nearby,* from which shreds of meaning, sound, or content are picked up that for the person have a connection with the first. With unclear or unstable boundaries, concepts become fluid, allowing for *loose associations* between one thought or concept and another. In addition, some highly charged or valued ideas act like a sponge in the stream of thought, absorbing extraneous material, which makes them larger and larger, thus enhancing their cognitive dominance. These are the "complexes" of Jung: strong, absorbing nuclei that come to govern the patterns of association.

Perhaps the loosest connection is *clang association:* The mere sound of a word elicits a like-sounding word, and between the two some quasi-meaningful connection is forged. "Cool" sounds like "fool," and if these two are linked by sound, they must also have some deeper connection: Maybe "fools are cool-headed," which "proves that the insane are really *full* of wisdom while normal people have lost their heads."

To the question, "What is a cushion?," the patient answers,

"A bouncing enjoyment." Is this response instigated by the childhood memory of a pillow fight, or does it capture the erotic luxuriousness of a soft pillow? In either case, the association is *loose* because it leaves out the shock-absorbing function of cushions; instead it attributes animation to them so they can bounce, and shifts their function from utilitarian to aesthetic or recreational.

Looseness of association can also be part of *looseness in maintaining the intended frame of reference* or realm of discourse. When "How far did you go in school?" is answered with "About two-and-a-half miles," the questioner's intention is mistaken or negativistically distorted by spiteful punning or clever play on words. It is sometimes difficult to distinguish between organic concretism and schizophrenic literalness, but this example shows that the schizophrenic patient can move from one frame of reference to another, sometimes quite whimsically and adroitly, assuming an "as if" attitude that the organic patient would find beyond his power. "Did you have your parents on your side?," the patient is asked. Now the patient looks up and down the left side of his body and studies it intently. The point in this example is that the patient is not concretistic in the sense of being stuck to the presentation of the phenomenal world, but has the ability to concretize *words* and to literalize the language in which he is addressed. He freely interchanges sign and signified, thing and symbol, language and referents, so that communication falters and the examiner is bound to feel that he has no rapport. Listening with the third ear, the examiner knows that he is dealing with a very complex thought process, buffeted by contrary feelings, ambiguous threads of meaning, and fragmented ideas— unchecked by the reality of the workaday world and the intended frame of reference of the examiner's questions.

Thought Organization and Its Disturbances

Having reviewed concept formation and the precision of thought boundaries, we are ready to turn to thought organization for a closer look at its formal features. Thinking is a very complex activity with many parameters; in health as well as in illness it is organized so as to achieve characteristic patterns. There are diverse modes of thought, attuned to the thinker's purpose and his subject matter, and most people are capable of moving from one mode to another in order to let their thinking fit the occasion. Except for the developmental factor: Ontogenetically as well as phylogenetically, some forms of thought are an achievement that requires special readiness. As Werner,[33] Piaget,[34] and others have shown, peoples and individuals have to take certain developmental hurdles in the progression from primitive to advanced thinking. And even when those hurdles have been taken, thinking may regress again to lower forms, either involuntarily under the impact of great stress, or as a playful regression in the service of the ego.

From a clinical viewpoint, the following parameters of thought are relevant:

Secondary process	————	Primary process
Reality oriented	————	Autistic
Realistic	————	Dereistic
Rational	————	Irrational
Logical	————	Illogical
Coherent	————	Incoherent
Directed	————	Loose
Conscious	————	Unconscious
Conceptual	————	Symbolic
Communicable	————	Unspeakable
Consensually validated	————	Whimsically private
Objective	————	Subjective
Sensible-plausible	————	Bizarre

Clinical observations suggest that each of these pairs is better handled as a continuum than as a set of discrete choices. For thought is stratified, combining different levels of organization, each with different modes. The seemingly simple and straightforward thought "I am I" may contain strands of "I'd rather be than not be," "I am an awful creature," "Thank God

I am not like my father," "Don't take me for somebody else,"
"I have this excruciating pain," "You think I am male, but I
know I am female," "Nobody knows the trouble I've seen,"
"Watch out, Whitey," and a host of other fleeting feelings and
images and values. These parameters are not all the same;
each denotes a special quality, so that the words in each column are not interchangeable. Yet they do overlap more or
less and share certain values, so that the words in the first
column add up to the clinical judgment of "healthy" or "normal" thought, whereas the words in the second column give
rise to judgments of thought pathology or abnormality.

The diurnal cycle familiarizes all of us with two very different modes of thinking. In the waking state we are capable
of thinking in terms of *ideas* with conceptual properties, in the
formation of which words play a large role and whose linkages
are guided by canons of reasoning. In sleep, and in the trans-
itions to and from sleep, our thoughts turn into *images* with a
pictorial rather than verbal character, which separate and
combine not by canons of reason but by displacement, condensation, and symbolization, which offend the logical rule of
noncontradiction. This "primary process," as Freud called it, is
not chaotic—it only seems so from the point of view of the
secondary process. It is an order *sui generis,* fit for dreams,
feelingful states, and certain artistic pursuits. Using this distinction, and differentiating the two basic building blocks of
thought, namely ideas and images, we arrive at the grouping
shown in Table 1. Note that the boundaries between the four
sections are permeable, in acknowledgment of the continua we
assume; this fact allows locating an observed thought pattern
at greater or lesser proximity to any of the four dimensions.

Zone A contains the typical thought patterns of normal,
healthy traffic with the world and communication with our
fellow men. It involves checking with the way things are,
rather unreflectively and undifferentiatedly as in common
sense, or with great precision and refinement as in science. It
is grounded in a shared world, open to inspection by everyone. It allows verbalization in language that can be understood. Its concept of truth is rational, public, and accessible to

TABLE 1
PATTERNS OF THOUGHT ORGANIZATION

	Ideas	Images
Secondary Process	**A** empirical common sense scientific logical intellectualization paucity of ideas repression dissociation denial	**B** poetry allegory myth guided imagination common symbols repression
Primary Process	**C** flight of ideas superstitions fixed ideas illusions delusions incoherence bizarreness ideas of reference paranoia	**D** reverie dreams hypnopompic and hypnagogic images private symbols autistic fantasy

anyone who cares to look, think, and draw conclusions. But this zone also contains the psychiatric symptom of *intellectualization,* a special coping maneuver or defense mechanism in which a normal function is used excessively and in isolation from other functions (such as emotion, engagement in object relations, or action) so as to avoid exposure to anxiety-arousing stimuli. Intellectualization is a flight into thinking, amounting to hard cognitive work on intellectual propositions or conundrums: "What if all marriage laws were abolished?," or "Who sinned first, Adam or Eve?," or "Does goodness have any chance in a world governed by the survival of the fittest?" As these questions show, behind their cool intellectual generality may lie a hot individual concern in which the thinker has some stake. Nevertheless, the intellectualizer may address the question very rationally and have clear ideas.

Mishaps in the secondary thought process can occur without necessitating a shift to the primary process. The *paucity of ideas* found in organic conditions, particularly the aphasias, is a reduction in the availability of ideas. As one aphasic patient, highly aware of her condition, once said to me: "I can't think of anything at all any more!" Precisely to the extent that this impoverishment is felt as a handicap and experienced as an ego-alien curbing of erstwhile capacities, the style of thought within its limited range remains loyal to reality and maintains its communicative properties.

More complex, and more likely to entail some regression, are the dynamic shrinkages of thought content produced by *repression* and *dissociation*. These defenses eliminate ideas from the stream of awareness, forcing them into a different stratum of consciousness where they remain active and may produce symptoms, e.g., parapraxias, affect storms, somatic conversion reactions. These eliminations may leave the rest of thought intact, although strong repressive efforts tend to have a general dulling effect, rendering the thought process somewhat vague, unclear, and imprecise.

Denial is also eliminative, but it involves a specific distortion in affirming that the unpleasant or unacceptable fact of experience does not exist and therefore cannot gain the status of an idea. On account of this negative falsification of reality, denial is a serious pathological indicator that comes close to primary-process thought.

Zone B denotes thought patterns with a foothold in reality and much regard for interhuman communication, but whose building blocks consist predominantly of images rather than ideas. These thought patterns enlist fantasy, which, in more or less narrative fashion, establishes truth by letting it evolve in the form of a story, a plot, a happening, of acceptable plausibility or aesthetic satisfaction. *Allegory* elucidates meanings and ideas by the use of vivid and well-understood images; *myths* are not wild fictions but have a "deep structure," as Lévi-

Strauss[35] would say, which makes a discriminating point about reality that has adaptive value for a whole people. The living, *common symbols* of a community condense an intuitively grasped truth important to all its members. Much of the business of everyday life is conducted on the basis of commonly held images considered socially or culturally real—especially the rituals that regulate social transactions, the forms of address, and the paths of access we have to other people's feelings and convictions. On account of these common understandings, we do not have to take someone's saying "The world is coming to an end" literally as a cosmic disaster, but interpret it on empirical grounds as a signal of his feeling blue today. The empirical ground is that all of us have recourse to a special form of thought and language when we have profound feelings or wish to convey a moving thought.

Between the primary and the secondary process and between idea and image lies that delicate experience of a patient related by Hayward and Taylor:

> The first time I cried, you made a terrible mistake; you wiped away my tears with a handkerchief. You had no idea how I wanted to feel those tears roll down my face. At last I had some feelings that were on the outside. If only you could have licked my tears with your tongue, I would have been completely happy. Then you would have shared my feelings.[36]

This is from a schizophrenic patient's account of her psychotherapy—she is much better now and reflects on an earlier episode. She conveys something quite understandable, and quite moving in its sincerity; most of us can easily empathize with her experience. But she did, in the original episode, confuse feelings and bodily expression; she concretized tears and the therapist's licking them as the only way of sharing an emotion. A poet could have said the same thing with symbolic intent, alluding to body language as an appeal to the reader's capacity for symbolic thought. An important message would have been conveyed in aesthetic form. But this patient wanted no symbolic niceties or aesthetic finesse: She wanted tactile participation and exchange of body juices, as in complete symbiosis. While her wish may be understandable, her demand on the therapist disregards his status as a separate person, let alone his role as a professional person. Now put in the language of secondary-process thought, after the fact, the patient's reflection makes sense and conveys a plausible message, but during the event her thought was governed by the primary process.

In introspective techniques, as in *free association* and *guided imagination,* it is possible to keep the mind conspicuously open to its own thought content so as to be receptive to whatever comes up. This need not imply a weakening of reality testing—it may be done with the intention of letting the ego observe with maximal objectivity and without prejudgment the mind's spontaneous productions. Aspects of this attitude are perfected in the technique of phenomenology, letting things be without categorizing, without intellectualization, and with as little intrapsychic defensiveness as possible, so that some psychic reality can be "lit up" with intuitive clarity. One sometimes finds this approach in the Rorschach protocols of people who have undergone intensive psychotherapy, particularly psychoanalysis, resulting in a marked disinhibition that can be assumed at will, and often engaged in with some amusement. This requires, of course, a delicate balance between the strength of the observing ego and the strength of the fascination of the image. When the balance shifts so as to weaken the observing ego, we approach the primary process.

Many images are memories, and some memories are traumatic. In eliminating such images from consciousness, *repression* narrows the range of available images. And since repression tends to overshoot its goal, or to set up ripple effects, it is not only the traumatic image that becomes a blank, but any number of associated images also, to the point where a general obnubilation of thought may ensue (the famous *abaissement du niveau mental* of Janet[37]). Coupled with heightened activity of the primary process, to which the repressed images are relegated, the clear distinction between wakefulness and sleep may give way to intermediary states of consciousness—*somnambulism* or *trance states.*

Zone C comprises primary-process manifestations in which ideas are prominent. In *flight of ideas,* ideational activity is potentiated by existential concerns and absorbing problems that need solution: "Am I damned or saved?"; "When everything is closing in on me, can I find any exit?" Grandiosity is often part of it, resulting in scornful judgments of common propositions and attitudes, with much preachiness. Here is a fragment of a senile patient's flight of ideas recorded by Gesell:

> The mystery of life is solved: Harmony, Holy Bible, Nature, Reason. "Look up" elevates. "Lie down" rests. "Bow down" degrades. A man must obey Nature's laws in order to be happy. God has winked at man's ignorance too long already.[38]

And so on, in an effusive outpouring. Ideas, phrases, and aphorisms come rushing in, sometimes combined by chain associations, or clang associations. Some central concern may stand out and form a golden thread through the whole series, but scattering is not uncommon. Lofty abstractions abound; highly charged words are frequent, and a certain amount of punning may occur. Speed of thought is greatly accelerated; there is no time to pause and consider, to reflect.

What *superstitions* and *fixed ideas* have in common is that both are refractory to argument and disproof. The craze for unidentified flying objects finds many "true believers" immovable in their conviction that creatures from outer space are spying on the affairs of Homo sapiens, to plot its eventual extermination. No objective assessment will shake their fixed idea—their minds are set on it for better or worse. If coupled with great apprehension, at times bordering on panic, the idea becomes a belief, a superstition that posits malevolence to be warded off by rituals or magical counteractivity, charms, or amulets. To "knock on wood" playfully, so as to share with an audience the vestiges of his common magical ancestry, is one thing; to do it privately, unobserved, and in dead seriousness, is something else. In superstitions, fear is on the surface; in fixed ideas, it has succumbed to intellectualization, with a denial of realistic alternatives.

Fixed ideas can be seen as *obsessions:* Seeing a sharp object entails the forceful fantasy that one will cut oneself with it, complete with a vision of the bloody wound; climbing a dark stairway automatically precipitates the fantasy of meeting a robber. Fixed ideas are like *intrusive thoughts* in that their occurrence is beyond conscious control: The idea "comes by itself," self-validated by its repetitious emergence. With suspiciousness added, fixed ideas may become *ideas of reference:* "People are talking about me"; "My husband is in love with someone else and the two are plotting my downfall"; "The neighbor upstairs is seeking every opportunity to ridicule me." While these things may or may not be true, or contain some germ of reality, the patient loses all sense of proportion by assuming that others are totally preoccupied with their bad intentions, as if they had nothing else to do.

Delusions are intellectual houses of cards. Whether fragmentary or elaborately systematized, delusional ideas are fragile constructions in which the "stuff" of thought is real enough for the patient, but unchecked by the obvious features of observable reality, logic, and consensual validation. To surrender to the thought that one is Napoleon or Hitler when he is only Joe Doe is a break with reality; to speak and act like Hitler and emulate his mannerisms is a further break that elaborates the first one.

A middle-aged woman patient, for years a puzzle to the staff, interspersed seemingly normal sentences with striking neologisms. She referred to the Quonset-hut canteen on the hospital grounds as the "Ro-ro-rotunda"; to the occupational therapy quarters as the "Po-pope's home." And so on. Of pyknic body type to begin with, she had become quite obese as she was fond of snacks between meals. She even chewed bubble gum, lustily blowing globules through her puckered lips. Was the "rotunda" an allusion to the round roof of the canteen building? Did it allude to her own roundness, augmented by the overfrequent intake of canteen food? Did it allude to the bubbles blown from gum obtainable in the canteen? Why the triplication of the first syllable? Was it an arithmetical concretization of these three possible meanings? And why the name "Pope's home"—the first syllable duplicated—for the occupational therapy space in which she spent many mornings and afternoons? It took years to discover that this woman, a late convert to Catholicism, maintained an extensive delusional system: She thought she was married to the Pope, thus spending much time in his home (twice daily), and having the run of the Vatican and St. Peter's, whose structures she imposed on the humble hospital buildings (e.g., rotunda). In addition to the enumerative reasons for duplicating and triplicating the syllables of some words (roundness of the canteen roof, her own body, her obesity, the gum bubbles, etc.), she may have had ritualistic reasons, including Trinitarian symbolism, for these odd neologisms. At any rate, she had reorganized her whole world to conform to a wish, flouting the elementary features of reality and seriously obstructing communication with her fellow men. She had nestled herself into an autistic existence in which highly idiosyncratic, if not solipsistic, ideas took radical precedence over facts and shared ideas. Given her faulty premises and the tremendous elaboration of her fantasy world, she proved refractory to the messages from the real world that could have corrected her wishful thoughts.

Before this woman's delusional system was discovered, examiners found her utterances *incoherent* and her ideas *bizarre*. That is indeed what they sounded like on the surface, until their subjective "sense" began to be understood. Incoherence and bizarreness are only descriptive designations, representing an immediate impression that the patient is "out of touch" and "makes no sense." Ideally, the sense in the nonsense is to be discovered by finding the self-construct and the world construct that underlie the rambling appearances.

Certain ideas are laden with great apprehensiveness and convey profound suspicions, which the person is at once pinpointing and trying to ward off. We have already mentioned ideas of reference, which convey the conviction that one is the target of someone else's malevolence. These may be seen as a great exaggeration of the common social sensitivity capsuled in the phrase, "What will people think if I . . .?" Kretschmer[39] described in telling German the *sensitive Beziehungswahn,* literally meaning madness consisting of ideas of reference in (hyper)sensitive people. From here to *paranoia* is only a small step: What starts as an apprehension and a suspicion becomes a focal concern with one's own person as a victim of evil forces in a world full of enemies, with hypervigilance to attacks and plots and machinations lurking around every corner. In a friendless world, the paranoiac projects his own basic aggression as well as his vengefulness onto other people, usually in sizable groups (all men, all women, all Jews, all food vendors, all homosexuals, etc.), and frequently onto cosmic forces, as well as authoritative social systems (police, doctors, Church, the law, etc.). To make these projections possible, the targets of projection have first to be depersonalized, so that, say, Mr. Barker, the upstairs neighbor, is no longer seen for what he really is, but turned into a cliché or screen that can receive the projection. I think this is the first, and ominous, reality distortion from which many other distortions follow in rapid sequence, reminiscent of the myopic vision that comes to prevail when one person despises another one with implacable hatred and vengefulness.

Finally, in *zone D* the primary process emerges primarily in the form of images. Unlike the imageful thoughts of the secondary process, which are largely diffused throughout a culture via its literary and artistic media, the imagery of the primary process is rather private and tends to remain utterly subjective. *Reverie* includes the daydream, that temporary and partial escape from the real world by indulgence in the spontaneous play of fantasy that creates a more pleasant, soothing, or idyllic state, free from nagging problems and disagreeable duties. Reverie also allows a temporary reidentification of the self: One can imagine that he is older or younger, more powerful or beautiful than one really is, that one is of a different gender, or has a different station in life. Reverie offers temporary alternatives to reality which, when the person returns to the concentrated waking state, may even help him solve some actual problems. The images it produces may be creative, like Kekule's vision of the benzene ring, which solved a chemical puzzle. Alas, in most daydreams the accent remains on the *flight* from reality: The fantasy images enlisted are all too satisfying and thus produce habituation to such flights, which makes the return to the reality of the waking state even more painful.

Of particular psychiatric significance is the reiterative, compensatory reverie that in frequency, duration, or energy becomes so demanding as to interfere with productive work. As in masturbation fantasies, the withdrawal from reality may become so extreme, and the satisfactions such a good "ersatz," that reality and its objects are no longer sought as sources of gratification.

Freud saw *dreams* as the royal road to the unconscious and as the most telling manifestation of the primary process. Though not devoid of traces of reality content (day residue, subliminal alertness to signals from the environment and the body), the latent dream thoughts (impulses, wishes, affects) obey in the dream work an altogether different set of rules from the logic of the waking state, in the first place by their typical transformation into pictorial form, and in the second place by the technique of image forming, which depends on condensation, displacement, and symbolization. For example, part may stand for whole, ground for figure, something may be expressed by its opposite, one part may substitute for another, symbols may roll dozens of hazy meanings into one obscure, tangled message. If one could know all the building blocks of dreams, all the transformations they undergo by the diverse forces (e.g., impulse, censorship, repression) impinging on them, the manifest dream would, of course, "make sense"—after an arduous job of translation that puts the primary-process pictograms into the discursive language of the secondary process under the requirements of logic. It is clear that the primary process is appropriate to the dream, and apparently quite adapted to the biopsychological function of dreaming, which is normally an entirely intrapsychic affair confined to moments in the sleep cycle. The psychiatric point to be made is that the primary process may become dislocated from the dream and come to function in the waking state also, spilling over into the sphere of interpersonal communication and object relations.

This process occurs in *autism.* In flagrant cases, the whole world of people, animals, houses, trees, food, body organs, waste products, things, forces, and movements becomes a loose amalgam of fluid appearances. Nothing is simply itself with the usual contours, boundaries, thickness, and resistances. Everything can be taken for something else, assume different names and attract strange attributes, by the processes of condensation, displacement, and symbolization. People become tigers, clock hands become hatchets that chop off heads, a handshake becomes a killing, a hospital canteen becomes the dome of St. Peter's, a tear is to be licked as a way of sharing sadness, a bestial grunt signals "Would you tie my shoelace?" The whole of life may thus become an enacted dream, superimposed on the discrete world recognized by the secondary thought process, in which A is always A and not B, in which words have stable meanings for different speakers, and in which thinking (in ideas or images) serves the ultimate purposes of action and respectful understanding of anything's essence, with acknowledgment of its objective existence.

Again, while dreams and *hypnagogic and hypnopompic imagery* are normal manifestations of the vitality of the primary process in all of us, most likely with an adaptive and restorative function, their effects may fall short of these desirable goals. Instead of equilibrating internal disharmonies, dreams may upset our balance, and hypnagogic images may haunt us and interfere with our falling asleep. Hypnopompic images may make us cross for the first few hours of the morning, putting us in a brooding mood. This reaction does not come from their structure (governed by the primary process) but from their content, retroactively apprehended in the framework of the secondary process. The suffocating panic of nightmares may leave the person exhausted the next day, set him up for a bad mood or an anxious preoccupation, all of which may color his reality perception while he is awake. In this sense one may speak of symptomatic dreams, dream pathology, or abnormal dream activity to which the examiner should be alert as instances of thought disturbance, if only because of the excessive push of thought from pressing conflicts they bespeak.

Stratification of Thought

At the end of this chapter we must face some knotty problems that beset psychiatry today, and are part of its historical growth from a narrow specialty dealing only with the flagrantly mad to a broad discipline applicable to almost everybody, including cases of marital discord, school failure, sexual disturbances, and such behavior as stealing and lying. Let me list a number of questions and propositions frequently heard today in clinical work in regard to thought disorders.

1. Many clinicians seem to assume in practice that "thought disorder" is *ipso facto* diagnostic of schizophrenia. This notion implies the corollary that neurotic disturbances (being in some way "milder") are free from thought disorder. European clinicians observe that schizophrenic reactions are more frequently diagnosed in America than in Europe, precisely on the basis of the presence of some thought disorder which is often poorly described—as if "thought disorders" were an all-or-none phenomenon. They point out that this practice represents a misunderstanding òf the intention of such psychiatric pioneers as Kraepelin and Bleuler.

2. Phenomenologists are likely to point out that thought disorder is not a unitary phenomenon and that it cannot be graded on an intensity continuum such as mild, moderate, or severe. Rather, it is only a collective name for very diverse thought patterns, each of which is worth studying and describing in great detail inasmuch as it may be the royal road to grasping the essence of a person, an illness, a disorder, a world view, or an existential situation. In this vein, correlations may be sought between typical thought styles (or specific thought pathologies) and recognizable psychiatric (or neurological) syndromes. To some éxtent I have used this approach illustratively in this chapter, e.g., by linking flight of ideas with manic states, narrow concept formation with obsessive-

compulsive conditions, looseness of associations and conceptual boundaries with incipient loss of reality testing as in schizophrenic syndromes, etc.

3. If neuroses are considered relatively mild or benign in comparison with the alleged severity of the psychoses, one is tempted to locate and confine thought disorders in the domain of the psychoses, precisely as the criterion that turns anxiety states, phobias, obsessions, conversion reactions, etc., into madness. Accordingly, the neuroses tend to be seen as covert and intrapsychic and the psychoses as overt and interpersonal forms of illness. This viewpoint inherently belies the severity of some neuroses and character disturbances and denies that these conditions can entail bungled or deranged thinking— which is grossly out of keeping with the lessons learned from psychoanalysis. Moreover, it ignores the fact that madness is not always manifest, and it rides roughshod over the question of evidence: What do we take as evidence of thought pathology—behavior, interview material, hearsay from other informants, happenings in stress interviews, psychological test data? And if psychological test data, from which tests? Does evidence of thought disturbance on an intelligence test have the same weight as odd Rorschach test productions, when the latter test can be taken—and given—with the mental set of maximum openness to fantasy activity?

4. The term "overideational personality" has been mistaken to mean much the same as "schizoid personality," with the clinical lore about the latter tacitly transposed to the former; both terms implying a disposition to schizophrenic decompensation if derangement is to occur. The analogy is false, if only because "schizoid personality" is derived from the quality of a person's object relations and prevailing defense mechanisms, whereas "overideational personality" is a description derived from the large role and intense cathexis of thinking (of almost any sort) in any person's life. "Overideational" may cover the flighty thinker, the keen logician, the speculative metaphysician, the romantic poet as well as the person given to obsessions and ruminations, the brilliant manipulator, and the bright adolescent whose curiosity about

thought and its modalities leads him to venturesome explorations of the inner world. None of these highly cathected attitudes toward thinking is necessarily schizoid, let alone "preschizophrenic."

It would seem to follow from these four points that a precise assessment of thought processes must first yield *adequate descriptions* of the patient's *habitual* modes of thought, the deviant thought patterns he adopts *under stress*, and the *diverse styles of thought* (normal or pathological) he is capable of using under different conditions. Most of us can consciously adopt different thought patterns, depending on the task at hand, the social situation we are in, and the goals we wish to reach. In fact, capacity for playful variation of thought styles is no mean asset, as Shakespeare knew. Perhaps the worst condition is to be frozen to one form of thought, whichever that is, to suffice for earning one's living, rearing one's children, praying, making love, and reading poetry.

Time and again in clinical work we see that patients, alleged to "have a thought disorder," think and act crazily in one situation, only to think quite correctly and with good common sense in another situation. It seems to me that this observation and the other issues raised in this section give the hint that the ideal assessment of thought functioning should result in statements delineating the *stratification* of thought patterns to be found in anyone's life. This is likely to be a *hierarchical* stratification, with levels of thought grouped in order of prevalence: first the most commonly adopted patterns, next the patterns used under different degrees of stress, then the patterns used on rare or very special occasions, etc. Such a hierarchical sequence may be compared to lines of defense, and the total configuration may be taken as the person's thought strategy.

Chapter 7

Assessing Part Processes: Language and Communication

From a common-sense point of view it is fitting that the chapter on thought be followed by a chapter on language, for it is generally assumed that a person first "has a thought" and then conveys or expresses it in language. There is, however, a more sophisticated view, which holds that much of a person's thinking is determined by the language he has available; in particular, that the categories of his thought are prestructured by the words and syntax of the language he uses. An important corollary is that some ideas or concepts are simply *not* thought because the culture does not esteem them, and its language has no words for it. Thus thinking is somewhat limited by the language apparatus within which it occurs, as well as slanted toward those ideas for which the language has words. Eskimos have many different words for snow and ice, so that they see the various modalities of snow and ice as altogether different entities, speaking of them as distinct substances. Spanish has two words for "being," each felt to be a different condition, state, or process, and thus leading to differentiated thoughts about being. "Gentleman" is a British phenomenon presupposing British culture—there are no French or German gentlemen. In other words, any language is, among other things, a particular grid pressed on the phenomenal world, chopping it up into discrete bits that form the "stuff of thought" for the speakers of that language. Despite great similarities between the grids, no two are exactly alike.

What holds for cultures and their languages also holds for special subcultures and their lingo, argot, dialect, and local verbiage, as well as for technical and artificial vocabularies. Only psychoanalysis knows of "repressions"—and spots them, when the word guides the thinking of the analyst about his patient. Only behaviorists know of "reinforcement"—and see it at work in a confusing mass of behavior bits. "Schlemiels" are discovered by Yiddish-speaking observers in Jewish surroundings—not by farmers in the rural vastness of the Midwest. Christian Church members think of "salvation"—secularized Soviet engineers do not. There is women's language and men's language—correlated with women's thought and men's thought. Juvenile language knows of "trips" and juvenile thought engages in them, with a different outcome from the trips of older people, who generally use the word—and the idea—for a Sunday afternoon ride in the country, with clear consciousness and wholesome food in the picnic basket!— Enough to indicate that the relations between language and thought are mutual, not unidirectional.

It appears that language also steers thought by the frequency with which certain word groupings occur, e.g., in clichés, verbal stereotypes, habitual sayings, and catch phrases. The power of language is of great moment in the psychology of prejudice (racial, ethnic, political, or sexual), where slanted words mean biased thoughts. By the same token, pious language breeds sanctimonious thought. At the level of speech, the sound quality of a word may load thoughts in a certain direction, as in clang associations; or even produce unexpected novelties of thought, as in rhyming.

As a clinical example of the interdependence of language and thought, the case of a 57-year-old man with presenile dementia comes to mind. Whenever I asked questions requiring a proper name for an answer, e.g., "Who wrote Hamlet?," he responded almost invariably with "Jesus Christ"—seriously, after painstaking search, and obviously at his wit's end. An

all-purpose verbal cliché seemed to be used to fill his thought
and memory gaps. More tellingly, when on a sorting test he
had grouped together some small metal objects including a
lock with "Made in USA" engraved on it, he gave the following rationale for his grouping: "Because you can lock things
with it . . . belongs to the United States of America . . . and for
which it stands . . . all nations . . . justice for all . . . in the name
of the Father, the Son, and the Holy Ghost."

At the visual-motor level of operations, this patient made
an acceptable grouping that consisted of all metal objects. But
he could not conceptualize this sorting. Groping for an organized thought pattern, he regarded the lock and saw the
imprint on it (USA), which started a train of habitual phrases
taken from the Pledge of Allegiance, and in turn this hallowed
language pattern elicited another hallowed word sequence,
this time from a prayer formula. The switch from one to the
other implies some dim thought of the order: authority, powers that be, things that abide, safekeeping, etc., plus the effects
of rote childhood memories of overlearned phrases. Undoubtedly the patient's moral and emotional dynamics also loaded
the dice: He was born and reared in the Bible Belt, had
switched from farm to cemetery work, and felt oppressed by
(probably delusional) guilt feelings over having improperly
filled out his Army papers (many years ago), for which he
feared he would soon be arrested. State and church obviously
loomed large in his emotional landscape, but also figured
prominently on the tip of his tongue in a circular pattern!

A distinction must be made between *language* and *speech*.
Speech is the production of a special sort of sound, involving
vocal cords, tongue, palate, lips, and other features of the oral
cavity—hence the act of speaking may be disturbed by any
functional or organic defect in any of these organ parts, from
hysterical aphonia to cleft-palate nasality or the slurred speech
characteristic of advanced multiple sclerosis. Or, without any
difficulties of morphology and neuromuscular innervation, the
whole speech act may be suspended, as in autistic mutism. In
all these speech disorders, however, language itself is likely to
remain intact, if only in the ability to respond to reading and

the spoken word, to express oneself in writing or gestures, to engage in inner, subvocal dialogue, etc. Language disturbances, on the other hand, especially when they occur in the context of intact phonation and speech mechanisms, tend to be of central nervous system origin, as in the aphasias, or of central psychic origin, as in psychotic disorders producing verbal autism or word salad.

Although communication is one outstanding function of language, the span and meaning of the two are not identical. Much communication occurs through paralanguage—intonations, gestures, involuntary body movements and postures, and conventional and artificial signs as well as physical pulls, tugs, shoves, buttonholing, shoulder slapping, and stony-faced silences. As is obvious from these descriptions, much of paralanguage is body language, and the latter may be stretched to include pains and aches and other somatic symptoms, which form the patient's "presenting complaints" to his doctor and are now regarded as modes of communication or cries for help. It stands to reason that paralanguage is a very important signaling system in patient-doctor relationships, and that psychiatrists must become adept at it in their professional work.

All three—language, speech, and paralanguage—can be approached in a psychiatric as well as a neurological perspective, and often need to be considered in both perspectives at once. They involve ideational processes as well as skills, and since most of the skills have to be acquired, there is also the developmental consideration, which alerts the clinician to regression phenomena. We shall review these three processes successively, looking at each from various angles.

Language and Its Disturbances

Since the *aphasias* form a well-systematized clinical and research domain with useful conceptual spin-offs, let us start with these disorders and construct from them the scheme shown in Figure 1.

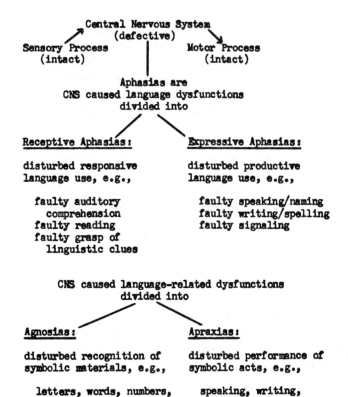

FIGURE 1

This scheme makes clear that language is an immensely complex process that comprises a number of discrete subprocesses, here fitted into the basic pattern of the reflex arc, with sensory acts at one end and motor acts at the other. Each subprocess can be selectively disturbed, or deficiencies can occur in special combinations of subprocesses.

By definition, *the aphasias* are of central nervous system origin and pertain to *primary* linguistic dysfunctions. Sensory defects such as deafness or blindness (whether central or peripheral), which prohibit adequate linguistic intake, or motor defects such as paralysis or chorea, which interfere with speaking or writing, are not considered aphasic disturbances, no matter how much they obstruct language behavior or linguistic development. A blind person cannot read ordinary print, but may be trained in Braille reading if his language functions are intact. A palsied patient who cannot move his tongue and lips freely will speak poorly, but can write or use the typewriter when his language function is adequate. The deaf-mute child will be slow in language development, but if he is otherwise intact and receives special training he may acquire sign language for expression and lip reading for understanding, much as Helen Keller overcame the effects of her blindness and deafness.

With the wider application of child psychiatry and under the impetus of the current interest in learning disorders, *dyslexia* is being given prominence as a rather widespread symptom. The term originated in work with adult aphasic patients who, with intact vision, failed to recognize words or letters; frequently they also wrote poorly (dysgraphia) and tended to reverse letters in reading and spelling, or showed unstable right-left approaches in their attempts to read and write. Today the emphasis is on dyslexia in children of school age who show marked retardation or gross inadequacies in trying to acquire the skill of reading, for which a great variety of alleged causes are advanced—by no means only proven neurological conditions.

Typically, two other groups of central nervous system disorders are classed with the aphasias, namely, the *agnosias* and *apraxias*. Although the first are dysfunctions of perceptual acts and the latter of motor acts (on account of which they may be described under "perception" and "action" respectively), they have a firm link with language in the sense that they involve interpretation of and skill in dealing with symbolic data— either receptively or productively. They too hinge on higher-order brain processes, and are to be diagnosed only when simple perceptual and motor defects can be excluded.

Accurate description and delimitation of the symptoms is the first law in diagnosing an aphasic (or, if milder, dysphasic) condition. If the language defect is gross, there is usually no difficulty in identifying it as predominantly expressive or receptive. *Receptive aphasias* show up as faulty response to the spoken or written word: the patient makes no response at all, grossly misunderstands, comprehends poorly, or responds only partially to selected items in the sequence heard or read, e.g., to a few nouns or verbs, skipping adjectives, adverbs, and other "small words" on which so much grammar and syntax are built. Frequently, the patient attempts to repeat a few of the examiner's words, with a puzzled and uncomprehending look on his face. One may find that spoken language is grasped auditorily, and responded to orally, but that graphic materials (letters, words, sentences, numbers, geometrical shapes, colors, pictures of objects, etc.—all or some of these) are not comprehended when seen. In that case one is dealing with an *agnosia*—to be specified according to the perceptual modality as well as the class of stimuli involved. For instance, word blindness is a selective visual agnosia; word deafness and tone deafness are forms of auditory agnosia.

For differential diagnosis, delimitation of the symptoms and an eye for their clustering are of great importance, even at the purely descriptive level. Poor response to arithmetical items and operations, including failure to recognize printed numbers, may constitute an *acalculia,* which is sometimes a delimited disorder (without gross aphasia), and in turn may be exacerbated by a *left-right disturbance,* which throws the reading (and computations) of the decimal placement order out of kilter. (The patient may take 387 for seven-eighty-three, or seven-thirty-eight, or just seriatim as seven-eight-three).

Turning to the other side of the reflex arc, gross *expressive aphasic* defects are manifested either by complete absence or great paucity of spontaneous speech (typical in the motor aphasia involving Broca's area) or by overt oddities in language production, e.g., impoverished sentences (telegram speech with many gaps), single words intended as a sentence (e.g., "Eat?" meaning "When is dinner time?"), groping for words, heavy gesticulating, mispronunciations or gap-filling clichés used as an all-purpose tool in communication. Here again, distinctions and clusters must be noted. Patients with pure Broca's motor aphasia can ordinarily write and gesticulate.

To the expressive defects belong all forms of *paraphasia,* a general term standing for mistakes in pronunciation, omissions of sounds, reversals of syllables, and other obvious errors in speaking, and their parallels in writing. The patient may say "scare" for a square, "tangle" for a triangle, change the word order in his sentences, or leave out the small "grammar" words, such as *the, a, if, however, but, not, my,* entirely. In extreme cases, this difficulty leads to so-called telegram speech.

Patients with *word-finding difficulties* can often circumlocute or indicate their intention by gestures. For instance, a patient needing the name "Truman" in answer to a question pounded her hands in irritation over her inability to find it, saying haltingly: "Oh . . . Democrat—can't say his name . . . from Missouri!" The same patient, having to describe the missing part (funnel) in a picture of an ocean liner, promptly put her finger on the gap in the drawing, saying: "The . . . middle, eh . . . eh . . . what's in the middle . . . it's . . . a sail . . . no, these . . . it lets out the energy . . . it's round . . . the steam!" In response to the question "Why do people pay taxes?," she went through the following excruciating verbal gyration: "It pays for the U.S. . . . for the . . . starts with . . . American history . . . or . . ., no, no . . . like we're having . . . the government . . . it starts with H . . . the other starts with S . . . House of Representatives and Senate!"

Inability to write, or very poor skill at it (after adequate schooling and in the absence of motor disturbances), is *agraphia* or *dysgraphia,* which can be a circumscribed defect as well as part of a larger expressive-aphasic syndrome. It can also occur in the otherwise nonaphasic *Gerstmann syndrome,* which consists of left-right disturbance, acalculia, agraphia, finger anomia (inability to name the fingers of one's hand), constructional apraxia (difficulty in making configurations, say, with blocks or tinker toys or jigsaw puzzles), and, often, a visual field defect (hemianopia). It is noteworthy and psychologically interesting that several of these deficits involve the body scheme, especially the hand, at multiple levels of meaning (left versus right; arithmetic as derivative of digits, i.e., fingers, made abstract in the digital-decimal system; naming the fingers; working with the fingers), as if the Gerstmann syndrome were a complex symbol disorder of hand and space relations. The existence of such symptom configurations means that the examiner who spots, say, an acalculic deficit, must systematically weed out other possibilities such as agraphia, left-right disturbance, etc. The whole range of associated functions must be surveyed and tapped.

The apraxias are, by definition, disorders of acquired skills. Accordingly, one might describe motor aphasia as an apraxia of speaking, agraphia as an apraxia of writing, etc. While this usage is not the typical one, it would make the examiner aware of the function under consideration as the outcome of a developmental process and, by implication, any deficit of that function as the result of dedifferentiation, primitivization, or regression.

Dedifferentiation appears plainly in such broad language disorders as *central aphasia, amnesic aphasia,* and *Wernicke's aphasia.* In a way, these designations were meant to correct earlier views, according to which the aphasias could be minutely subdivided into the discrete part-processes of language and correlated with specific brain sites responsible for their dysfunction. They imply a profounder view of language and brain functioning, which recognizes that most aphasic patients also suffer from difficulties in comprehension, thought, abstraction, or memory, and must often completely restructure their basic relations to the world, undergoing a noticeable personality change at various levels of organization. Cognitive emptiness, irritability, labile affect, spells of crying or anger, withdrawal into solitary brooding, and the reemergence of childish behavior are likely to occur, bespeaking a fairly massive regression. One of Goldstein's[40] patients could not freely produce names of specimens within a class—animals, plants, etc.—or even think of them, but was forced to revivify an old, concrete memory of a childhood visit to the Berlin zoo, which he literally "read off" through his mind's eye, saying painfully, slowly: "... *the* polar bear, *the* grizzly bears, *the* brown bear, *the* antelope ...," etc., or something to that effect, reporting what he successively saw when he walked with his father through the zoo's entrance lane. His response is not just an unorthodox form of retrieval and name production, but a wholly different way of thinking. Thought of this order is no longer symbolic, and neither is the language used. Words now refer to the perceptual world of concrete items, and the names of things are seen as one of their properties. For instance, it may happen that after a patient names one color chip "brown," he is unable to assign this name to another brown chip (of the same or similar hue) because he considers it to be the exclusive property of the first one.

Thus language not only *is* a symbolic process but also *reflects* a symbolic process, namely, thought. In this sense, language is a symbol of a symbol. This relationship also works the other way: If language is the symbol system in terms of which we do so much of our thinking, thought is a symbol of a symbol.

Hence *the pervasiveness of deficiencies in mental retardation.* In many forms of retardation (excluding cases of specific, circumscribed deficit such as aphasia or cerebral palsy) thought is low in abstraction level and poor in concept formation; it is concretistic, oversimple, and tied to perceptual, motor, and emotional activities. Similarly, the retardate's language is based on a small vocabulary and simple sentence structure, consists of much naming, and tends to remain embedded in perceptual, motoric, and emotional acts. Hence also the large place given to language behavior in estimates of intelligence, and the popular tendency to equate intelligence with verbal skills. Poor vocabulary, poor verbal comprehension, and poor grammar in a growing child are indeed classical signs of developmental arrest, tending to doom the thought process to an elementary level. Not infrequently the child may compensate for his language (and thought) deficiency by much chattering, garrulousness, having the heart on the tip of the tongue, and explosive utterances accompanying his affect states. But compensation is not the only reason for such excessive (though simple and stereotyped) verbalizations; they also bespeak the greater impulsivity that ensues when language and thought are too weak to interpose themselves as an intricate symbolic world between perception and action.

We learn from these observations that language is one of the foremost ego functions and ego builders; and conversely, that language is likely to be used as a most important coping tool in the ego's management of organismic equilibrium.

Perhaps the grossest use (one might say misuse) of language as a coping device is to strip it of its communicative features, make it enigmatic instead of clear, and in that way ignore or frustrate the hearer. For instance, a patient responded to questions about his work by saying: "Selling pitchers of worms." It took some doing to relate this verbal puzzle to two jobs he had held. One was selling bottles ("pitchers") of an animal health food (denigrated as "worms"); the other was selling aerial photographs (pictures, disguised as "pitchers") of farms (disguised as "forms" and coalesced with "worms"). This language fragment employs clang association, aims at concealment, teases the hearer with its negativism, uses the device of punning, and condenses two distinct reality fragments into one glib verbal phrase, thereby establishing a seeming conceptual unity that turns out to be only a similarity of affect, namely, that the patient felt disgusted by both jobs.

This patient used ordinary English words, but gave them private *autistic* meanings. His phrase illustrates the wisdom of Sullivan's[41] remark that one should not presume to understand a patient who seems to speak normally, for normal language may be used for autistic purposes. Less concealed linguistic autisms are neologisms, word salad, and anything else that is overt gibberish. In fact, recognizable words or word fragments may be relinquished entirely, in favor of grunts, shrieks, and other primitive vocalizations, in which case we have *mutism* accompanied by prelingual emotional overflow phenomena.

It is to be noted that all these clinical phenomena refer to expressive or productive language. What happens to receptive or responsive language behavior in such cases? Can we assume that the patient takes the language spoken by people around him and the written language that comes to his attention in the normal way, responding to their objective meanings and taking their obvious intentions for granted? I think not. We have already seen (Chapter 7) that one patient responded to the question whether his parents were "on his side" by looking up and down the left side of his body, utterly mistaking the speaker's frame of reference. Paranoid patients read hidden meanings into innocuous phrases. The meaning of a doctor's order may be grossly misheard or distorted.

Short of such gross functional language pathologies are linguistic oddities coupled with psychiatric symptoms, as well as linguistic styles characteristic of personality patterns. One of the symptom-related language characteristics is the tight-lipped *guardedness* of suspicious or paranoid patients, which greatly reduces their spontaneous speech; and when they speak, their word choice tends to be overprecise and pedantic. In marked contrast is the *pressure of speech* that accompanies anxiety states and may embody an urge to confess in response to acute guilt feelings. In depressions (if not agitated) there tends to be a *dearth of* language behavior; with other mental processes, it succumbs to the general psychomotor slowing that prevails. In phobic reactions one can find gaps in the language flow, representing the strenuous *avoidance* of fear-laden or taboo words, as if the mere enunciation of a word (say, "snake") could bring the feared object into the patient's presence.

We expect to hear *pedantic,* stilted, overprecise, and overformal language productions from compulsive personalities and people with tendencies toward intellectualization or isolation of affect. "I beg you to collect these several items of personal property" is the stilted phrase a disturbed woman used for "Please come and pick up your things."

Verbosity has many roots. Linked with pedantry, it occurs in persons who feel under internal pressure to make a show of their intellectual superiority. Linked with garrulousness, it appears as the incessant chattering of narcissistic personalities who must be the center of everyone's attention even when they have nothing of substance to communicate. With glib turns of phrase and fleeting foci of attention, verbosity marks the restless language behavior (including gestures and many accessory body motions) of hypomanic patients.

States of overexcitement tend to affect language in two contrasting ways. On the one hand, the flow of speech seems to be accelerated, and word choice is loaded with superlatives, intensity words, and exclamatory phrases, accompanied by gesticulations; sometimes disinhibition leads to swearing or vulgarities. On the other hand, the linguistic process may be stalled, with the resulting frozen state of near mutism accompanied by motor overflow phenomena: primitive motions of various body parts, such as pounding, twitching, or pacing the floor.

Blocking is the earmark of obsessional patients: The verbal flow is stopped short in the middle of a phrase or sentence, there is an anxious groping in the sudden silence, punctured by "eh . . . eh," or "but . . .," usually followed by a new start at verbalization and the introduction of a different idea, which deviates from or contrasts with the previous one. The result is a fragmentation of both the flow of speech and the thoughts conveyed. Milder forms of obsessional thinking show up in a distinct verbal style, full of subclauses and such qualifying words as "but," "however," "although," each new phrase taking back what the previous phrase has asserted. It is the language of ambivalence, in which the mechanisms of isolation and undoing pervade the language (and thought) process.

Emotion-laden words and terms with empathic impact akin to superlatives ("terrific," "wonderful," "frightful," "so lovely") characterize the language of hysterical patients. To the observer, these words, emphatically declaimed, have a hollow ring; the listener senses that the patient's emotion is of incongruous intensity or quality in relation to the idea conveyed. He is likely to believe that the affect-laden words mask shallow feelings, or are products of displacement from other, repressed, ideas whose emotional charge intrudes into consciousness, escaping the ego's defensive vigilance; or that the patient is going through the verbal motions of emotional display in order to capture feelings that have been repressed and have thus produced an artificial emotional dullness.

Language can be endowed with *magical power*. In that case, words are chosen that conjure up the powers with which the person wishes to be aligned, or whose power he seeks to use for attack or defense. The words that serve these functions tend to have cosmic connotations: life, soul, All, death, devil, semen, birth, mind, generation, the names of all astral bodies, and of course any conceivable deity or demon. A patient says: "Power is rising up—I get much strength from it." Another patient, afraid of cardiac failure, speaks of "the hearty food" that will "bring all of us down."

Magical expectations about language also produce selective avoidance of certain words, particularly those referring to *taboos* and to objects of *phobias*. To pronounce "hell" might make the heavens cave in; to speak of a "bull" in the pasture would subject one to sexual contamination in fantasy. Phobic reactions to snakes or mice often entail traces of panic at the mere mention of these creatures' names, which subsequently drop out of the patient's vocabulary.

Finally, there are the milder, and common, neurotic language mishaps known as "slips of the tongue," which signal a return of the repressed by faulty word choice or telling alterations of the intended word to produce surprising new meanings. Better controlled, in the sense that they do not produce sudden disruptions, are the habitual or situational *language mannerisms,* which strike the observant listener as a dead giveaway: the "believe me . . ." of a liar, the "frankly speaking . . ." of a person bent on concealment, the "I don't mean to interfere . . ." of the meddler. Verbal phrase and dominant character trait here stand in apparent contradiction: Conscious message and unconscious signal strike an odd, ambiguous bargain from which the clinician reads attitudinal conflict or pronounced emotional ambivalence.

In regard to *object relations and self-image,* a turn of phrase can suggest fragments of the speaker's positive or negative identity. The married man who speaks not of "my wife" but of "my son John's mother" sets a distance between himself and his spouse, and may identify himself with the family's children. The spouse who narrates marital events with many "I's" and few "we's" reveals a weak marital bond. Accents and dialects can be maintained, or even nurtured, to suggest strong identification with the group of origin. New accents and phraseology can be adopted to stress upwardly mobile class identifications as well as to distance oneself from one's former affiliations.

Active versus passive verb usage ("I went to live in Memphis" versus "I was moved to Memphis") is a fairly reliable clue to the activity-passivity dimension of a person's life and his feelings of mastery. Similarly, "It happened to me that . . ." bespeaks a more ego-alien experience than the robust phrase "I decided to . . .," which tells of ego-syntonic acts.

Speech and Its Disturbances

Though the spoken word is part of language, for which reason the preceding section contains examples of uttered phrases, the act of speaking is a more or less circumscribed process having its own variables. Regardless of the content of what is said, the production of speech sounds is a complicated act that requires considerable skill in coordinating several somatic systems. Many developmental steps lie between the infant's birth cry and the adult's mature, sexually differentiated, and culturally adapted speech patterns. And many mishaps are possible on this developmental journey, traces of which are left in gross or subtle qualities of a person's speech.

Apart from otolaryngological problems and aphasic symptoms that affect speech in various ways or make it altogether impossible, a multiplicity of voice clues register on the psychiatrist, psychologist, and neurologist as they listen to their patients, and affect their clinical judgments. Maybe most of these clues are registered unconsciously because speech and hearing are automatized to an exceptional degree. Even 'so, these clues will elicit some evaluative response. Other clues, like loudness and gender qualities, are quite consciously perceived and responded to. Which are the clinically significant variables of speech and the useful clues?

Sex differences. Speech development is more rapid in girls than in boys, and articulation defects such as stuttering are far more common in males than in females. Dyslexia too is more frequent in men than in women. Thus there is reason to assume that certain aspects of language and speech functioning are sex linked. The most obvious gender difference in speech is *pitch*, i.e., the sound-wave frequency of vocalization that produces high or low tones. Despite considerable overlap (and culturally determined tolerance for ambiguity), women speak in higher registers than men. Consequently, deviations from the expected male and female ranges (if not reducible to laryngeal defects) strike the hearer as odd, raising questions about sex-role identification. Particularly in children, whose identification with either parent is still tentative, periods of low-pitched speech in girls signal attempts to emulate the father or brother, whereas in boys high-pitched speech indicates an identification with the mother or sister. In late adolescence and adulthood, when gender identities are more stabilized, marked pitch-range crossing can be taken as a symptom of covert homosexual conflict, if not as a sign of overt male-passive or female-active homosexuality.

Volume. Since speech volume is the product of a delicate coordination between impulse and control, requiring calibration to the inherent norms of diverse social situations, loudness deviations bespeak faulty impulse control. Upsurges of affect, such as anxiety and rage, lead at first to an increase of volume that is most conspicuous in yelling and shouting; with further increases the whole voice system may become choked off, and the affect discharge takes place through autonomic pathways. A contrary result of great affect strength, handled by selective inhibition of laryngeal air flow, is functional aphonia, in which volume is reduced to the minimum, short of actual muteness. Apart from these very gross disturbances of volume, there are many milder deviations that provide clues to personality organization and coping styles. A habitually loud voice does correlate with self-assertiveness, if not aggressiveness, as the soft voice does with shyness or excessive meekness. Comparison of the speech volume of persons with athletic, leptosome, and pyknic body type shows an increase in decibel range in that order; despite considerable overlap among the three groups, there is some suggestion of constitutional-temperamental differences.

Making sounds takes energy. Aside from the expressive and communicative functions of speech, the act of speaking offers opportunities for drive discharge and affect release. The scream is a notable example of aggressive or sexual drive release at the most primitive phonemic level. Under stress, most people talk more, or talk with greater agitation, in either case feeling good about the tension release that speaking provides, regardless of the content. Infantile babbling and the garrulousness of young children soon after they learn to speak also show that speaking, like all acquired skills, yields a pleasure in functioning that augments its use. In addition, speech can be eroticized so that the act of speaking gives sexual gratification, just as the infant's sucking—which can be seen as a partial oral precursor of speech—gives erotic satisfaction. The eroticized speaker not only loves to hear his own voice, which is obvious enough, but likes the oral motions involved in the speech act. The aggressive speaker, who orally explodes, spits, thrusts, or blasts, finds both release of aggression and sadistic satisfaction in speaking. In these cases, drive release is coupled with drive binding, for the speech apparatus has become a highly cathected or preferred tool for gaining pleasure as well as avoiding pain.

These and other psychodynamic considerations have given impetus to the work of Rousey and Moriarty,[42] who have attempted (in a hitherto uncharted field) to correlate specific abnormalities of articulation with various intrapsychic or interpersonal conflict situations, using a developmental framework with special fixation and regression levels. Rousey and Moriarty believe that phonetic and articulatory stages in learning to speak are embedded in stages of instinctual differentiation and ego development, and that traces of the conflict and emotion prevailing at any stage may become attached to a child's speech mechanisms and remain there for years to come. Configurations of impulse and defense would then be discernible in specific forms of faulty articulation.

According to Rousey and Moriarty, in the first six months of life, vowels predominate in the infant's phonations; in the same period drives and affect states are experienced and become differentiated. Vowels and basic drives are intimately associated in this stage. Consonants, which require far greater phonetic coordination than vowels, are practiced later, coincident with the various stages of ego development and the articulation of specific defense mechanisms. Thus the proper mastery of all speech processes, which typically occurs between the ages of five and seven years, is not merely a matter of good motor development; it also involves emotional integration. Barring organic-mechanical speech defects, faulty articulation in the later years thus provides clues to fixations.

While minute phonetic analysis requires audiological laboratory techniques and the competence of a speech pathologist, certain quite obvious speech distortions can be registered by any alert clinician, without special apparatus or competence.

Regarding phonetic *substitutions,* Rousey believes that substitution of *w* for *r* bespeaks demandingness—often correlated in school children with underachievement—anal conflicts, and an obsessional style of thought. Substitution of *f* for the voiceless *th* sound ("fank you" for "thank you") suggests confusion in sexual identity, in both girls and boys, due to a disturbed relation with the father. Substitution of *d* for the voiced *th* ("dem" for "them") stems from oral aggression. Sexual trauma, real or fantasied, may leave a trace in substitution of *v* for the voiced *th.*

Lisping, in adults, bespeaks the retention of an infantile position in life. The frontal lisp (subsitution of *th* for *s*) is found in persons with a strong pull toward narcissism, who nevertheless give a surface impression of meeting more mature demands. The lateral lisp (a slurping effect due to air spilling over the sides of the tongue) suggests a pathological degree of narcissism, often associated with sloppy and messy behavior.

Tongue thrusting is a phallic signal, expressing aggressive intrusiveness and competitiveness; if it is maintained throughout adolescence and adulthood, it is likely to reflect unsolved problems in superego development.

Whistle sounds in the pronunciation of *s* are taken as a phonetic sign of anxiety—it is not a static phenomenon, but fluctuates with experienced anxiety levels.

Other easily detected voice qualities may have clinical significance. In both sexes notable *restriction of the pitch range* (less than one fourth of the expected range) occurs in severe depressions; milder restriction can be taken as a general sign of constriction of erotic impulses and feelings. *Breathiness* (a mild form of dysphonia or aphonia) is a voice symptom of denial and repression. *Harshness* and *nasality* suggest aggressiveness. These are some of Rousey's findings.*

While battles have raged about the explanation of *stuttering*, it is fallacious to declare that it is merely an organic disorder and overlook the obvious fluctuations of this speech disorder depending on whether the person is alone or in a group, likes or dislikes the persons he is speaking to, is verbalizing conflict-laden or conflict-free ideas, his degree of fatigue or excitement, and the degree of secondary gain he derives from the handicap. Predominantly tonic, or clonic, or mixed forms may be discernible, and may be characteristic of the person's general style of motor behavior.

Neurologists have all but pre-empted the term *dysarthria* for speech disorders of central organic causation. In its literal meaning, this word is synonymous with articulation disorder, but today the latter leaves room for distinguishing between

---

*I have reported Rousey and Moriarty's main findings in order to alert the general clinician who is not a speech pathologist to the kind of observation one can make about speech, so as to sharpen his acumen. It seems to me that, in isolation from other clinical observations and psychological test data, speech articulation alone is too small a sample of behavior to warrant the categorical genetic and dynamic inferences Rousey and Moriarty draw.

organic and functional features, including the emotional residues that Rousey finds in speech defects. In so complicated a skill as speech, however, it is rash to declare any deviance as either purely organic or purely functional. But certain speech patterns and speech alterations, predominantly induced by mishaps in the central nervous system, are of diagnostic significance to psychiatrist and neurologist alike, if only for a crude differential diagnosis that will affect the process of referral between specialists.

It is probable that conditions of respiratory insufficiency or abnormality also affect speech production, inasmuch as speaking hinges on air flow. In chorea and Parkinson's disease, in certain palsies and myasthenia gravis, the patient's speech may be *halting, tremulous,* or *staccato,* and of reduced volume.

The laryngeal system and the functions of the oral cavity can be disturbed by a variety of central nervous system disorders that conspicuously affect articulation. The *thick, slurred* speech of a patient with delirium tremens or of a patient coming out of a major epileptic seizure is easy to recognize. Cerebral palsies can produce a variety of articulation defects depending on the degree of ataxia, athetosis, spastic paralysis, or rigidity present. In cerebellar ataxic dysarthria, speech becomes *explosive,* often with halting between syllables or slurring. Speech in spastic dysphonia is described as *harsh,* with startling *pitch variations* ranging from extremely high to extremely low.

It is widely recognized among aphasiologists today that a clear-cut separation between dysarthric and aphasic symptoms cannot be made. The clinical picture is often blurred; the technical nomenclatures are very confused, and a thorough conceptual understanding of speech functions requires interdisciplinary knowledge rather than the territorial claims of particular disciplines that have prevailed for so long.

Finally, we must include in this section a ritualized regression of speech that is seen by some as a supernatural gift or an asset: *glossolalia.* Whatever use is made of *speaking in tongues* and however hallowed the practice may be in the context of a religious belief system, the fact remains that it is an articulatory dissolution of speech acts in which phonetic mastery is relinquished in favor of a kind of spontaneous infantile babbling. The clinical significance of glossolalia varies with the context in which it appears. For those who have engaged in it as long-time members of Pentecostal groups, who saw their parents and religious leaders practice and extol it, its meaning may be primarily one of libidinal good feelings, a sign of grace, and a means of avowing their loyalty to a cherished group and their identification with a set of beliefs. For those who turn to it at a late age and against the premises of their family's belief system, the act is bound to assume the character of a protest or narcissistic innovation, with a commensurately larger share of aggressive drive dynamics. In either case, glossolalia stands in marked contrast to the clever tinkering with language sounds found in *Alice in Wonderland* and Joyce's *Finnegans Wake,* on which considerable intelligence is expended. Many games can be played with language and speech sounds; clinically, the singular quality of glossolalia lies in its being a dedifferentiation of organized speech, i.e., its regressiveness.

Paralinguistic Mannerisms

It may be said that *all* behavior is communicative, whether communication is intended or not, and whether the specialized media of language and speech are used or not. People can signal to each other through gestures, body postures, silences, sighs, shouts, groans, the color or pallor of their cheeks, the glint in their eye, the scratching of body parts, the way they sit in chairs, their gait, and the way they dress. All these have message value, and the message they convey may or may not be congruent with the spoken message: Paralanguage may underline the spoken word, contradict it, amplify or qualify it, provide its context, or substitute for it.

Some paralinguistic phenomena, such as pointing with the finger, shoving somebody out of the way, or putting one finger on the lips while saying "shsh" as a demand for silence, are clearly under voluntary control. These phenomena contain the whole class of *conventional gestures,* accepted and ritualized within a culture, each having a codified and unambiguous meaning shared by sender and receiver. In fact, the acquisition and transmission of such gestures presuppose a verbal system that legitimates them and can describe their propriety. Not so for *involuntary gestures:* The extended index finger that dangles from a relaxed hand hanging over the arm of a chair is not an act of pointing to the floor; a scream of pain is an abrupt overflow phenomenon of the autonomic nervous system; and a public speaker's squeezing his nose between thumb and index finger is an unintended giveaway of his embarrassment rather than a purposeful communication. The doctor who places himself ponderously in the best overstuffed chair in the room and the patient who hesitantly perches himself on the forward edge of a hard seat are conveying potent messages, but very likely not the ones they consciously want to transmit. Their unconscious comes through, whatever the messages they send by their words.

In keeping with the sequence of topics in this chapter, we should first attend to a variety of *nonverbal vocalizations.* An obvious class of these behaviors is formed by laughing and crying, whose typical index value of joy and sadness needs no explication. But one can laugh inappropriately, for instance while talking of sad things; or one can smilingly convey a shocking message to someone else, in which case a trace of sadism complicates the verbal statement. One can cry at a happy ending, thereby showing how much one had identified with the drama's protagonist, or manifesting one's great relief after a painful abreaction of a traumatic event, now worked through to the point of pleasure at its cleansing effect. Or one can laugh and cry in rapid alternation, as in labile affect states, or as an expression of great ambivalence.

Another class of involuntary vocalizations comprises giggling or snickering and sobbing or whimpering—two contrasting sets of sounds having to do with pleasure and pain respectively. Giggling and snickering frequently have aggressive overtones to the extent that they contain ridicule, or glee over someone else's misfortune. Sobbing is plainly a vocal gesture of woe; whimpering adds a plaintive, if not passive-demanding, note. Both are akin to moaning and groaning, but in the latter reactions the voice is more prominent and its tonal quality more richly modulated, with possibilities for dramatization.

Hollering typically consists of clear-cut words uttered very loudly; in yelling and the scream, words are absent. In these communications *in extremis* natural expletives replace the common phonemes of one's language: They are "Ouch!," "Auuw!," or "Hey!"

It is the body, and not a conventional code, that rules the sounds of yawning, belching, and flatus: potent messages each of boredom, disgust, and disregard of taboos when introduced into civil encounters. Similarly, but without the use of any system of sounds, the body conveys the message of "shutting out" or withdrawal when a person's eyelids droop during a conversation or when he falls asleep during a lecture.

The body as a more or less autonomous message system is the subject matter of *kinesics*.[43] This subject comprises a virtually endless series of observations one can make about *gestures, postures,* and *facial expressions,* and the way these acts affect the processes of communication and empathy. The importance of these acts lies in the information they convey to the examiner, such as the slow gait and drooping posture of the depressed patient, the heightened muscle tone of the hyperalert paranoiac, the profuse gesticulation of some hysterical patients, or the frozen posture and "uh-uh's" of the obsessional person. Involuntarily, the examiner may follow his patients in some of their kinesic acts: When the patient's arms are crossed, the examiner may soon cross his; when the patient yawns, the examiner may empathically start yawning too. For this reason, close self-scrutiny of one's own involuntary body reactions is an indispensable step in learning to watch the subtle signs emanating from the patient's body. Kinesics is still a young discipline, and perhaps more art than science. This section has therefore been confined to a few gross observations and some hints that each reader can learn to elaborate in his own years of practice. More observations about body language and behavioral styles will be made in the chapter on action.

Chapter 8

Assessing Part Processes: Emotion

Difficult as it is to capture the essence of emotion in scientific language, I find it fitting to open this chapter with a poem by Emily Dickinson:

> The Heart asks Pleasure—first—
> And then—Excuse from Pain—
> And then—those little Anodynes
> That deaden suffering—
>
> And then—to go to sleep—
> And then—if it should be
> The will of its Inquisitor
> The privilege to die—[44]

There it is: the great, abiding, overarching scheme whereby all feelings are apprehended—pleasure and pain. And since emotion is closely interwoven with motion, this scheme is also one of action: pleasure is *sought,* pain is *avoided.* By this basic scheme much of life gets structured. In Chapter 2 our sketch of the person had the word "Satisfaction" writ large on it, culminating in the arrowhead's continuous move toward objects, i.e., satisfiers. The poetess elaborates the other side: "those little anodynes" of the defenses, which mitigate pain, including withdrawal into sleep and the extreme position of longing for death.

A more formal way of stating this idea is to say that emotions are characterized foremost by their *hedonic tone*, i.e., the kinds of pleasure they give or pain they cause. By definition, no emotion is hedonically neutral. Anger, anxiety, awe, bliss, cheer, dread, fear, fury, gladness, gloom, grief, hate, joy, loathing, love, rage, resentment, sadness, shame, sorrow, terror (to give a purely alphabetical enumeration)—each has its own unique quality of subjective experience that sets it apart and makes it more or less describable. Even contentment and lethargy have specific tones, "quiet" as they are. One can reduce the hedonic tones to the two main qualities of pleasure and unpleasure/pain, and envisage mixed hedonic forms in which pleasure and pain blend or occur jointly in some proportion.

Attempts to classify emotions have led to a search for significant dimensions of emotion. One of these is the *excitement-quiescence* polarity, which is nearly identical with the distinction between *tension and relaxation*. Exactly what these words refer to is not so easy to specify: Both polarities can be taken in an objective sense (referring to overt behavior) as well as a subjective sense (the way they feel to the person). Tension and relaxation refer more specifically to muscle states of increased or decreased tonus, a viewpoint that recognizes the close links between emotion and the skeletomuscular system. The French used to differentiate between *emotion choc* and *emotion sentiment*, in recognition of the fact that some emotions have a shocklike effect or overwhelming impact (such as grief, startle, rage), whereas others have a more lingering quality that allows clear conscious registration and a certain amount of dwelling on the experience (e.g., sorrow, hope, jealousy). The dimension of *approach-withdrawal* embeds emotions in molar behavior sequences or attitudinal states, situating the person in his environment. In all these attempts at classification a continuum between two opposite poles can be assumed.

While these distinctions have some clinical relevance (they are so obvious and basic that they are built into the theories of mood-regulating drugs), the practicing clinician is likely to focus on other dimensions of emotion. For instance, emotions should be scrutinized for their *time* patterns. Many emotions have a gradual ebb and flow character, requiring some time to build up and to fade away. This aspect is particularly characteristic of moods, which tend to linger on for long stretches of time. In fact, a person's emotional life over time appears to yield a complex curve: a slow curve of waxing and waning basic moods (e.g., gloominess, cheerfulness, more or less chronic anger, lassitude, or anxiety) on which a faster curve of specific emotions of shorter duration is imposed, creating more accentuated peaks and valleys or to some flattening of the mood curve. This view prepares us for other parameters of emotion: Moods are often considered as *endogenous* processes, whereas short-term emotions are more closely linked with *exogenous* factors, i.e., are responses to specific precipitating conditions. For instance, Kraepelin's concept of mood disorders (depression, mania) presupposes abiding predispositions toward gloom or elation or long-term cyclic alternations between the two, relatively independent of current stimuli. They are attributed to glandular processes and lifelong character traits.

Another clinical dimension of some importance is the *intensity* of any emotion. Feelings can be weak or strong; in clinical parlance these terms are often equated with superficial or deep. Here again we have a semantic problem: Does "weak" mean "hardly felt" or does it refer to its behavioral visibility? And what is a "superficial" feeling? One clinical chestnut of great durability holds that hysterical patients, given to effervescent gestures and rather spectacular facial displays, experience feelings only superficially. In this view, what meets the eye are *histrionic* bits of behavior taken to be simulations of the expressive movements of affect rather than trustworthy indicators of felt emotions. There may be truth in this observation. The patient may have repressed certain vital affects so radically that he is no longer in touch with them, and yet is human enough to long for them, trying to recapture their hedonic tone by going through the motions of their typical motor accompaniments. Or else the repressed affect breaks through in a sudden symptomatic motor pattern, expressing the "wisdom of the body," while the patient's dissociation from its feeling tone is maintained. The opposite impression is given by the *flat affect* of certain patients, typically very compulsive, obsessional, or schizophrenic, who lack emotional expression, even such involuntary reflex signs as tears, tremulousness, or facial color changes, when presented with highly charged ideas or confronted with stimuli of known emotional potency. Intense or prolonged psychic pain may produce a numbing effect. Said Emily Dickinson:

> There is a pain–so utter–
> It swallows substance up–
> Then covers the Abyss with Trance–
> So Memory can step
> Around–across–upon it–
> As one within a Swoon–
> Goes safely–where an open eye–
> Would drop Him–Bone by Bone.[45]

Here repression is at work, obliterating the affect from consciousness and producing a trance state—maybe somnambulism. More severe and radical is the numbness of catatonic stupor described in the following Dickinson poem:

> After great pain, a formal feeling comes–
> The Nerves sit ceremonious, like Tombs–
> The stiff Heart questions was it He, that bore,
> And Yesterday, or Centuries before?
>
> The Feet, mechanical, go round–
> Of Ground, or Air, or Ought–
> A Wooden way
> Regardless grown,
> A Quartz contentment, like a stone–
>
> This is the Hour of Lead–
> Remembered, if outlived,
> As Freezing persons, recollect the Snow–
> First—Chill—then Stupor—then the letting go—[46]

Do these patients really feel nothing? How did the expected intensity of their feelings get lost? Are they perhaps hiding their feelings by curbing their expression? Or have they successfully shut off the flow of signals from the outer world by a radical withdrawal? Can feelings as such be effectively repressed, or can one repress only the ideas and memories that carry them, divorcing idea from emotional charge while that charge yet remains somewhere in the recesses of the mind? And in that case, is that charge not *felt* in any sense and in any hedonic modality?

Before we can go into these questions we must look at some other parameters of feelings. Closely linked with intensity of feelings is the notion of *stimulus thresholds,* the counterpart of which is *arousal readiness.* If emotions are signs of actually occurring body processes (James's[47] famous "Tears roll down my cheeks—I am sad"), or signals preparing us for adaptive action in the world (rage as preparation for attack, fear as the precursor of flight), or even when they are construed as phylogenetic atavisms (Darwin[48]), or as overflow phenomena of the autonomic nervous system's emergency reactions (Cannon[49]), there must be some threshold at which the stimulus takes effect, giving rise to awareness of a specific feeling tone and a perceptible body reaction. Not all stimuli reach this level—not only because they may be intrinsically too weak, but also because the state of the organism is unresponsive.

One aspect of the interaction between stimulus and organismic readiness is of great clinical importance: the *appropriateness of the emotion to the stimulus* in hedonic tone, specific quality, or intensity. Briefly, on the basis of experience we expect some prevailing correlations, and are struck by exceptions. We expect a painful event to induce sadness, a threat of pain to elicit withdrawal or flight, or at least some wincing. A joyous happening should produce a smile or two, some bubbliness, an approach reaction, and maybe a demand for more. These rules are sometimes flagrantly broken, which typically strikes the examiner as rather uncanny. A person may laugh (not bravely, but eerily) when he experiences pain. A persistent smile may accompany a patient's narration of gruesome events in his life. Talking about a loved one recently deceased, a person may snicker. Given a gift, a person may get angry. Some people become flustered or actually depressed on being promoted to a desirable position. In all these cases the expected emotion (expected, that is, by statistical rule or by the observer's empathic reaction) is replaced by another, often contrary, feeling.

Finally, there is an observable *rhythm* or *pattern* variable in emotions. In some patients, the basic mood changes have a *cyclic* character, so noteworthy in manic-depressive disorders. Before the advent of effective anticonvulsant medicines, some epileptics showed a definite *periodicity* of tension buildup, increasing irritability, and angry moods, culminating in a seizure. This observation led Janet[50] to the wistful thought that if one could find a way of inducing seizures, some nonconvulsive patients might be helped to gain a better or healthier balance—an idea that later eventuated in the various shock therapies. Some persons maintain a striking and unusual stability of basic feeling throughout the vicissitudes of life: They are always cheery or always gloomy, no matter what stimuli come their way.

Our ideas about normal oscillations in the flow of feelings and of normal rates of change between one feeling and another become severely shaken by the phenomena of *ambivalence*. Ambivalence is an odd emotional pattern and a distorted rhythm, consisting of rapid and sudden flip-flops in expressions of love and hate. Staccato fashion, a friendly handshake is abruptly overtaken by a facial snarl, in turn replaced perhaps by a charming word. Such alternations between components of opposed feelings of love and hate are too quick, too abrupt, too frequent, to fit the expected and healthy patterns of emotional modulation. The two emotions seem to vie for expression, with quickly shifting fates. But ambivalence can also take the form of a compound expression, so stratified as to contain the opposing affects simultaneously. Such compounding is exemplified in the hearty, friendly handshake that is also an aggressive, painful squeeze, or in the compliment that is also a verbal stab. Ambivalence should not be equated with mixed feelings. In the latter, the person holds opposed feelings in consciousness and can explicate their origins or reasons, being able to state the pros and cons of an issue that grips him. In ambivalence, one of the two basic feelings is conscious while the other is unconscious—the latter leading to symptomatic expression rather than a modulated response. Ambivalence is the coexistence of antithetical emotions acting with some degree of independence of each other. Put differently, the emotions are insufficiently fused or blended, inadequately checked so as to mitigate their effects. Such absence of fusion (or emotional synthesis) is characteristic of young children whose reactions to the imagined "good mother" and "bad mother" tend to be quite *ad hoc* and abruptly alternating. In this sense, a marked ambivalence in the emotional behavior of adults is an important indicator of regression or fixation.

Are emotions culturally conditioned? Their expression certainly is, and maybe their admission to consciousness also. American males do not hug and kiss each other in public; Mediterranean men do. Shame is painful for everyone, but an ordeal for some peoples, e.g., the Japanese, who after "loss of face" feel impelled to kill themselves. Expressions of anger are taboo in certain religious circles, and feelings of lust, let alone their expression, tend to be regulated in almost all cultures, but with striking differences. Much of the "generation gap" is a matter of culturally accentuated differences in the expression of emotions, and in the nurturing of subjective feelings as well.

A Psychodynamic Approach to Emotion, Especially Anxiety

In clinical appraisals, certain emotions take the limelight. General anxiety, specific irrational or disproportionate fear, great sadness or gloom, rage and hatred, conspicuous and irrational elation, apprehension about body functions, profound guilt feelings without apparent cause, deep shame, boredom, and spleen are emotional states that patients—or someone else!—complain of. They are typical symptoms of emotional distress, by themselves or in conjunction with other symptoms. They are all unpleasant—even the exaggerated elation that will soon bring the patient to reversal into sadness or exhaustion. By and large, intense or prolonged subjection to these feelings is experienced by the patient as disintegrative in its own right, or else is taken as a sign of disintegration occurring in other mental or body functions.

The striking clinical feature of these emotions is that they influence thought and action. They appear to be motives that alter conduct in certain directions. This feature of emotions is captured in the term "affect." Affects behave like energy systems, seeking release or discharge when tension exceeds an optimum level. When active, they dominate inner life (in perception, thought, etc.) and also produce many involuntary somatic processes (e.g., tremors, blushing, lacrimation), which make their presence overt.

This *driven* and *driving* function of emotions figured prominently in McDougall's[51] hormic psychology, to which Freud was attracted. In this conception, instinctual drives have three aspects: (1) cognition—a selective perception or a selective stimulus triggering the hormic upsurge; (2) emotion—a particular feeling tone fit for each drive, creating a unique inner state; (3) conation—a specific pattern of action tendencies or actual conduct that releases the hormic tension.

Phenomenologically, feelings are of course just feelings: *sui generis* subjective states registered in specific qualities such as sadness, languor, or hatred. Affects are those special feelings that have great impact—some power to overcome the person. They beset the stream of consciousness and the body's baseline of customary well-being. Psychodynamic theory treats feelings, and particularly affects, as the subjective mental representations of drives. Drives are the basic or ultimate motives, i.e., the biopsychic energy systems that are the "movers" of all behavior. Emotions (affects and feelings) are the signals of these drives, allowing them to come to awareness as purely psychic content. By some feat of inner translation, drives are presented, registered and felt as emotions in the stream of consciousness. Who or what makes these translations?

The "mysterious leap from the mind to the body" remains as mysterious as ever, but it is conceptually plausible to see the ego as the translator. The ego is the "seat of emotion," as Freud's later writings have it. It produces and registers states of feeling as signals, turning the energy processes of drives into messages that can be heeded for the purposes of adaptation. In this sense, feelings are a kind of language (as poets have always known) in which a dynamic state of being is conveyed to an inner perceiver who is also an actor—in effect, a manager aligning the organism's inner environment with the world or outer environment. By and large, positive feelings (pleasure signals) indicate that satisfaction is at hand, whereas negative feelings (pain or unpleasure signals) bespeak dissatisfaction, frustration, danger, or maladaptation. The latter call for special coping measures such as fight, flight, or action to alter the situation. And very often, negative feelings elicit special defenses against experiencing the unpleasant signals themselves any longer than necessary.

This fact is especially true of *anxiety,* so prominent in clinical situations. Produced by the ego as a special signal of danger, or as a kind of alarm, anxiety also prompts the ego to instigate measures for abolishing the alarm signal. These measures are *defense mechanisms,* a special class of a much larger group of coping devices that deal with stress. Defense mechanisms are intrapsychic operations which seek to mitigate or abolish anxiety in all its forms, including guilt feelings (as superego-induced anxiety) and shame (as a product of ego-ideal demands). Apart from its function as an alarm signal, anxiety apparently has a special "sting" that elicits such defenses, not characteristic of other negative feelings such as sadness, grief, or boredom. These emotions too are painful states that the ego will seek to mitigate, but its way of coping with them typically entails acts that are far more complicated and far less stereotyped than the defense mechanisms against anxiety—for instance, seeking diversion in work, having recourse to narcotics, or going on a spending spree.

One must also make a distinction between the healthy ego's hearing the anxiety signal and promptly engaging in effective action to abolish it, and the less than healthy phenomena that prevail in clinical cases. In the latter instances, anxiety signals seem to be ringing on, too long, too loudly, or too erratically because the ego's actions are ineffectual or inappropriate or have unwanted side effects. Clinical anxiety is not normal anxiety—it is in some way maladaptive.

Defenses, then, are ways of doing something about anxiety, which, having fulfilled its original signal function as a warning of danger, now needs to be eliminated. The sleeper who hears the sound of his alarm clock must do something. Short of shutting off the ringing and waking up to do a day's work, the sleepy person has a few other choices, albeit some of these seem rather far-fetched. He can shut off the alarm and go back to sleep. He can put a pillow over his ears to deaden the sound and no longer hear the ringing. He can defy the sound in the hope of eventually becoming numb to it. He can make himself believe that it is the neighbor's alarm, not his, and therefore none of his business. He can start singing loudly, so as not to hear the bell's ringing. He can say to himself: "I really hear nothing—it is only a chimera." He can distort the signal by the fantasy of its being a lark singing in his garden. He can try to listen to the bell's harmonics, ignoring their fundamental, extracting *Eine kleine Nachtmusik* from them. Or he can work the stimulus into a dream and not wake up at all. In some such ways, the ego can use various defenses against persistent anxiety. Of course, each defense has its particular price tag in energy expenditure and side effects.

Before the defense mechanisms can be described, we should consider the question why there is such a preponderance of negative affects in clinical situations. The answer is that most patients are, by definition, conflict-ridden. But that answer is rather cryptic unless it is amplified by a delineation of conflict. Conflict always involves several parties in strife or struggle with each other. Who or what are the warring parties whose strife is signaled as anxiety (or other painful affect) by the observing and managerial ego? Without ignoring struggles *between* persons, the psychodynamic viewpoint calls attention to struggles *within* persons: It focuses on intrapsychic conflict between intrapsychic parties. From the clinically prevailing battle lines, psychoanalysis slowly developed some ideas about the warring parties, eventually recognizing them as substructures of the personality, already described briefly in Chapter 2: id, ego, superego, and ego ideal. Being functionally specialized, each of these structures has, as it were, its own rules and procedures, its own tasks to accomplish, and its own gratifications to demand so as to remain viable. We denoted the ego as the managerial party, the synthesizer of the whole of personality. This role puts the ego in the position of needing reports from all other intrapsychic parties, and of course from the outer world (objective reality) as well, in order to establish working agreements between the demands of all, in relative harmony, in good balance, and with a fair apportionment of satisfactions. Note that the ego must be attuned to *all* participants in the life process; unfair partisanship or favoritism would undermine its managerial adequacy.

Aided by this imagery, we can now look at the various defense mechanisms as intrapsychic coping devices for anxiety management that betray, each in its own way, a certain kind and degree of partisanship, always keeping in mind that the primary target of each defense is a particular unpleasant *affect* whose impact is to be mitigated. The direct object of an intrapsychic defense is an anhedonic emotion, and it is the unpleasure of it that elicits the defense.

Defense mechanisms can be classified in various ways. We are focusing here on variables of *exclusion* (elimination, subtraction), *substitution* (replacement, addition), and *transformation* as the basic techniques of defense.

One exclusionary move is *repression*. It eliminates a painful affect from consciousness and excludes its associated occasions from memory. It is a motivated forgetting that subtracts painful items from the data bank of available memories, moving them as it were into "dead storage." That fact does not mean the end for these items—the storehouse has its own rules (the primary process that governs the unconscious), which allow displacement and a massing of energy charges, by which some items can break out again, disguised as symptoms. Another move is *denial*. It too is an act of exclusion or subtraction, but it also involves an element of rebuttal or protest: A painful fact or feeling is declared not to exist despite its obviousness (to others). Its reality is not granted, *because* it is painful; it is scotomatized out of existence because of the patient's preponderant dedication to the pleasure principle. This is the crudest form of denial, not to be equated with denials supported by bravery, or the denial in fantasy where painful truths are only temporarily obliterated in compensatory reveries. It is the automatic, reflexlike functioning of repression and denial that bring out their subtractive character. The moment the act of forceful forgetting becomes a conscious effort, as in *suppression*, some focus on the item to be eliminated is implied, and thus some awareness of it.

Appearances notwithstanding, *introjection* also entails a subtractive maneuver. On the model of food ingestion, introjection brings into the person a good or bad object, entire or partial, which then becomes a part of the self. In its most primitive form such an incorporation takes away the object's externality and objective existence; the object is now dominated by the infantile omnipotence of the undifferentiated id and proto-ego, precisely because its objectivity would be too anxiety arousing. If the external object is bad, it presents a formidable threat; if it is good, its uncontrollable presence, its instability, or its distance entails the threat of loss. This archaic mechanism of introjection is to be sharply differentiated from the developmentally higher forms of identification, imitation, and selective copying that keep the external object intact, proceed by nonincorporative modes, and are less driven by signal anxiety.

Projection is an additive or substitutive defense, in the sense that it adds to the external world certain features of the person himself—and keeps them there very much in focus as a point of concern. The original problem that caused anxiety is by no means taken off the person's mind. It persists in consciousness, but now as an external rather than an internal danger. Anxiety is thus transformed into a fear of something that can be pinpointed: "The police are after me," "Watch out for homosexual seduction," or "UFOs crowd the air to extinguish me." Different kinds of projection relate to different developmental levels. The most primitive kind is, like introjection, caught up in the infantile omnipotence of thought, with very little self-object differentiation. It is analogous to oral spitting or vomiting, as introjection is analogous to oral ingestion. Higher-order projections may occur when superego structures are operative and produce guilt feelings; in that case the expulsion technique may be in the anal mode. The projections involved in communal prejudice against racial, ethnic, or social groups may assume a competitive, phallic character. Projections are also involved in supernatural world views that populate the skies with gods or demons and all kinds of imaginary beings. Somewhere on this scale of projections is a transition from the specific defense mechanism of projection to projection in the looser sense of externalizing the products of the imagination.

Among transformative techniques of defense, the mechanism of *isolation* is instructive. Here is an example in the form of a story a twenty-year-old college student produced to a stimulus picture of a somewhat ambiguous human figure slumped down by the side of a bench near an object on the floor often seen as a revolver (a picture that often stimulates suicide fantasies):

> Facing a future of despair and loneliness and apparent hopelessness . . . I want to say . . . the individual . . . (but I think you want me to denote it somehow . . .) the individual shrinks . . . from the social interaction of which it has been a part. The realization of the alienation inherent in modern society in the face of increased mechanization and impersonalization of the social machinery produces an internal conflict between the social needs of the individual and an attempted expression of creative and meaningful work . . .
>
> The intense loneliness developing concurrently in the face of this impersonalization may produce a total withdrawal unless the individual can find a means of expres-

sion. (Now I suppose you want a result)...I could not necessarily give a decisive result...Only with a re-alization ... a development ... of individual creativity may a meaningful existence be developed.

However painful this man's predicament was or is, we hear only the faintest echo of emotion. He has separated the painful affect from the occasion that hurts him, and from its direct associations. He now talks only about ideas, in an extremely laborious, quasi-philosophical, abstract way, nearly devoid of feeling. He strengthens the attempted isolation of affect from idea by *hyperintellectualization* and seeks maximal distance from real beings of flesh and blood by dwelling on disembodied clichés. The experienced connections between concrete occasion and painful affect are dissipated. In fact, isolation is rarely limited to specific traumatic events and particular anxieties. It typically operates as a general device that blunts *all* emotions; it shifts the ego's functioning toward cognitive processes, resulting in obsessions, whose alternations between belief and doubt echo the muffled ambivalent feelings.

There is a kind of repression that not only eliminates a painful affect but turns it, or the behavior associated with it, into its opposite—a *reversal of affect* or *reaction formation*. Usually, the resulting feelings or attitudes have a forced character, which alerts the observer to the fact that an extra quantum of energy is being enlisted for the upkeep of the behavioral "front." Through reversal, feelings of spite or hatred may lead to attitudes of loving concern—but of a smothering kind that also implies some denial of the angry impulse. By reaction formation, feelings of great dependency may lead to displays of brave self-assertion—but conspicuously overdone. A fear of heights may lead to heroic efforts at mountain climbing—but with so much drivenness that phobic traces remain visible in the *counterphobic* reaction.

Somewhat akin to reaction formation is the mechanism of *undoing*. It occurs in guilt-ridden persons who are prone to compulsions and ritualistic acts. Undoing is an attempt at restitution through an act that is the opposite of a previous act that has produced anxiety or guilt feelings.

For instance, a trusted and elderly bank employee who was responsible for the vault's safekeeping found himself, just before his retirement, overcome by episodes of doubting whether he had really closed the vault at the end of the day. Walking home from work, he stopped halfway in near panic, thinking that he might have left the door of the vault open. So he walked back to check. Finding it securely locked, he nevertheless had to open it first, and then close it again. Such episodes occurred with increasing frequency, so that the man found himself quite depleted by his time-consuming engagement in this ritual.

This example also suggests that the defense may be better described as "doing and undoing" rather than as merely "undoing": The secret, unconscious wish to leave the door open must momentarily be indulged, quickly followed by the restitutive act of closing it.

What has been said here about these basic defense mechanisms needs amplification to show their fixity and sweeping impact. First, these defenses are not the products of conscious deliberation and do not occur with felt effort. They occur as *automatisms* of which the person is unaware—although he may become aware of their consequences and side effects. Second, these defenses are also operative in the diagnostic and treatment efforts, impeding the patient's self-assessment and the therapeutic process in the form of *resistance*. The operation of the defenses makes the patient resist self-disclosure, resist reality testing, and resist any change in his *status quo*. Third, the defenses and their attitudinal aftermath are repeated as *transference* patterns in the patient's relations to the diagnostic and treatment staff, as if he rehearses with them the salient features of his past and present object relations.

These *dynamisms of repetition* have an important consequence for the diagnostician assessing emotions. In many cases, particularly those in which the defense mechanisms work with some efficacy, the patient's emotionality is observable not in its natural or raw state, but only as disguised or transformed. In an acute anxiety reaction the autonomic symptoms of trembling, sweating, or dyspnea are obvious, though the affect as felt may be weak; in any angry outburst, behavioral or verbal, the affect of anger is quite overt. In many depressive states the emotion of sadness, despondency, or gloom stands out for all to see—but certainly not in all forms of depression. Feelings may be thoroughly disguised, screened out, or dampened—both from external recognition and from internal awareness.

While an organized and articulated use of certain defense mechanisms against the experience of anxiety is tantamount to symptom choice and hence correlates with specific neurotic or psychotic syndromes, anxiety (or guilt feelings or shame) is not always the pivotal emotion in symptom formation. Any and all unpleasant affects may become targets of defense, and the defenses are not confined to the specific mechanisms thus far presented. For instance, in *identification with the aggressor* the person who feels victimized by an attacker comes to adopt the role of the attacker not merely to avoid the painful position of being a victim, but also to give vent to his own sadistic impulses, for which he now has an important rationalization. A position of *self-sacrifice* and conspicuous *self-renunciation* can relieve fear of competition as well as release masochistic leanings. In some deep regressions the pleasure ego holds sway, as it does in some severe character disorders fixated to long overindulged primary narcissism. In such cases a great variety of unpleasures evolving from reality testing and pressures for growth are warded off largely by avoidance, manipulation, and persistent passivity. The more conspicuous affects in such persons are lustful rather than painful—indeed it is often their relatives who are saddled with the negative feelings that the patient's manipulative behavior elicits!

In clinical practice one sees quite a few patients who deny that they have any problem, do not feel "tied up in knots," do not seem to be "falling apart," and do not present conspicuous amounts of negative affect. Some may be guilty of serious crimes, but attest to no guilt *feelings* whatever. Some have seriously transgressed, socially or morally, or have shown profound lapses in loyalty, but seem to experience no shame. They are nonchalant during interviews, or argue vehemently about legal matters and protest the idea of a psychiatric diagnosis. Their emotional tones, subjectively experienced as well as objectively displayed, do not seem to fit their predicament or the events that brought them to psychiatric attention. Frequently, their deeper emotions, hidden behind a facile façade, must be elicited by the examiner's determination to put them under special stress, e.g., by confrontation, withholding privileges, or assigning unpleasant and frustrating tasks.

Such cases raise the issue of *capacity for emotional experience*, and of selective *tolerance* for certain emotions. Autonomous as emotions are, since they are rooted in vital biopsychic processes that push themselves through, come what may, people do not have equal tolerance for any and all emotions. To some persons, the specific emotion of, say, grief is quite *ego alien:* they feel overcome by it. To others, grief may be an *ego-syntonic* feeling with which they have learned to live. Said Emily Dickinson:

> I can wade grief—
> whole pools of it . . .[52]

Is this a matter of habituation, diversity of life experiences, or congenital sensitivity thresholds? Some children are recognized at birth as "vulnerable babies"; others are quite hardy. Pedagogues would emphasize the importance of experience—adequate exposure to diverse satisfactions and frustrations as essential to the emotional growth of any person. Clinicians do see evidence of individual thresholds of sensitivity, but also know that formerly ego-alien emotions can become synthesized into ego-syntonic feelings.

There are epileptic phenomena consisting of pure feelings suddenly welling up in the patient and then abruptly abating, often accompanied by some of the motor corollaries of feelings; fits of almost vegetative anxiety without apparent cause, or fits of rage comparable to the sham rage that can be experimentally produced in animals by brain stimulation. "Fits of fear," said Hughlings Jackson,[53] "not fear of the fit." Typically, such fits feel entirely ego alien to the person having them. Limbic and insular discharges may be invoked as proximal causes of these seizures, but does that mean that the feelings are entirely foreign bodies within the patient's personality? Yes and no—they are surely *felt* as alien to the conscious ego since they do not fit in the self-percept. But, like dreams, they are meaningful events—if not to consciousness, then to the unconscious. Such cases teach the important lesson that *emotional processes are not to be equated with the phenomenology of consciousness.* While consciousness undoubtedly contains feelings in their diverse hedonic qualities, and whereas phenomenologists (e.g., Sartre[54]) insist that feelings must be *felt* in order to merit the designation, the fact is that some affects bypass consciousness altogether, taking a direct path to the motor system where they find discharge. In this sense, much of the "emotional life" of a person comes as a surprise to him. He has to infer unregistered feelings from certain behavioral acts he finds himself engaged in.

Some of these acts one finds oneself doing are *regressive,* even to oneself. The person recognizes that he "let himself go," at odds with his customary control and without his usual conscious modulation. Uninhibited discharge is the primary-process model of affects: the affect appears as the subjective equivalent of drive, whether libido or aggression. The secondary-process model of affects is the one elaborated in this section. A delay of drive gratification is imposed that alters tension thresholds (for instance, by the anticathexes of the defense mechanisms) and translates drive tensions into signal affects in deference to the reality principle and the relative autonomy of the psyche's subdivisions, all of which demand adaptation.

It is inherent in the psychodynamic view of emotions that the emotions per se are an active part of the developmental process. Emotions mature just as much as thought and perception mature. They become diversified and refined and assume multiple functions in their own right—they are not merely controlled and channeled by the regulatory ego as if the ego were essentially opposed to them. In the course of growth, emotions come to participate in the increasing stratification of all mental life, functioning concomitantly at conscious and unconscious levels, each with different qualities, and simultaneously at the perceptual and motor ends of the action spectrum. This view of emotions implies that regressions and fixations can occur; in other words, emotional dedifferentiation.

Problems and Opportunities in Assessing Emotions

In the assessment of a patient's emotions the clinical observer will find it useful to keep the parameters of emotional growth in mind, for much of his evaluation is geared to age-specific norms or ideals, and he is often faced with issues of regression and fixation. The emotional life of a toddler is not as diversified as an adolescent's; the middle-aged person's feelings should be more differentiated than those of the pubescent boy or girl. What are these developmental parameters of emotion? Briefly, the following:

1. from diffuse, instinctual activity bursts to delayed, purposive, controlled acts;
2. from gross motor activities to the covert activity of thinking;
3. from direct engagement in deeds to verbalization;
4. from impulsive affects that overwhelm the ego to ego-syntonic or tolerated feelings put to adaptive or creative use;
5. from smooth muscle and glandular (somatic) reactions to striped muscle responses, including speech and gestures;
6. from inhibited, censored, defended-against emotions to consciously registered and modulated feelings;
7. from a coarse love-and-hate polarity with its attendant ambivalence to a rich pattern of variegated feelings allowing for complex combinations and subtle tones.

Each of these represents a distinct dimension of emotional development. Each also involves a timetable of growth, some shorter, some longer; some take as long as the whole life span. Their keynotes are differentiation and synthesis.

To illustrate the import of these parameters, consider the difference between a childish tantrum and, say, a college student's participation in a protest march. Both acts are dominated by aggressive feelings. The first is a brief burst of feeling without target, for want of which the person's own body becomes both path and object of discharge; the act is rather isolated from preceding and subsequent acts, and the angry feeling totally dominates consciousness for the duration of the tantrum. The second behavior is likely to be embedded in a mosaic of other feelings, with selective discrimination between ideas, objects, and targets of aggression, and with distinctions between feelings of spite, rancor, hate, bitterness, animosity, disgust, dislike, resentment, etc., each linked with ideas having slightly different feeling tones and leading to differentiated action patterns. A good part of the aggressive action is verbal, or in other ways symbolic, undergirded by selective feelings of amicability toward like-minded members of the protesting group. Our protester can introspectively dwell on his aggressive feelings, sorting them out, taking some distance from them, channeling them into diverse patterns of action. An enormous amount of emotional differentiation stands out in contrast to the simple tantrum, not only in resultant action and levels of expression, but also in the subjective experience of hedonic tones.

By the same token, differences stand out between the overwhelming emotion of the rapist blinded by his impulse, and the modulated, if not planned, emotional processes of one person wooing another during a lengthy time span, eventuating also in an act of sexual union—but with what qualitative differences! Impulsive pawing of a desired person enlists cruder feelings than those leading to tenderly verbal and infinitely varied expressions of "I love you," well-timed and flexibly calibrated to the needs and personhood of the beloved. The overwhelming anxiety of panic "feels" different from the realistic fear one might have of a hot stove or a poisonous fruit. The fist fight entailing large muscle groups gives aggressive feelings a different tone from a debate with an adversary, which entails the small muscle groups of speech mechanisms and gestures, and a great deal of ideation that gives the hatred an altogether different tonal range. Depression is a cruder, more pervasive, and more primitive (and irrational) package of feelings than sorrow for a known transgression or sadness over an actual bereavement. Suspicion is not paranoia, not only because many suspicions are justified, but because the states of consciousness in the two cases are of different orders: The paranoiac is utterly dominated by the threat of his projections coming home to roost, whereas the person having a suspicion can concomitantly experience many other feelings, and put his suspicion in perspective. Repressed feelings are not consciously registered with fine phenomenal attunement to their shadings and qualities, but come through as a nebulous awareness of diffuse tension, or as inexplicable and unwanted mood dispositions—very different from consciously registered and appropriate emotions. The somatized anger in gastric ulcer is not felt as anger, but as pain and digestive discomfort, which in turn skews the patient's responsiveness to any and all other feelings.

Maybe the single most important gain that results from all parameters of emotional development is itself an emotion, namely the *feeling of freedom*. This feeling is certainly complex, with many dimensions, not to be confused with objective or metaphysical definitions of freedom. One of its dimensions is openness to experiencing any and all emotions aroused by the events of life, taking delight in the pleasurable ones and tolerating the unpleasurable ones that must be, without immediate defensiveness. Such a feeling of freedom both enhances an introspective savoring of emotional varieties and widens the scope of emotional expression, with increased governance over purposive action. It enhances spontaneity as well as deliberation, and fosters communication. For all these reasons, a definite feeling of freedom is an earmark of mental health, and its felt increase a sign of betterment. In contrast, its felt absence or diminution accompanies all psychological symptoms and is probably the most important motive in assuming patienthood and seeking treatment (or eventually accepting it, if imposed).

A special problem inheres in the clinical ·assessment of emotions. Here, more than in the evaluation of any other part process, the examiner should be aware of the preponderance of *interactional phenomena.* Both he and the patient *emit* feelings to each other. Both he and the patient *display involuntary as well as voluntary signs* of emotion. Each *responds consciously and unconsciously* to emotional clues from the other. In regard to emotions, there is no clear-cut role division between the examiner and the examinee. They are constantly exploring and testing each other, at some level of awareness, and both are also likely to explore themselves through *introspective musings.* Are there any systematic approaches that would help the examiner arrive at solid observations and keen judgment?

Yes. The first step toward objectivity is provided by the fact that *emotions have physiological accompaniments not easily controllable by voluntary effort.* The very anxious person sweats, trembles, and tends to have difficulty in modulating his voice. The very sad person is slow in most of his motor activities, including speech, and tends to be tearful. The very angry person has high muscle tone, makes facial snarls, and is given to explosive speech. There are abundant facial clues, from pallor to cyanosis, from eyes popping to aversive glances, from frowning to an engaging openness, that betray emotional dispositions or states. There are also postural clues: the way a person walks or stands, sits or slumps; his capacity for quietly relaxing as against the need to fidget, squirm, or display an utterly taut and tense muscle system. Ordinary suspiciousness becomes visible watchfulness and hypervigilance in the paranoid patient who keeps scanning his environment and the examiner for potential threats. While the "reading" of emotions from such physiological clues often falls short of scientific certainty and precision, there is no doubt that one can sharpen one's observational acumen about such clues by long and varied clinical practice.

The virtue of learning to read this kind of body language of emotion is that it provides a path of access to patients inept at verbal communication, and those who have muffled their own registration of feelings by extensive defense. It also brings the observer in touch with that special stratum of emotion consisting of affects: the drive-linked passions that tend to be dominant sources of motivation, shaping a good part of the patient's behavior. Inasmuch as such passions reveal something of the primary process, the reading of body language, like the interpretation of dreams, is a royal road to the unconscious.

A second clinical approach to emotions consists of *pointed conversation*. This notion may strike the reader as trite, but it is not, if one realizes that some examiners lean toward a clinical mystique in which the patient's words are a priori disdained and the clinician himself emerges as the megalomanic expert on the patient's feelings. While it is true that any patient's verbal statements may only describe his conscious feelings, or express defenses against affects, many emotions are well expressed by the patient, and some are simply inaccessible without his verbalizing them. Such states as grief, feelings of loss, emotional emptiness, spleen, shame, guilt feelings, and certain fears are eminently expressible in words and can be consciously conveyed. The psychiatric cliché "How do you feel today?" should never be made a mockery by the clinician himself not heeding the patient's full answer.

A third approach frankly enlists an interpersonal phenomenon already hinted at earlier: *empathic reverberations* in the examiner of the patient's emotions. Mothers and their infants share each other's feelings directly by their partnership in a symbiotic unit, and many adults retain some capacity for such direct sharing. Clinicians develop this capacity, if need be, by a regression in the service of the ego that is part of the use of the self as a diagnostic tool. A patient's sadness, even if absent from his conversation and motorically disguised, may deeply affect the examiner, who feels sad, eerily, without any awareness of distinct signs or signals of it and without rationally drawing inferences. Empathy supplements *in*spection of the patient with *intro*spection of the examiner. By carefully reading his own feelings, the clinician may discover the leading feelings of his patient, often with an astounding convincingness that is pragmatically verified.

But the empathic process is two-pronged. Not all feelings are sympathetically shared, producing identical emotions in the partners. Some feelings of the patient may elicit powerfully antagonistic, antipathetic, or otherwise remarkably different feelings in the examiner, such as irritation, aversion, loathing, anger, pity, or anxiety, that are not commensurate with what the patient experiences. Both are moved, but by different emotions; the interpersonal reverberation consists of a shared *intensity* of affect, touching an equal depth. In such cases, the examiner's self-scrutiny entails a more complicated inference process: He must know through self-analysis what feeling in the patient trips off his own antagonistic emotion.

A fourth technique of assessing emotions evolves from the psychodynamic recognition that emotions are muffled, disguised, or transformed by *defense*. At first blush, the catatonic patient assuming a statuesque posture does not look anxious, but bizarre; the phobic's tenacious avoidance of elevators, mice, or doorknobs looks not like fear but like silliness. A hysterical fit before a small audience on a hospital ward looks like a put-on, almost an enjoyable theatrical pantomime. The college student mentioned earlier, using isolation of affect so widely, sounded so cold and distant that one would not attribute any feeling to him—he gave the impression of being a robot. The counterphobic, daredevil acrobat appears so certain of his acts that one would consider him fearless, without the least concern about being maimed. In all such cases it behooves the examiner, through skillful observation, to penetrate the patient's *behavioral façade*, taking it as *a compromise of affect and defense*. He has to ask himself what the patient's feelings would be if they were not disguised or altered by defense. He has to disregard for the time being the patient's use of repression, denial, intellectualization, isolation, reaction formation, etc., so as to surmise or discover what emotions the patient is struggling with, or what he would experience (and might experience with less ego vigilance, as in his dreams, or in fatigue) without his prominent defenses. What raw anxieties, shame, guilt feelings, self-loathing, panic, and other psychic pains lie behind the defensive bulwark—and occasion-

ally sneak through the defense lines in the form of symptomatic acts, dreams, parapraxes, somatic symptoms, nightmares, or explosive behavior!

A fifth approach resembles the cognitive technique of the
fourth: It too consists of temporarily disregarding or subtract-
ing the effects of modifiers on feelings, but in this case the
modifiers are *pharmacological*. With a plethora of tranquilizers
and mood-modifying drugs on the market, and the prevalence
of self-medication, the moods and feelings of many patients
presenting themselves for psychiatric examination are unnatu-
ral, i.e., artificially disguised or transformed. I remember the
case of a middle-aged woman, a year earlier bereft of her
husband, who on presentation was on no fewer than eight
prescribed drugs, all of which had the effect of so toning
down or modifying her natural feelings of bereavement and
loss that she had had no opportunity to mourn! All we had to
do was slowly and judiciously take her off medication so that
she could come to grips with her real feelings—which she did
promptly and in due time as a normal, adaptive course of
mourning. Indeed, what are the patients' real feelings in a
drug-manipulated culture? What new, unfamiliar, or even un-
natural feelings are induced by hallucinogens and other drugs
that alter consciousness? What old feelings do the new feelings
replace? What promising, healthy adaptations to pain, and
what normal functions of pain as warning signals of realistic
danger, are nipped in the bud by sweeping recourse to pain-
killers, even for minor discomforts?

On the other hand, the patient's positive response to
thoughtfully prescribed energizers and mood-altering medication can retroactively verify the clinician's initial hunch about
the mood or affect he sought to deal with, which is particularly striking when the feelings were initially quite disguised.
When a depressed patient perks up on energizers, the initial
guess about a blue mood was probably right, even when the
patient was unable to describe or express any particular feeling and only manifested a behavioral lassitude.

A sixth approach to emotions is *historical*. A keen observer
may come to think that only the feelings enacted and experi-

enced in the here and now, under his observing eyes, are real. This assumption overlooks the fact that emotions can be remembered and often receive added impetus from the past, inasmuch as current feelings are states of reliving old feelings. If anything is continuous in life, it is the emotions. The examiner should therefore pursue the patient's *emotional history* by interviewing him about his typical emotional reactions to landmark happenings in his life: how he felt when deprived or frustrated, what he experienced when he was blamed, how he reacted to the loss of loved ones, what feelings were engendered by success or praise. He should also elicit the patient's awareness of certain continuities: Does his current reaction to stress resemble previous reactions? Does the patient himself see a typical emotional response pattern? And does he appropriate it or does he tend to disown any pattern?

Most importantly, clinical examination of emotions involves a keen eye for just those *contradictions in behavior* that stand out in psychopathology. Is there a notable disparity between a patient's words about feelings and his gestures or body reactions? How do his words stack up against his deeds? How does his face look and his voice sound while he is narrating a sad or gratifying life event? Does he laugh while in distress, or cry at the happy ending? Discrepancies of this kind are not only symptoms of marked ambivalence, they flow from the complex stratification of all mental life, yielding multiple signal systems all operating at once.

Last, but not least, the examiner of emotions tends to be handicapped by the limited vocabulary of feelings. Exposed in college courses to the pain-fear-rage triad, and later to the libido-aggression and depression-elation dualisms, the professional mental health worker is tempted to use shorthand expressions, reductionistic phrases, and an all too coarse classification of emotions. All too often a patient is declared "depressed" before the fine shadings of his feelings have been explored. Yet sadness is not depression. All too quickly a patient is described as "paranoid" when he is only suspicious— and maybe for good reasons! Yet suspiciousness is not paranoia. In short, the examiner who wants to do justice to his patient's feelings must explore their subtlety and complexity, and to do that, he must have a rather rich vocabulary for the multitude of human emotions. To attune him to diversity, and to aid him in the correct use of descriptive terms for feelings, this chapter ends with "A List of Words Descriptive of Affective Reactions," drawn up by Barrington.[55] This list is certainly not the "last word" on describing feelings, but it may be a helpful step in the right direction.

A List of Words Descriptive of Affective Reactions

by BYRON L. BARRINGTON

As part of the study of the verbal behavior of therapists, a list of words was needed which would include most of the common descriptions of emotional reactions or feelings.† As far as the author could determine, no such list was available in the literature and it was therefore necessary to compile one. The development of this list was rather time consuming and it is therefore reproduced here for the convenience of anyone interested in a list of words descriptive of feelings.

To develop the list, four clinical psychologists were asked to write all the words they could think of which describe feelings. This list was then supplemented by looking up these words in a thesaurus and adding to the list all related words that described emotional reactions. These two procedures produced 434 words directly referring to affective reactions which are given in Section 1 below. A second group (Section 2) was also compiled of 64 words which referred to the elicitation of, or implied the presence of, a specific emotional response.

Because of multiple meaning, some words were included only when used in a particular context, e.g., when preceded by the words "felt," or "feeling of being." In Sec-

---

†For a report of this study see *J. of Counseling Psychology*, Vol. 8, No. 1, 1961, pages 37-42.

tion 1, where relevant, the context is specified by indicating in parentheses those other words which had to be associated with the word in question for it to be classified as having an affective reference. To save space the associated context words are abbreviated, with the meaning of the abbreviation given at the [beginning] of Section 1.

In Section 2, some words were included only if they referred to, or implied, a reaction by a person. Two examples of such words are "calm" and "upset." In the list, such words are designated by an asterisk. Two asterisks following a word indicate its inclusion in Section 2, except when it is used in a context qualifying it for Section 1. It will be noted that the Section 1 words are divided into various subgroups. These are rather arbitrary categories set up to permit more rapid localization of a word on the list. Because of their arbitrary nature, the value of these subcategories for any other purpose is questionable.

SECTION 1. WORDS RELATING DIRECTLY TO AFFECTIVE REACTIONS

Key: (f) "felt" or "feel"; (fo) "feeling of"; (fob) "feeling of being"; (fla) "felt like a"; (so) "sense of"; (sob) "sense of being."

UNHAPPINESS
blue
bad (f)
badly (f)
dejected
dejectedness
dejection
depressed
depression
despair
despondence
despondency
despondent
disappointed
disappointment
disconsolate
discouraged
discouragement
dismal

distressed
gloomy
miserable
miserableness
mournful
sad
sadness
sorrow
sorry
sullen
sullenness
unhappiness
unhappy

PERSONAL WORTH
acceptable (f)
conceit
conceited

good (f)
important
needed (f, fob)
pride
priding
proud
respect for
respect
valuable (f)
valuing
worthwhile (f)
worthy

DISORGANIZATION
amazed
amazement
astonished
astonishment

astounded
baffled
bewildered
bewilderment
confused
confusion
disintegration (fo)
dismay
dismayed
disorganized (f)
disorganiza-
  tion (fo)
distressed
dizziness
dizzy
fogginess
foggy (f)
fuzziness
fuzzy
light headed
mixed up
perplexed
puzzled
shock
shocked
surprised
torn apart (f)
torn up (f, fob)
uncertain
uncertainty
unsure
unsureness

IMPATIENCE
dissatisfied
dissatisfaction
fed up
frustrated
frustration
impatient
impatience
restless
restlessness

LIKING
admire

admired
admiration
admiring
affection
appreciate
appreciated
appreciation
care
cared
crave
craving
desire
desiring
friendliness
friendly (f)
liked
like (as verb)
liking
interest
interested
long for
longing for
love
loved
loving
prefer
preferred
regard for
respect
respected
respecting
want
wanted
wanting
wish
wishing

EMPATHY
empathy
empathic
empathizing
pity
sympathy
sympathetic
sympathizing
pitying

DISLIKING
animosity
antagonism
antagonistic
aversion
bitter
contempt
contemptuous
despise
despised
despising
detest
detesting
detested
disdained
disdainful
disgust
disgusted
dislike
disliking
don't care
hate
hated
hating
hostile
hostility
loathe
loathing
repugnance
resent
resentful
resenting
resentment
vengeful

WORRY
alarmed
bother
bothered
bothers
concern
concerned
disturbed
doubt
doubtful
doubting

suspicious
suspicion
troubled
worried
worry
worrying

HAPPINESS
amused
amusement
cheerful
delightful
enjoy
enjoyment
enjoying
gay
glad
gladness
good (f)
grateful
gratification
gratified
great (f)
happier
happiness
happy
joy
joyful
jolly
pleased
pleasure
wonderful

ANGER
aggravated
anger
angered
angry
annoyed
exasperated
exasperation
furious
indignant
indignation
infuriated
ired

irked
irritated
irritation
mad
maddened
provoked
resent
resented
resentful
resenting
resentment

TIREDNESS
apathetic
bored
drowsy
dull
exhausted
exhaustion
fatigue (except as
    verb)
fatigued
indifference
indifferent
lazy
laziness
lethargic
lethargy
listless
listlessness
sleepiness
sleepy
tired
tiredness
wearied
weary
weariness
worn out (f)

STRENGTH
able (f, fob)
accomplishment
    (fo, so)
brave
capable (f, fob)
competent (f, fob)

confident
confidence
courage
courageous
hope
hoped
hopeful
independent (f,
    fob)
independence (fo)
mastery (fo)
strong (f, fob)
stronger
useful
secure (f)
security (fo, so)

WEAKNESS
awe
awed
bashful
bashfulness
caught (f, fob)
dependence
dependent
depending
helpless
helplessness
hopeless
hopelessness
inadequacy (fo)
inadequate (f, fob)
incompetent
    (f, fob)
inferior (f, fob)
inferiority (fo)
inhibited
inhibitedness
impotent
shy
shyness
timid
timidity
tied down (f, fob)
trapped (f, fob)
weak (f, fob)

ENERGETIC
alert
alive (f, fob)
eager
eagerness
energetic
enthusiastic
enthusiasm
excited
inspired
optimistic
peppy
peppier
wide awake

JEALOUSY
envy
envious
jealous
jealousy

FEAR
afraid
apprehension
apprehensive
dread
dreading
fear
fearful
fearing
frightened
horror
horrified
insecurity
insecure
panic
panicky
scared
terrified
terror
wary

GUILT
ashamed
embarrassed
embarrassment

guilt
guilty
humiliated
humiliation
shame (so, fo)
shameful
regret
regretted
regretting

ANXIETY
anxiety
anxious
anxiousness
moody
nervous
nervousness
on edge
tense
tenseness
tight
tightness (f)
upset (except as
verb)

COMFORT
at ease
calm
comfortable
content
contented
contentment
contentedness
peaceful
peacefulness
pleasant
pleasantness
pleased
relaxed
satisfied
satisfaction
unconcern
untroubled
rested

DISCOMFORT
discomfort
discontent
discontented
self-conscious
uncomfortable
unpleasant
unpleasantness

REJECTION
alone (f)
left out (f)
loneliness
lonely
lonesome
rejected (f, fob)
rejection (f)
unloved (f, fob)

ACCEPTANCE
accepted (f)
acceptance (fo, so)
consoled (f)
loved (f, sob, fob)
wanted (f, sob,
fob)

WORTHLESSNESS
foolish (f)
lacking (f)
silly (f)
worthless (f, fob)
useless (f, fob)
uselessness (f, so)
unimportant (f)

PATIENCE
patience
patient
resigned (not as
verb)
resignation (not as
noun)

DETERMINATION
certain

determined	anticipating	PAIN
determination	cynical	hurt
sure (except as	reluctance	pain
"yes")	reluctant	painful
	sensitive (f)	
OTHER	sick (f)	
anticipation	tempted	

SECTION 2. WORDS RELATING TO ELICITATION OF SPECIFIC EMOTIONAL RESPONSES

alarm	bewildering	disappoints
alarming	bore	disappointing
alarms	bores	discourage
alerts	boring	discourages
alerting	bothering	discouraging
amaze	bothersome	disintegrates
amazing		disinteresting
amuse		dismaying
amuses	calm*	dismays
amusing	calming	distress
antagonize	calms	distresses
antagonizes	cheer	distressing
antagonized	cheers	disturb*
antagonizing	cheering	disturbing
annoying	confuse	dizzying
annoys	confuses	dulls
angers	confusing	dulling
astonish	consoled**	
astonishes	consoling	
astonishing	comfort	eases
astound	comforts	easing
astounds	comforting	embarrass
astounding		embarrasses
awakened	delight	embarrassing
awakens	delights	enthuse
awing	depress	enthuses
	depresses	excite
baffles	depressing	excites
bewilder	detestable	exciting
bewilders	disappoint	exhaust
		exhausts

*When used in reference to human reactions.
**Except as used in Section I.

fatigue (as verb)
fatigues
fatiguing
frighten
frightening
frightens

gladdens
gratifies
gratify
gratifying

hateful
horrifies
horrify
horrifying
humiliate
humiliates
humiliating
hurting
hurts

inhibit
inhibiting
inhibits
inspire
inspires
inspiring

mixes you up

pains
panics
perplex
perplexes
perplexing
provoke
puzzle
puzzles
puzzling
pleases
pleasing

reassuring
relax
relaxes
relaxing

sadden
saddens
saddening
scare
scares
scaring
scary
satisfy
satisfying
satisfies
satisfactory
shame**
shames

shock*
shocking
surprise
surprising
surprises

tempting
tenses
terrify
terrifies
terrifying
tire*
tires*
tiring
trouble*
troubles*
troubling

upset* **
upsets*
upsetting*

wearies
wearying
worries
worrisome

Chapter 9

Assessing Part Processes: Action

The moment a clinician meets a patient he is presented with forms and qualities of action. Much as he may wish to listen to and talk with his patient, and however dependent he is in his daily work on verbal communication, his eyes come greatly to the aid of his ears, and are sometimes his only source of observation. He sees a smile or a frown, a docile posture or an agitated gait, the sagging limpness of a depressed person or the restless flitting about of a hyperkinetic child. He sees one person sitting tautly on the edge of his chair, another reclining luxuriously in the full circumference of his seat, a third standing stock still for hours in a weird stance, a fourth unable to pick up his fork and spoon at the dinner table because he feels compelled first to sway his arms rhythmically in the air as if he were conducting an orchestra.

The variety of activities the word *action* covers is large. Least dubitable are the manifest activities of striped muscle groups, large or small, that quickly come to notice. More difficult to discern and judge is covert action, such as unreleased muscle tension, a fist clenched but not pounded, jaws taut with concealed grinding of teeth. Covert action also pertains to the activity of smooth muscles, which does not meet the eye at all; and in a more remote sense it may include thinking, feeling, internal speech, and óther invisible processes. I shall disregard the latter here since they are discussed elsewhere in this book. Without stretching the concept too much, we might say that action refers to "what one does and how one does it," or, in a behavioral framework, the predominantly motor responses of an organism to any external or internal stimulus.

Because it is such a large category, action can be approached from many different points of view, of which the following are important to a greater or lesser degree:

overt versus covert
voluntary versus involuntary
natural versus symbolic
alloplastic versus autoplastic
immediate versus delayed
integrated versus fragmentary
mature versus primitive
reflex versus complex
impulsive versus controlled
adaptive versus nonadaptive
libidinal versus aggressive
deft versus maladroit
mediated by central versus autonomic nervous system
goal-directed versus scattered

Quite a few other aspects will come to mind, but, consistent with psychodynamic personality theory, we will first deal with action from the following points of view: (1) the energetic aspect; (2) the economic aspect (i.e., expenditure of energy); (3) the control aspect, including skill; (4) the developmental aspect; (5) the symbolic aspect—all of which allow a meaningful grouping of clinical data and will prompt the examiner to observe purposively.

Energetic Aspects of Action

There is no action without energy, however we define the latter and whatever we postulate about its sources. Muscle action takes sugar, brain activity takes electricity, and mental activity takes psychic energy. The latter may be assumed to be a neutral force, or diversified qualitatively into libido (from Latin: pleasure) and aggression, allowing for various admixtures. The main point is that life has, both subjectively and objectively, a *hormic* (from Greek *horme:* impulse or impetus) quality felt as push or upsurge and prompting a person to *do* something. The push is more or less strong, and the resulting action more or less vigorous. Quite obviously, there is a quantitative variable in action, from which an observer makes guesses about the actor's momentary energy quanta and, if he knows a person for a long period of time, guesses about his characteristic energy level or basic energy endowment. Experience shows that some people are vigorous in all they do, whereas others appear rather inert or apathetic in all their undertakings. It is therefore plausible to assume that natural endowments of energy vary, probably correlative with various endocrine processes and basic metabolic rates.

Clinically more significant, however, are *fluctuations of energy level over time,* both in terms of a normal developmental sequence and as functions of special psychological or pathological conditions. We all know that the young are more energetic than the old; this fact alone may explain the higher frequency of flurries of aggression in the young than in older people, which all governments put to use in selecting people for military duties. Men have greater muscular vigor than women, which, along with heavier bone structure, gives men the appearance of greater strength. But does that mean more energy? Probably not, for women may distribute and deploy their given energies differently, for instance in concentrating on fine control over motion, on mobilizing and expressing feelings, or in more detailed forms of social interaction. Adolescence entails an increase in sexual drive level and often a total hormic upsurge, which poses problems of managing all these energies.

Fatigue is, by definition, a temporary state of critical depletion of energy, usually related to a known cause of great expenditure, and with the expectation of forthcoming replenishment through a period of rest or a good night's sleep. Not so lassitude, lethargy, and apathy, which tend to be felt (or observed) without obvious acts of spending. Barring somatic reasons (such as infections or blood dyscrasias), these states can be seen as resulting from invisible strenuous or prolonged mental work such as brooding, mourning, worrying, or the exertion of energy-demanding control over intolerable impulses. They point to conditions of intrapsychic conflict in which one group of energies is pitted against another, or massive energies are invested in defense. In other words, what appears on the surface as apathy or nonaction may be intense action, hidden from view; more or less like the periodic standstill of two deer fighting with antlers locked. Such considerations show how quickly one moves from views of energy per se to an economic view of its expenditure. Assumptions about basic energy resources in any person are highly inferential, but the clinician must make them in order to do justice to the individual differences he encounters. Much of the older theories of *temperaments* was an attempt to deal with lifelong patterns of zest or apathy, vigor or sluggishness, drivenness or lethargy.

Marked *decreases* in a person's customary energy level should be counted as symptoms. These can be primary, as in the presenile dementias and other organic conditions, as well as in certain forms of depression. They can be specific to a particular drive, as in a decline or loss of sexual libido without the involvement of other energy functions, or as in the lessening of pugnacity that one finds in older people who have psychopathic histories of rampant aggressiveness. More frequently, however, significant changes in energy level are secondary symptoms, particularly in the neuroses. The noteworthy *abulia* of many neurotic patients and their chronic complaints of fatigue and feelings of depletion are likely to be the result of their costly, strenuous coping devices, many of which also prevent them from replenishing their energies at the natural source, which consists of gratifying engagements with other people, recreation, and exposure to diverse stimuli that act as nutriment for the mental apparatus. The more one worries, the more time one spends on compulsions, the more one invests in hypochondriacal fantasies, the more one cuts oneself off from the "goods" of object relations, nature, and culture, which provide zest and narcissistic gratifications.

Can conspicuous energy *increases* also be symptomatic? It is not likely that they occur as primary symptoms; they are nearly always secondary to disinhibition. While manic episodes entail enormous vigor in muscle use, loudness of voice, and swiftness of the stream of thought, this seeming increase in energy can be understood as a release from former inhibitions, the sweeping away of all controls by a profound regression, which sets hitherto bound energies free for unencumbered use in the service of drive expression. In principle, all regressions could produce such seeming increases in energy. Leaving aside these phenomena, however, most increases in customary energy levels would be signs of betterment, in which portions of conflict-bound energy become available to the ego's conflict-free sphere.

Economic Aspects of Action

What does one do, stylistically, with the energy one has available? Are there spendthrifts and hoarders, wastrels and misers, in the management of psychic energy, with most people falling somewhere in between these extremes? Of course there are. Some people constantly wear themselves out, always walking fast, gesticulating wildly, working day and night, always busy with something, always ready to volunteer for causes; their handwriting is large and expansive, their body contacts with others frequent. Others appear stingy in all their motions and doings: their script is cramped and minute, they rarely touch anybody, they stand perfectly still while talking or lecturing, are given to sitting or lying down, abstain from all unnecessary involvement, and are always trying to "preserve their strength." These are styles of life, patterns of psychoeconomic management. They tend to be lifelong patterns, and they have some correlation with psychopathological syndromes. That is their clinical import.

Extreme stinginess with psychic (and sometimes motor)

energy is a feature of obsessive-compulsive conditions and of the more severe pathologies that are grafted onto these conditions, such as catatonic stupor and schizoid states of emptiness, detachment, or "frozen" ambivalence in which neither of the contrary feelings tips the balance. On the whole, these patients are cautious about taking spontaneous action of any kind, hypercontrolled, and most of the time feel quite exhausted by their affective stalemates and intrapsychic defenses. Many of them are also manifestly afraid to act—phobic about approaching anyone or anything, scared of committing themselves to anything. Any decisive or consummatory act is to be avoided, for it is thought to entail guilt feelings, retaliation, or world disaster. Their key word is "inhibition," and their technique consists, by and large, in avoiding overt action and engaging in covert thought. Or else they avoid consummatory action in favor of preparatory activities, remaining stuck halfway in the normal unfolding of any action sequence: With the utmost control, they engage in rituals (compulsions), which may temporarily alleviate some anxiety but do not bring gratification. One might say that these patients have a problem in energy release: when an excitation arrives in their awareness they promptly seek to block its natural response.

A male patient in his forties, admitted to the hospital in a state of acute bewilderment, was led into the examining room where he kept standing at the door, frozen and without making eye contact. After lengthy coaxing he inched to a chair into which he finally seated himself, remaining mute and nearly immobile, except for repetitive arm and hand movements of a highly stylized sort, which appeared to be gestures of shielding his eyes and stopping his ears. He remained in this posture for 45 minutes, totally uncommunicative. His leaving the room was as slow as his coming in. In subsequent interviews the patient came around to revealing that he heard sounds as of a bell ringing, smelled the scent of embalming fluid, and saw human corpses decomposing. These hallucinations were pronounced when he came into the examining room, but had also been present at other times. He took the room for a morgue. Only by standing up straight could he prove to himself and others that he was alive, a compromise ritual that also expressed his obsession with the notion that he was already dead.

How different these patients are from the *profligates* who seem to lack any inhibitions, whose every impulse is quickly acted on, and whose drivenness is manifest to everybody. In the so-called impulse disorders the ego cannot tolerate delay of a promised satisfaction; the tension of unfulfilled desire cannot be borne; thinking is not substantial enough to interpose itself between stimulus and response, and time is almost completely confined to the present moment. In manic states overactivity pervades nearly all modalities: Motor movements are large and fast, speech is loud and voluble, laughter is more than hearty, the vital body processes are accelerated, and even social interaction is of an ebullient, slapdash kind— all typically followed by great exhaustion. The economics of action can be "read" from many kinds of activity, involving large and small muscle groups, and ranging from walking and physical labor to talking, writing, eating, and the handling of pictures and blocks on psychological tests.

Applying the economic viewpoint to mental activities and combining it with psychodynamic parameters allows us a glimpse of the *energy expenditures involved in ways of coping with stress, including defense mechanisms.* Every act costs something in energy, and that cost should be considered in relation to the satisfactions each act secures and/or the pain or unpleasure it wards off. To keep up repressions requires anticathectic energy; to deny unpleasant parts of reality may require little immediate energy but opens one up to serious confrontations later, which may then require costly maneuvers; a counterphobic ploy requires strenuous and daring action; identification with the aggressor requires the infliction of pain or harm on somebody, with grave risks of retaliation; withdrawal may require relatively little energy but effectively cuts one off from natural sources of replenishment of energy and thus, in the long run, leaves the ego depleted. We all know how exhausting prolonged or intense worrying is. Compulsions require time and energy, both wasted on preliminary activities which, while holding some feared calamity at bay, do not provide positive gratifications.

In a word, the economic aspect of action requires serious consideration and must be part of the clinician's evaluation. Since it leads to a view of the ego's style and skill of tension management and its adequacy as the person's "executive," we shall return to the economic principle in a later chapter.

Control Aspects of Action: Skill

The clinician is not only interested in what a person does, but in how he does it—with what degree of skill, how well controlled, how well coordinated, and with what degree of success in meeting his goals. The control aspects of action are of obvious importance in neuropsychological assessment, since motor phenomena are obvious indicators of brain disorder. Paralysis, paresis, contractures, cogwheel rigidity, tremors, gait disturbances, and postural defects are generally conspicuous enough, but there are many less visible or minor motor disturbances, which the patient may try to cover up and which require an observant eye. Many young people come eventually to clinical attention because of their awkward motions, their ineptness in mastering skills such as writing, their discoordination in gymnastics classes and sports, their frequent falling or stumbling, or their persistent difficulties in learning a craft that requires fine movements. The precise opposition of fingers and thumb, adequacy in grasping anything, releasing an object swiftly from the grasping hand—any or all of these acts may meet with difficulty in patients suspected of a minimal brain damage syndrome, in many cases of mental retardation, and in many otherwise "normal" persons who retain in such motor awkwardness some vestige of developmental arrest or a limited dysfunction. And since many of these young patients, when in school, may also show striking weaknesses in certain scholastic subjects or get entangled in interactional problems with teachers or peers, they often present a problem in differential diagnosis: emotional disorder or learning defect? In such cases the clinician must be an astute observer of the minutiae of motor patterns.

But there is a clinical payoff in carefully watching anyone's motor skills, for how else can one distinguish between, say, a neurotic compulsive ritual, a catatonic stance or posture, and a sequence of motions in a psychomotor seizure? And how can one estimate in what way a person comes to terms with that natural basis and substrate of all his experiences—his body— except by carefully noting his ease or dis-ease in using any part of it? Control of action involves levels of organization and levels of awareness, a sense of purpose, and some knowledge of the communicative value of motor acts. A finely honed gesture is one thing, a jerking arm flared out in an aggressive manner at an opponent is something else—in intention, control, and meaning as well as state of consciousness. The ego is foremost a body ego, rooted in perceptual and motor functions charged with pain and pleasure.

A man in his early thirties had spent literally 25 years of his life compulsively whittling away at his ten fingernails, to the point of agonizing pain and severe disablement. He started out as a nail biter, then began to pick up knives and eventually razor blades to "improve" the feel and look of his increasingly disfigured fingers, totally unable to restrain himself. In his school years he missed classes on account of this compulsion; later he had to absent himself from work and began to shy away from social events, because of both his awkward appearance and his irresistible urge to sculpt his nails to the point of bleeding, no matter where he was. In full consciousness, this urge followed him like his shadow; yet the wielding of razor blades, files, etc., required attention and skill. With the possible exception of his original childhood nail biting, the sculpting was not a primitive reflex action but required the highest central nervous system levels of organization and extreme care not to exceed his tolerance for pain. It is a case of controlled motions within an unstoppable act, an impulse whose force is not scattered in an explosive release but is harnessed into a patterned compulsion with deft movements.

This vignette highlights several meanings of control: (1) the capacity to stop, intercept, or delay an impulse: (2) the skill in making motor means serve selective ends; (3) the power of voluntary decisions and acts to supersede primitive or irrational motor sequences; (4) cortical guidance of subcortical innervations. One may add that "control" also means the stylistic approximation of any act to some cultural norm or pattern of meaning.

One could group pathologies of action according to the mode of control that appears to be deficient. *Inadequate capacity for delay* is inherent in the so-called impulse disorders: The ego's foresight and time-binding functions are weak in proportion to the impulsive search for instant gratification. *Inadequate skill in combining means and ends* of action is found in mix-ups between the preparatory and consummatory phases of an action sequence, such as in sexual perversions where elements of foreplay displace the gratification of coitus, and in compulsive rituals that prevent rather than facilitate the consummatory response. Obsessional thinking that goes around in circles without ever coming to a resolution or decisive end can be placed in the same category of dyscontrol. *Failure of voluntary action to guide and modify primitive motor impulses* is seen in hebephrenic silliness, mannerisms, and catatonic conditions, as well as in many automatisms and tics, in tonic or clonic stuttering, and in sexual dysfunctions such as ejaculatio praecox. Cortical inadequacies and subcortical mishaps would comprise all epileptic phenomena, from the diffuse and massive motor discharges in *grand mal* seizures to the selective atavisms of psychomotor seizures and the brief suspension of voluntary control in *petit mal* attacks.

That *action is subject to social norms* comes through conspicuously in those bits of behavior or penchants called abrupt, intrusive, maladroit, overbearing, "bull in a china shop," gauche, blunt, assaultive, etc. No matter how well coordinated and skillful a person may otherwise be, if his action lacks polish he is likely to be seen as a misfit, eccentric, or worse. A good many schizoid persons come eventually to psychiatric attention because of this kind of social dyscontrol over their actions, behind which the referring persons may well detect great loneliness, alienation, or shyness; in other cases they will wonder about aggressive or manipulative traits. The sexual perversions, especially exhibitionism and voyeurism, come to notice precisely because of this lack of social control over action.

Developmental Aspects of Action

Normal development entails systematic shifts in the patterning of motor activity. Whereas adults narrate verbally, young children enact their stories motorically while they talk. In Coghill's[56] famous experiments with salamanders, the young newt shows a massive diffuse body reaction to any stimulus; older specimens show only a local response in a limb or body organ. In Werner's theorem of motor development, the first phase is one of diffuse globality; the second is one of articulated action of partial systems, which are rather fragmentary; in the third phase, integrated action involves the whole but with articulated coordination of the parts. In the adult, action assumes the characteristics of a good gestalt.

This normal progression also involves a *new balance between thinking and acting,* in which thinking (rational thought as well as fantasy formation) becomes increasingly a preliminary to, or a substitute for, motor activity. "Don't act—think!" is the parental watchword. That phrase contains several exhortations: "Don't waste so much energy in movements but let your brain do some quiet work," "Don't rush in, but do some planning first," "Do consider the consequences of what you are about to do," "Don't upset the apple cart," "Check your impulse and give yourself (and us) some time." All these statements hint at the relation between action and motives or drives, and appeal to a need for the integration of action with other part processes of the ego. A balance is also needed between alloplastic and autoplastic behavior: Neither the self nor the others should become the preponderant or exclusive object of action. Autoplastic exclusiveness gives rise to psychosomatic symptoms, autoerotic compulsions, or depressive reactions; alloplastic overemphasis entails externalization of conflict through vice, vandalism, crime, or constantly unsuccessful social relationships in which others feel victimized.

Moreover, the sequence of development of libidinal and aggressive strivings shows in rough outline an important *object shift:* The first object is one's own body and the nascent self and the parts of others that are incorporated as introjects; the later, mature object choice turns toward other people as distinct and autonomous entities. Egocentricity slowly gives way to allocentricity; primary narcissism gives way to healthy self-regard coupled with respect for others, and the energy investments spread from a few hypercathected caretakers (and the self) to a larger number of persons, ideas, values, causes, and things in a graded series of cathexes, with some flexibility of transfer from one category to another. Drive aims can be inhibited or transposed, making sublimations possible.

These main lines in the development of action alert the clinician to the phenomena of behavioral regression. Given some vulnerabilities and enough stress, acquired patterns of action can be abandoned for the safety or relative ease and painlessness of older ones. It is, of course, in the psychoses that we see the most *drastic regressions of action:*

> On admission, the patient was extremely quiet, unable to initiate any action by herself. When others insist, she may follow simple instructions. She walks with rigid posture, dragging her feet constantly and directing her hands forward, slightly flexed, but without movements, like a robot. Occasionally, she stops in the middle of her pacing and appears confused. Soon after admission she fell into a state of disorganized motor excitement, throwing herself against the door and rolling her brassiere up around her neck. A few days later she became very quiet again, but engaged in bizarre actions: Sitting in a chair, she slowly slid forward until she lay on the floor. After she was helped to get up, she repeated this sequence many times.

This patient displays the postural sulking of a negativistic child with occasional tantrums; her mutism makes her motor behavior all the more telling. Whether we deal with the nonaction of complete withdrawal, the quiet action of excessive sleeping, the inner action and physical tension of hyperalert watchfulness, the restless action of frantically pacing the floor, the handwringing of an otherwise immobile person in a state of depression, or the inappropriate giggling of a hebephrenic girl assuming the posture of a nymph—in all these cases some parameters of the normal development of action have been undone. The acts described are concentrated on the self or the body, their libidinal or aggressive intent is all too transparent, their purpose is no longer to communicate or alter a part of the environment, the Gestalt of action has succumbed to a few parts that predominate. Curiosity, playfulness, humor, and exploratory behavior are abandoned in favor of small, solipsistic motions such as rubbing body parts, fidgeting with clothes, clasping the hand around small things such as pieces of string or food, or sheltering oneself from the looks of others by covering the face.

But there is plenty of *regressive action in the neuroses* too. The melodramatic gestures of hysterical patients are childish and naïve, lacking the finish of stage actors; and so are the sighs, whimperings, and gigglings that accompany the flow of their words. The flight, screaming, or clinging of phobic patients when they meet the feared object or situation are quite primitive, like those of a toddler. Automatisms and grimaces of any person under great tension tend to be rather atavistic—eye blinking, lip smacking, throat sounds, or puckering of the mouth. The halting action of obsessional or blocked patients not only lacks flow but at times amounts to serious fragmentation without a conclusive end-state. The rituals of compulsive patients are often based on childhood admonitions taken literally: "Wash your hands," "Don't touch dirty things," "Fold your hands and close your eyes while praying," as if they were goals in themselves, and tests of total obedience.

Early libidinal zones may again take precedence in the patient's actions. We have already seen the dominance of orality in many automatisms. Regressions to anal preoccupations and acts are no less frequent. I remember a severely depressed middle-aged patient who stationed himself at the entrance of the hospital lavatory to inspect the equipment after each use, for he was afraid, he said, that other patients would stuff the toilets with newspapers, causing a calamitous overflow of dirt through the whole premises. At the same time, he engaged in lengthy bowel-evacuation and self-cleaning rituals, which drained his body, time, and energies.

Under the developmental aspects of action we should also pay heed to those small, habitual, involuntary gestures that give away early strivings and remain as vestiges of childhood identifications: the feminine gesture of putting the hand to the lips or before the mouth, the masculine leaning of the chin on the cupped hand, the snapping of fingers accompanying a verbal command to give it urgency, intrusive buttonholing, or overtly pointing the finger at other people.

Symbolic Aspects of Action

Symbolism enters into action in at least two ways: (1) by endowing certain motor movements with surplus meaning that makes them participate in some transcendent power; (2) by subordinating certain movements to cognitive grasp of linguistic symbol systems. To the first group belong rituals and a great many aesthetic motions and ceremonials; to the second belong such acts as writing and other praxic-manipulative movements that function within the framework of language and other conventional systems of notation. Each group has its normal and abnormal uses, its hypertrophies and deficiencies.

Rituals, ceremonies, and liturgies are part of communal life and are guided by social norms, based on considerations ranging from ultimate meanings to decorum. For at least some of our actions, most of us operate within such ceremonial frameworks: in table manners, in the courtroom, in church, at parties, in scientific meetings. These frameworks all involve stylized acts, special modes of speech, deft gestures, knowledgeable maneuvering between the private and public zones around any person's body—in a word, *manners,* subject to taboos and of a quasi-sacred nature, which we take for granted. Is there a pathology of such symbolic acts? Yes, there is, and it consists largely of two modifications: privatization of rituals, and a shift from more or less elegant and playful execution to mechanical performances of great drivenness. In both respects, moreover, meanings are disengaged from their historical or communal moorings and re-embedded in personal whimseys, as in the case of compulsions and a good many phobic avoidance rituals. Phenomenologically, such acts are characterized by much attention to the minutiae of movement, often with an emphasis on repetition guided by some magical numerological formula: three times, five times, seven times, etc. I remember a severely compulsive patient who had to introduce such utilitarian acts as washing, shaving, eating, going to bed, or sitting down in a chair with hand and arm motions as if he were conducting an orchestra, always in counted series; another patient carefully wiped the rim of his drinking glass three times, each time folding the napkin so as to have a clean surface to wipe with. Such rituals are a demanding activity, carried out with extreme care and anxiety, lest the slightest mishap annul their hoped-for effectiveness or bring about a calamity. The same is true for catatonic dramatizations of action and posturing. In much more attenuated form, mannerisms and automatisms are also private rituals, highly mechanized and carried out with drivenness, often as a prelude to a voluntary act, such as the preliminary grimacings of public speakers, or the shuffling of silverware before a meal.

Sometimes these rituals can be further specified in terms of symbolic meanings. The motions can be predominantly oral; they can reveal a preoccupation with dirt and cleanliness; they may be phallic or intrusive; they may be in some sense masturbatory or aggressive. They may be aesthetic, exhibitionistic, or theatrical, or they may have pious and liturgical features picked up from religious ceremonies.

An entirely different class of symbolic acts, and their pathology, involves cognitive mastery of linguistic symbolism. The apraxias and dyspraxias fall into this category. For instance, the agraphic patient knows how to handle pen and paper and has no paralysis in the pertinent musculature, but he cannot write recognizable letters or words. He can be induced to draw strokes, even up-and-down strokes, and he may be able to draw, but he is stumped when it comes to actual writing. The patient who combs her hair every morning without help is unable, on command in the middle of the day, to demonstrate her combing motions. "Mock motion," the voluntary performance of routine acts when not actually needed, is out of the question because the "as if" quality of the proposition "to comb" prevents the act. I have already dealt with the apraxias in the chapter on language behavior, because of their linguistic origins; I mention them here only to place them in the supplementary perspective of the pathology of symbolic action.

Expressive Aspects of Action

When all the preceding systematic aspects of action have been taken into account there remains another approach to action, one that has to do with its expressive qualities. Action conveys feelings and messages; it communicates intentions and motives; it conveys a style of life, a vision of the self and others, whether consciously or unconsciously. And these expressive features of action have a powerful influence on the observer. The motions of a hand, the blink of an eye, the stooped posture or the brisk gait, are so many self-presentations and so many forms of communication.

The fact that people know so little about their own self-presentations through their action patterns suggests that unconscious influences are great, making the assessment of action all the more rewarding. Fundamental attitudes and personality characteristics come through, often registered by the observer as unconsciously as they are emitted by the actor.

For instance, certain patterns of movement will strike us as *masculine* or *feminine*. Precisely which motions suggest either gender may be hard to describe: Their signal-value may not be definable, but their total pattern, with its fine nuances, often conveys an indelible impression, which by and large will prove to be a trustworthy observation shared by many others. When the impressions conform to the person's actual gender they are rarely noted or reported, but when they deviate and are felt to "belong" to the opposite sex they quickly come to awareness. Such gender-specific action patterns may be discerned in the selective preference for large versus small muscle groups, in manners of stooping, kneeling, and the positioning of legs while sitting, in the angularity or roundness of the curves described by the movements of limbs. These patterns give clues to the less conscious aspects of a person's gender identification.

A primordial biological distinction evident in the animal world gives human action the qualities of *fight or flight,* the latter sometimes ushered in by the postural pattern of suddenly *freezing up* to complete, but tense, immobility. While pugnacity is so overt that it cannot be mistaken, belligerence is often more verbal than behavioral—in fact, it is not uncommon to find verbal fight combined with physical flight patterns. Argumentativeness, protest, and agitated diatribes, impressive as they may be during an interview, do not necessarily spell out readiness to fight. They may be "trial actions" implying a good deal of inhibitory control over motor activity, barely concealing the patient's proneness to leave the field of battle and settle for a meek withdrawal. Precisely these contrasts between verbal and motor behavior are clinically important. Blocking, freezing up, and other phenomena of acute conflict in which contrary forces are pitted against each other reach their extreme form in catatonic conditions, including stupor, which have therefore been likened to the tense standstill reflex reactions of squirrels and the "playing dead" reactions of opossums.

Motor self-presentations convey, of course, much about a person's basic proclivities for either *activity or passivity.* Large, quick, and energetic movements, particularly those that emerge spontaneously in situations that do not call for them (i.e., outside of sports, recreation, etc.), bespeak an active posture toward life, whereas few, small, slow, and weak motions and a penchant for sitting or lying down are typical earmarks of a passive disposition. But much depends on the setting and the occasion. Reaction formation tends to play havoc with these variables, catapulting people with passive tendencies into great displays of activity, which leave them frustrated or exhausted afterwards. Activity and passivity tend to be heavily regulated by the superego, which attaches praise or blame to either choice, and thus we find many persons straining to appear active, even hyperactive, against their natural dispositional grain. Hence also the flurries of activity alternating with periods of passivity seen in people who are greatly conflicted about the pattern imposed on them by years of training.

From a social point of view motor behavior is regulated by norms of class, caste, gender, fitness for the occasion, decorum, etc. Action is subject to social ritualization. Hence action patterns are to be assessed in terms of *conformity or deviance,* including *defiance.* Conformity can be overdone, through strained efforts at excessive containment, primness, delicacy, feigned elegance or ceremoniousness. Defiant action exudes an attitude of protest, a willful breaking of taboos, for whatever noble or ignoble purpose. To go around unkempt with a conspicuously slouched posture and tired gait, or to walk with a swagger and great braggadocio, are only different ways of conveying the message that one does not care for the prevailing rituals of action. Patterns of defiance of some alleged "establishment" also tend to become quickly ritualized in their own way by group formation, which demands conformity to the mores and manners of the clique while prescribing conspicuous deviance from the dominant patterns. This aspect of action is thus beset with identity and identification fragments, which provide clues to a person's self-image.

Unmitigated drive tendencies can give a *conspicuously erotic or aggressive* tone to a person's actions. The healthy norm or the mature ideal does not consist in a forced choice between these two, but in effective sublimation and neutralization. The examiner must be clear about his observational standards: The clinical situation, by definition, emerges from a person's help-seeking behavior, and is thus guided by norms that are different from those prevailing in the marketplace, on the beach, or at a cocktail party. When a patient is flirtatious, coy, seductive, exhibitionistic, or erotically manipulative within a professional helping relationship, such manifestations of erotization should be given considerable weight. They are a clue to the dominance of erotic strivings and their style in the patient's non-clinical relations, and to the weakness of his control over libidinal impulses. These erotic bits of behavior are often lifelong patterns, tightly interwoven with the character structure and therefore by and large ego syntonic. They have failed to come under the dominion of *sublimation* in the various senses of that word, including shifts in drive aims, transposition of feelings and satisfactions from instinctual to ego levels, acculturation, and a sense of tact, taste, and appropriateness.

The same clinical reasoning applies to observations about aggressiveness in the patient's help-seeking behavior. Commanding gestures, bullyishness, intrusiveness, strivings for dominance, turning the interview situation into a chess game, cattiness, or arrogance bespeak far more tellingly than an occasional outburst of anger or rage the prevalence of aggressive drive dynamics in the patient's character, giving his self-expression an enduring tone from which cycles of social entanglements arise. These traits suggest a failure of *neutralization*, i.e., the tempering of aggression by libidinal satisfactions, by fusion with erotic valences, by transposition of primitive personal targets to larger social causes and constructive enterprises.

A Note on "Acting Out" and Existential Action

In today's clinical vocabulary "acting out" is an often heard term. For many (sloppy) users it is nearly equivalent to a pronounced alloplastic tendency—a flurry of ill-considered, mostly angry behavior, or a bout of abreactive release of excess tension. These are not the technical meanings of the term, and it should not be used for the behaviors just described.

Acting out is a technical term in psychoanalytic therapy, referring to some patients' proneness to interrupt the basic rule of verbalizing everything that comes to mind and, on the strength of transference feelings, enact or re-enact memories or fantasies outside the psychoanalytic hour. It has also become a designation for behavior against authority that is socially specifically forbidden, i.e., the transgression of a taboo, a sudden lapse in the patient's customary obedience patterns and modes of self-control. Lastly, it has come to refer to bits of behavior intended to lessen unconscious tensions in forms poorly adapted to reality, again flying in the face of an existing demand or contract for developing reflection and insight. In this sense, addiction, particularly in bouts, temporary flights into impulse neurosis, fugue states, and various episodes of vice or crime can be designated as "acting out" phenomena, provided they occur as breaks in the therapeutic contract which stipulates the patient's abstinence, sobriety, and maximum self-reflection.

In existentialist parlance, "act" and "acting" are words that do not typically refer to motor behavior, but stand for making decisions, taking risks, choosing, committing oneself, and courageously facing the consequences of one's decisions. The existential "act" is an attitudinal event, a self-disclosure, a moment of truth and candor, a leap of faith or an exercise of freedom. Thus its import cannot be adequately summarized in a few paragraphs in a chapter on "action" conceived as a specifically motor part process. If anything, it is a holistic event that can be understood only in terms of all the so-called part processes and integrative processes detailed in this book, and—for the existentialist—it supersedes all these matters in integrative significance.

Chapter 10

The Ego as Meeting Ground of Means and Ends

In Chapter 2 we described the ego as a particular structure of personality, functioning within and on behalf of the person as a whole to look after his wants, secure his access to the environment, maximize his chances of survival, obtain a modicum of satisfaction and well-being, and stave off as effectively and as long as possible the organism's eventual succumbing to the inertia of death. The latter entails vigilance to and coping with all the precursors, tokens, or symbols of life-denying propensities that Freud tried to capture in the experiential words *pain* and *unpleasure (Unlust)*, in his dynamic conception of aggression, and in his construct of the *death instinct.* Freud particularly emphasized the latter's relentless power and persistence, which give it a hormic thrust and make it appear like a drive. The pivotal biological role of the ego gives it a status that defies description in terms derived from a single point of view.

In Chapters 4-9 we stressed the gubernatorial or managerial aspects of the ego by describing the natural "tools" it has at its disposal for making contact with the environment, the various uses of these tools, and its dealings with the other structures of personality. Nature and culture have combined to make these tools useful, nay, indispensable; they consist of those human endowments, subject to growth and learning, that form the classical chapter headings of psychology—

perception, emotion, language, etc. These terms also form the rubrics under which a substantial part of psychiatric and neurological literature is organized (at least descriptively), and are, to boot, the most common-sense functional divisions of the human mind. Each of them allows for enormous differentiation, as we have seen. Each encompasses common and exceptional forms, typical and atypical uses, healthy and unhealthy applications, normal and pathological manifestations. For these reasons, the chapters on the "part processes" contain an intricate mixture of data, bits of processes, impressions, glimpses of "something there," and intimations of "something happening" that reflect the chaotic but intriguing manifold of things clinical. Whatever these chapters described, I hope they conveyed a fascination with the welter of clinical phenomena, sufficiently systematized to show some order in the chaos.

But the moment one asks what these "tools" are really *for*, what purposes they serve, what ends they are to meet, the vision of the ego as executive is bound to give way to the image of the ego as a servant. Like the ideal head of state in a democracy, the highest officer is also the humblest servant, having the common weal in mind. He is "under the law," under public scrutiny, and accountable; he is to hear the *vox populi* as well as the voice of reason; he is to avoid dangers and seize opportunities by being sharply attuned to both the "internal environment" of his country and the "external environment" of the world. He has to act in accordance with historical trends, traditions, and precedents; he must be informed by the past so as to respond to the present. He must maintain all kinds of loyalty and act in accordance with some communal spirit, or with a valued and proven vision.

This analogue of the high-placed servant puts the ego in a much humbler place than that of the operator who pulls the strings. Seen from this angle, the ego serves the person of whom it is a part and from whom it emerged in the organismic process of differentiation of labor and specialization of function. In that process, the nascent ego itself was subject to mishaps and vagaries of all sorts, making it more or less adequate to the tasks assigned to it in the wisdom of the organism. The growing ego needed distinct nutriment, a chance to practice its budding skills, protection from damage, and various spurs to transcend its stepwise achieved competences in favor of novel skills.

Thus for a person to be somebody, to function effectively, to mature according to proper timetables, and to grow in accordance with his opportunities, the adequate development of his ego is of central importance. If it is to perform all the functions ascribed to it, the ego must constantly practice them as they successively unfold, with the right balance at any given moment between its demonstrated competence and the next demands that nature or culture place on it. In the early years of life, that balance is largely regulated by external agencies, which come to the aid of the child's feeble self-regulations: the mother, the family, and the relatively small, selective, and protective world that forms the proper childhood milieu. Progressively, external regulation gives way to truly homeostatic processes by which the person functions with increasing autonomy at all imaginable levels, from reflex and simple cybernetic levels to those steered by the will and the sense of personal identity.

If there is truth in the adage that a nation deserves the government it has, one might reason analogously that the over-all adequacy of a person can be gauged by the kind of ego he has, i.e., its level and style of functioning, its pattern of competences and weaknesses, its skill or ineptness in the use of its tools, its repetitiousness or inventiveness in meeting life's unceasing situational demands and abiding purposes. But the ego's pivotal role and all the functions ascribed to it give it a somewhat ambiguous conceptual status. On the one hand, in a globally functional sense, because of its high place in the hierarchy of intrapsychic formations, "the ego" can be seen as a designation for the person as a whole, symbolizing his highest-level integrations and most holistic performances. On the other hand, in a structural sense (which has its specific functional aspects also), the ego is only a special intrapsychic structure that has to contend with other parts of the person (in fact, large segments of it such as the id, superego, and ego ideal), which not only have their own agenda, but in their way represent important aspects of the person not covered by the term "ego."

In both respects the ego needs nurture and practice. To discharge its regulatory functions well, its apparatus needs proper maintenance. To function with zest, it needs, like the rest of personality, satisfactions, which in its case amount to a feeling of success, perhaps derived from social responses and biological messages from the body. If a person is to have a sense of freedom, it can be experienced and become manifest only in his ego, through a feeling of buoyancy in synthesizing the demands and opportunities of the outside world and the other intrapsychic agencies: the id, superego, and ego ideal. Holistic in its top-level situation and its adaptational program, yet mechanistic in its particular procedures and the use of its tools, *the ego represents within the person the meeting ground of means and ends.*

This combination of means and ends will become apparent in the next several chapters. In describing various combinations we must heed some important distinctions. "Ego" is not an appropriate shorthand expression for "person." Only a person can have aims and goals, ends and outlooks, a sense of identity, a feeling of emptiness, or a sense of failure. The ego is to provide means to the person's ends, and only in being a good and diligent servant can it accrue the specific satisfactions that perfect its functional adequacy. The widest satisfactions are those of the person as a whole—those that enhance his sense of well-being, his lust for life, his caring capacities, his altruism, the meanings he finds in his existence. Other satisfactions are partial: the gratification of basic impulses, the friendly nods received from conscience when the person lives up to its norms and ideals. The ego is to secure and attain these satisfactions like a good provider and distribute them like a good steward, as it is to cope with stress, pain, and displeasure like a good defender and protector. In addition, it needs satisfactions of its own, which may be best described as building up a feeling of competence. That, too, is only a partial satisfaction, but an important one.

In seeking to obtain these holistic and partial satisfactions the ego has, in the last analysis, only one recourse. It must find them through engagements with objects in the environment, particularly other human beings. Primordially objects of drives, other human beings also become, in the course of personal development and civilization, the satisfiers of nonimpulsive longings: They provide nutriment for the workings of conscience; they give impetus to the formation of ideals; they stimulate and nurture the intellect, shape the ability to communicate, and provide a great many aesthetic pleasures. In a word, engagement in human object relations provides the ultimate satisfactions to all intrapsychic agencies: id, ego, superego, and ego ideal, and to the person as a whole, in a stratified order.

The ego contributes to this order and affects the distribution of satisfactions through its capacity to organize emotions. For the ego is also the site of feelings. It is the hub of experience where impulses, thoughts, memories, ideas, and tensions of all kinds are translated into emotions with specific qualities, which the perceptual consciousness registers as signals to which the ego can respond through specific, selective actions. Many longings, stirrings, inner promptings, pressures, and stresses reach consciousness in the form of specific feelings, whose tone prompts the ego to make a selection from its response repertoire. But any response, whatever it is, is very likely to take place in the arena of human relations, i.e., to involve objects, and thus to affect the quality and quantity of satisfactions that come the person's way. For instance, withdrawal into one's private fantasy world entails a diminution of the gratifications that could be had from a neighbor's love. A snappish remark is likely to elicit a snub in return, or a response of avoidance. An outright attack prompts retaliation. A response of fear may cause others to become overprotective toward us, infantilizing our already shaky composure. An embrace, on the other hand, will eight times out of ten elicit an embrace; a smile will come back like an echo, and a gift will bring forth a gift in return.

In this sense of producing spiral effects, object relations are both means and ends for the ego's task of maintaining a person's vital balance. Under the dynamic as well as the economic principle, a person involves himself in object relations so as to gain the satisfactions that are his psychic nutriment. But he can do so effectively only when he also provides his objects with the satisfactions *they* seek. Reciprocity is fundamental. We need others as they need us. Self and object go hand in hand, producing a ceaseless dialectic of means and ends.

In the next three chapters, we shall deal with the engagement in object relations by dividing the object world into three distinct categories. We shall first focus on other people, trying to make their enormous diversity manageable by selecting crucial clinical observations. Then we shall concentrate on the self: the image we have of it and the regard we have for it, the myriad ways in which we seem to love and hate it as we do other objects. Finally, we shall consider how a person deals with cultural goods, how he involves himself in things and ideas, and what satisfactions he seeks from cathecting them. These three categories are systematic aspects of the one process that sustains life. Integrative by its very nature, it promotes both personal and social integration and is therefore succinctly called the "integrative process."

Chapter 11

Assessing Integrative Processes: Relations to Other People

It is a basic fact of life that every person is conceived by two other persons and born from one of them, with whom he or she has been on the most intimate footing for nine months. After having shared as a fetus in the mother's blood stream in a symbiotic if not parasitic coexistence, the neonate not only has to face the world, but finds within that world a most equivocal object: his mother. She claims to know his deepest wants and share his innermost feelings, while also presenting herself as the first and most important "outsider." Her relationship with the baby is riddled with ambiguity and full of double messages: She is his primary object but also his auxiliary ego; she bends herself to his biological timetable while also presenting to him her own, different, cultural timetable; she is the closest object he has, but by her own ministrations presents herself rather fragmentarily, waiting for him to acquire a sense of object constancy. She is the one who satisfies and frustrates. Reciprocally, he satisfies and frustrates her; his closeness to her may frustrate her desire for singularity; his singularity will test the strength of her need to continue the oneness with him that they practiced together for nine months.

The fetus *has* his object and is contiguous to it; the neonate, no longer contiguous to his original object, must *seek, find, discover,* and *construct* it from little snatches of that "big, blooming buzzing confusion" in which the world presents itself, according to James, to the infant. The task mapped out for mother and child is, in Bowlby's words, coming to terms with *attachment* and *separation.* But neither of these words has a fixed meaning in this task, for the growth process does not involve a simple move from the first to the second state. The growth program does not demand maximum detachment from objects and maximum eventual separateness of the developing person. Instead, it demands a creative modulation of both attachment and separation, through various stages of growth, eventuating in the establishment of affectionate psychic bonds that act in space and time. In this sequence, *objects will come and go, but object engagement will remain.* In fact, the *praxis of object engagement* is what life is all about, and its style is the subject matter of psychodynamic theory.

What Is an "Object"?

In the preceding paragraphs, and indeed throughout this book, the word "object" was used when the context clearly indicated that "person" was intended. Is not this term an awkward, cold, inhuman substitute? Would anyone willingly refer to his loved ones as "objects"? Or, for that matter, would he even refer to his enemies as "objects"? After Buber,[57] dare we describe, let alone treat, any human being as an "it"?

Over the years, there has been an increase rather than a decrease in the use of the word "object" for "person" in dynamic psychiatry and psychoanalysis, and not from callousness! The word originated as a technical term in motivation theory; the postulate of drives that activate and channel behavior implies a goal: a state of satisfaction (pleasure) to replace a state of dissatisfaction (pain). The three main variables of drives described in Freud's "Three Essays on the Theory of Sexuality" are: (1) source; (2) aim; (3) object. A drive has a *source* in the somatic constellations and processes that form the biological "programming" of sex, hunger, thirst, etc. A drive's *aim* is set by the pleasure principle to discharge (painful) excess tension so as to attain a level of relative well-being (pleasure). A drive's *object* is anything by means of which pleasure or satisfaction is obtained. Thus *an object is a satisfier,* and it is in the first instance (though not solely) the satisfier of a *drive.* In adult sexual behavior, the satisfier (object) is a mate, as food is the object of hunger and liquid of thirst.

To clinicians and diagnosticians the technical term "object" serves as a constant reminder that they must evaluate human engagements from a functional point of view. Their first question about human relations is not metaphysical, ethical, aesthetic, socioeconomic, or political—though all of these can be suitable viewpoints to be used in subsequent rounds of the evaluative process. Their first interest is in finding out what satisfactions A seeks in engaging with B; how B functions as the *object* of A's drive demands. Equal attention is to be paid to B's functioning as an object of A's ego states, his superego norms, and his ego ideal's requirements. Thus *the satisfactions striven for are not simple; they are stratified* according to the complexity of A's total personality, in which drive demands, self-regard, and ethical, aesthetic, and all kinds of reality considerations play a role, including his philosophy of life. Indeed, the latter may well involve a critique of primitive drive satisfactions or objections to hedonism, to emphasize ethical motives; or it may stress reality factors that would give the edge to socioeconomic motives. Psychodynamic theory, however, will always focus on the kinds of satisfactions A seeks in his engagements with B, even when A alleges to be attracted to B for his own sake, from a kind of fascination with B in which the relation with B is A's avowed goal. My point is that the seeking of satisfactions and the seeking of objects, often described as irreconcilably different, are not a contrary pair of values or life goals, but a set of complementary operations, most likely two sides of one coin.

And so clinicians elect to use the technical term "object" to keep their diagnostic eyes on systematically relating a person's engagements with other persons to his diversified motives, values, and goals, in all of which his satisfactions and frustrations are of crucial dynamic importance. From this point of view people relate themselves to each other because they *need* each other, whatever else they may seek to accomplish in such relationships. From the hormic point of view they are *driven* to each other. From the psychoeconomic point of view they invest in and exchange energies with each other: They *discharge energies* on each other and *replenish their energies* from each other. From the structural point of view they engage with each other in processes of *internalization,* which *shape* and *build* the personalities that partake in the relationship. From the topographical point of view the relations between persons are cemented by *conscious and unconscious* determinants, which sometimes lead to profound ambiguities in the existing bonds.

While "person" is certainly a more appropriate and reverential word than "object," its very nobility may prevent the diagnostician from discovering his or her function in any interpersonal engagement. How to accomplish this -task systematically will be set forth in the next sections of this chapter. But we should first consider how the category of "objects" is clinically subdivided.

Some people are loners, by desire or by circumstances. Bereft of kin and friends, they may lead lives of great loneliness, waiting for company that never comes, perhaps nursing the memories of those they have lost. In the latter case, however, they may still be very much engaged with other people, albeit not meeting them in the flesh. They live with *imagos*—interior representations of people with whom they were once significantly intertwined: parents, siblings, spouses, children, friends, caretakers, etc. Such representations can be of two kinds: (1) a *psychic residue* of all that has been experienced with these significant persons, in the form of a network of associations, available to memory, rather accurately placed in a time/space coordinate and within the framework of reality, and more or less integrated into the subject's personality; (2) an *introject,* i.e., a more or less foreign body of representations that from time to time exerts an ego-alien influence on the subject's mind with which he feels he has to reckon—sometimes coming through in quasi-perceptual modes such as hearing these persons' voices, hallucinating their visual features, or feeling scrutinized by them. In the latter case, the introject's presence is felt as "being there" through its own momentum, eluding the subject's conscious control. It is evident from these descriptions that the first kind of representation has been influenced by secondary-process thought and allows for conscious reflection, whereas the second kind, the introject, has remained caught in primary-process operations. For this reason, introjects can manifest themselves intrusively, by unexpectedly encroaching on the stream of thought or by leading to symptomatic acts.

The situation of the loner, then, instructs us in recognizing two classes of objects: *internal* and *external*. From the angle of the subject, this classification reflects two referents of experience: *inside* and *outside*. This distinction also entails a developmental task that is apparently rather difficult for some persons. That task is to match and bring about a good fit between the internal representation and the external reality of any given object. For representations to be realistic, they must increasingly approximate the given, verifiable features of the flesh-and-blood object, with minimal distortion. Reality testing must be brought to bear on the external object so as to modify and update his or her original internal representation, at first heavily determined by childish longings and instinctual wishes, in the light of a more mature, secondary-process appraisal.

This consideration leads to another distinction between objects, best described in terms of *self* and *others*. For the self, too, as I shall spell out in greater detail in the next chapter, can be regarded as an object. Like other objects, it entails an internal representation as well as an external referent, both of which are strands of what is ordinarily referred to as the self-concept or the self-image. Both of these are affect-laden and charged with values, recognized in the concepts of self-esteem and self-regard. The self has an ambiguous epistemological status because it can be both subject and object in logical propositions and inferences. This ambiguity is increased by the fact that every person *has* (or *is*) a *body*, which is experienced now as an inside, now as an outside datum. In kinesthetic perception, the body is so intimately linked with the mind that both are experienced as "inside" the person; through the distance receptors we perceive the body as an "outside" entity on which the mind can throw its gaze, and which it can lump together with other external things.

Looked at developmentally, the body appears to be cathected very early as an object, particularly of primary drives and drive derivatives. It is probably the first object, or proto-object. Homoerotic activity, self-stimulation such as thumb sucking, and tantrums testify to this fact; it takes a while before other people become the preferred and steadily used objects for drive release. Phenomena of regression in adults tell the same story: In severe pathological conditions the acquired attachments to other people may be given up in favor of energy reinvestments in one's self and one's body, of both libidinal and aggressive energies. Even within the normal range, a physical illness or a traumatic psychic experience will tend to turn us back onto ourselves, making us temporarily withdraw our interest from external objects. The word *narcissism* alludes metaphorically to these alternatives in object choice: The more the self or any of its aspects is cathected, the less investment is made in others, and vice versa. Hence, socially speaking, the very narcissistic person is likely to have a *contact disturbance*. These alternatives should not be radicalized to a forced choice, however, for it is equally true that the quality of relations to external objects is codetermined by the quality of relations to the self-image. The ideal state is a matter of balance and proportion, not an either/or choice.

Table 1 is a schematization of the variety of objects according to the parameters thus far described. It sums up an acquired complexity without stating how, by what steps, in what phases or sequence, this acquisition was made. But a few hints about development are implied: Each of the internal images (which some writers also call objects) is subdivided into a primitive and a more mature form, according to its domination by the primary or the secondary process. In the more mature case, the primitive image is in some way corrected by feedback from the corresponding external object, or by being

TABLE 1

Objects	Primitively experienced	Maturely experienced
Self	fantasized internal self-image: e.g.,"I am omnipotent" internal self-image or self-representation: e.g.,"I am rather weak"	external self-representation, objective self, or social self: e.g.,"I have some competence"; "I am considered a good worker"
Others	introject: e.g., intrusive presence of father internal image of others: e.g., father-related thoughts and feelings forming an associative schema	external object: e.g., father

adjusted to the latter's objective features. In other words, the internal object representation (self or others) normally matures from a rather fragmentary, drive-determined, highly affect-laden, and very ambivalent set of associations to a more holistic, reality-tested, and more objective schema in which ambivalence has given way to modulated feelings. The latter achievement implies that some drive fusion has occurred, mitigating aggressive impulses and allowing for a degree of sublimation.

What precedes the charted entities? How do they come into being? Answers to these questions vary, and are rather conjectural anyway. There is much agreement that distinct inner representations of others—and hence articulate and stable social engagements with other people—do not develop until a distinct self-representation has taken shape. Does this mean that normally some elementary self-representation, perhaps concretely experienced as a body schema, arises first?

Probably so. The first articulated experiences are thought to formulate a sense of *me,* as distinct from a nebulous, diffuse *non-me.* At this stage, the *non-me* is not yet *other;* it is, rather, an undiscriminated *outside.* Within the global *outside* one object will slowly become differentiated as "mother" by way of the neonate's piecing together those fragments of "mother" (fragmentary in both time and space) with which he has successive contact. Only slowly do these fragments become a whole, and as this synthesis proceeds, the fragmentary experiences of me-ness will also round off into a more coherent idea of *me.* In all the stages of this process *individuation* and *separation* are constantly being put to the test, in seesawing motions as it were, by the nascent ideas of self and others, which are themselves changing at each point.

What are some of the mechanisms within this obviously dialectical process? Before the distinction between self and others has achieved some firmness, it is likely that some distinction between inside and outside already obtains. To the degree that it is as yet ill-established, the mechanisms of *projection* and *introjection* are facilitated. Through these mechanisms, for the neonate the mother's nipple and his own fingers touching his lips have a degree of functional equivalence. (In fact, it is reported that fetuses suck their thumbs, as if preparing themselves for later contact with an outside object.) Holding and being held, feeding and being fed, sucking and being suckled are not differentiated; they merge in experience. In the ensuing blur, the location and contours of anything are unclear. Things that are inside can be experienced as outside, and vice versa. A part can be taken for the whole; things can be felt as extending between here and yonder. For instance, the mother's breast can be experienced as being "within" the proto-*me,* and parts of *me* can be felt as "taken up" within the mother, who is felt as an ill-formed entity. And so affects and propensities arising within the infant are ascribed to ("located in") the mother—projections; and aspects or parts of the mother are ascribed to ("taken into") the proto-*me*—introjections.

Affects play an enormous role in these projections and introjections, for at the beginning of life they are highly polarized between pain and pleasure and between erotic and aggressive tones. These opposite tones provide raw experience with an emotional ordering schema in terms of *good* and *bad*. These words are shorthand for pleasant and unpleasant, love and hate, constructive and destructive, libidinal and aggressive, ultimately reducible to "life" and "death."

This good-bad polarity interacts with another one of primordial existential import: the polarity between *active* and *passive* modes of experience. These two words should not be used in "either/or" fashion, but broadly speaking, the infant moves in a few years from a rather passive position, in which his mother provides most of what he needs, to a much more active one in which he increasingly fends for himself. This transition requires mutual adjustments in child and mother and is, of course, step by step dependent on the successive growth of such ego apparatuses as perceptual focusing, motor coordination, articulate vocalization and language attainment, capacity for locomotion, and the eventual achievement of object constancy—both of self and others. One may even speak of "activity needs," which require their own satisfaction through practice, and one may point to the obvious "pleasure in functioning" that accompanies the early discovery and practice of each new capacity. In the meantime, however, the earliest emotional experiences are embedded in a framework of considerable passivity: The baby is undergoing libidinally toned ministrations by being fed, being washed, being warmed—in a word, being loved; and he is undergoing real or fantasized aggressive impingements, which may range from interruptions in his nursing schedule to blatant rejections. In the earliest phase, moreover, passivity as well as activity are qualities of experience that pertain largely to processes of the id, whereas in later phases the emerging ego adds a new level of experience by which activity and passivity become qualified. Primary-process longings for passive experience may then be counteracted by the active experience of a self-managing, competent ego, which stratifies the active-passive variable of all experience in a unique, complex way.

Since both activity and passivity are forms of adaptation, they will be reinforced operationally by their immediate yield of satisfaction or equanimity. Thus there is a high probability that one or the other will become a stylistic trait or a basic position in life. These two styles will strongly affect the process of identification also: They will not only selectively steer the child toward emulating either the passive or active features of the parents' character, but will also make him more or less hospitable to the earliest introjects. If the latter are indeed something like psychic foreign bodies within the infant's mental world, a passive attitude would amount to enduring them, or even promote the goal of learning to live with them, whereas an active attitude would seek their modification, by projection and other mechanisms. Either course is guided by pleasure maintenance and pain avoidance, until the reality principle refines the terms of pleasure and mitigates the sting of pain.

While the inside-outside and the self-other polarities together constitute a preliminary schema of the *world* and how it is organized, the good-bad and active-passive modes of experience combine into a schema for the organization of *affects*. The first two pairs are basically cognitive; the second two are basically emotional. Each combination is a framework for forming a type of judgment, to a degree parallel to Kant's notions of pure reason and practical reason respectively.

A synopsis of this section is presented in Table 2.

Number and Range of Relations to Other People

In psychiatric assessment, one of the first pictures to obtain is of the sheer magnitude and spread of significant interpersonal relations the patient is engaged in, i.e., the number of persons he is invested in as need-satisfying objects. Though quantity per se is no index of quality, it does give a rough clue to the patient's interpersonal situation. Is he a loner, a hypercautious contact maker, a bereft person forced into mourning and loneliness, or a person embedded in many sustaining re-

TABLE 2

Modes of Experience	World	
	Self	Other(s)
good-passive	primitive grandiosity of being center of nurturant attention wallowing in being loved	"This fountain of love is all for me" thriving on the soothing presence of the lover
bad-passive	overwhelmed by feeling hated or unwanted sweeping feeling of being mistreated	fear of being invaded, devoured, or absorbed feeling of being drained or attacked
good-active	grandiose creator of pleasure to love is to give satisfactions	mutual excitation of pleasure to love is to be loved and vice versa
bad-active	grandiosity of being a destroyer destructive manipulator	mutual destruction and infliction of pain on guard against attacks; no one can be trusted

Note: The first phrase in each box captures a presumed infantile experience; the second phrase denotes a characterological disposition of later life.

lations with kin and friends? If the person is an isolate, does he seem to be one by his own design, or has he been ostracized by his social group? Does the trouble lie in making contact with other people, i.e., in the seeking and finding of objects, or in maintaining and sustaining relations with the objects found?

The sociological distinctions between primary and secondary groups and ingroups and outgroups offer a further clue to assessing a person's range of object relations. Some persons are so embedded in their families that they confine their satisfactions to those obtainable in the primary group of spouse, children, parents, and other relatives, all of whom are cathected with great intensity, leaving little need, time, or energy for engagements with members of secondary groups. In some cases, the primary group is very large, embracing very diverse ages and greatly differing characters, all of which combine to make this pattern of relating less restrictive than it sounds. In certain artificially arranged communes, however, the primary group with whom one chooses to live can be confined to one age, one sex, one occupation, one uniform outlook on principles, values, and lifestyle, often coupled with a strong penchant for regarding all other groups not only as distant secondary groups but as potentially dangerous outgroups to be kept at bay with animosity or enmity. Both of these choices stand in contrast to the pattern of those who seek major engagements in secondary groups, finding large satisfactions in clubs, churches, or fraternal organizations, in gatherings with business associates or in recreation centers and sports events, all pursued to such an extent that they bespeak some turning away from intimate traffic with family members. Some people seek chance encounters with strangers, keen on quickly building up an intense relationship, which often proves to be short-lived. Some persons simply have no primary group in which to be embedded—it may have been cut off by death, fragmented and weakened by dispersion of its members, or the person may have broken away from it in anger or disappointment, either to hole up in a solitary existence or to seek new friends unselectively and often ineptly.

Indeed, how shall one distribute his affection, his memberships, his loyalties, his love and hate, his interest in other people? Are there any norms for the scope of one's cathexes and the spread of one's engagements with other human beings? These questions can hardly be answered apart from considerations of the quality of human relations. Hence the next several sections of this chapter.

Constancy of Relations and Depth of Emotional Bonds

Endurance in specific object relations can stem from freely and consciously practiced fidelity based on a deliberate commitment, or from being tightly and unconsciously bound by fixation to one object in great dependency. The latter is not only an archaic bond, but one dominated by an introject or an external object from which insufficient separation has occurred, with the result that the self-representation is also inadequately formed. While such archaic object relations may be deep and constant, they are so from helplessness, not from the person's freedom to cathect whom he wishes or from his moral determination. He is stuck with his object relation because he never learned or had the chance to separate himself from the principal object of his childhood.

A 21-year-old college student, recently hospitalized for being in a grossly disorganized state, with delusions of being Milton and at other times Shakespeare, of having died and been reborn, and of being a seraphim and able to fly, proved to have almost no positive attachment to anybody. Always aloof and suspicious, and recently adopting a nihilistic and sarcastic attitude, he had no friends in grade school or high school. His only friend in college, a roommate, married the girl in whom the patient had some interest, and then moved abroad with her. The patient responded to this double loss by trying to kill himself in skydiving, but failed. His only enduring attachments are to his own family, but these are very ambivalent and exploitative. He plays on their guilt feelings over his plight by demanding money, presents, and food. He tried to "buy" friends in college by passing out marijuana and played the role of "king of the hippies"—in great loneliness.

Few adults present as stark a picture as this. More often, the early object relation is partly (but only partly) abandoned through an *anaclitic* object choice: The person finds a mate who is, in respect to his needs and accustomed patterns of satisfaction, so much a replica of father or mother and their wish-fulfilling ministrations that the fantasies of father's or mother's immortality and abiding presence can be maintained. Little has been given up in shifting from a parental to a quasi-parental object; not much novelty was added by the spouse one selected; not much self-discovery took place in finding such a good substitute for the original object that one was so reluctant to relinquish. Though some separation took place, psychodynamic continuity retarded full emancipation. Although anaclitic object choices per se are by no means pathological, it behooves the examining clinician to assess carefully what gains or satisfaction the patient prizes most in his current object and to what extent this relationship allows him to maintain a significant childish dependence, a touch of masochism, a passive attitude, or an indiscriminate obedience pattern.

There is another fixation to an archaic primary object that can show striking constancy and depth of attachment: the *narcissistic object relation to oneself,* one's body, and all one's trappings, from appearance and character traits to property. While everybody needs some self-esteem and a feeling of competence, some persons are so concerned with nurturing their self-representation and guarding it against assault that they have little energy left to invest in other people; or if they do cathect others, they seem to use them for securing a veritable stream of flattery, praise, adoration, and other reassurances of their lovableness. What dominates is the need to be loved, a need that can be satisfied—at least partially—by bestowing as much libido as one has on oneself or by making sure that the libido of other people is flowing in one's own direction.

This pattern came through in a middle-aged minister, prone to temper outbursts that endangered his professional status. Passive and retiring in his interpersonal relations, he seemed overconcerned with pleasing others. He feels comfortable (with qualifications) only in his family setting, avoiding involvement in the lives of other people who seek his pastoral advice or help. He belongs to no organizations or clubs outside "mother" Church. Yet in his preaching and other public performances he is thrilled by the faces of people turned to him, as if these were mirrors in which he could admire himself. All his relations seem to be hierarchical: It is as if he were constantly addressing father and mother figures with deference. Even with his wife he experiences no intimacy, but demands a motherly show of affection from her, and if this longing is not gratified, he sulks, feigns illness, or throws a tantrum.

The prevalence of *primary narcissism*, by definition, militates against engagement in deep and abiding relations with others, except in those fortuitous circumstances in which the person has found one or more persons willing to demand little from the relationship, or ready to make self-sacrificing compromises. The narcissistic patient often has obvious trouble in maintaining enduring relations since he is incapable of the realistic give and take that most deep relations demand. Hypersensitive to blame, frustration, aloofness, or strictness, he is bound to be quickly disappointed when his desires are not gratified. And in his great fear of being abandoned, he may take the initiative—to maintain his self-regard—by abruptly abandoning those with whom he was tentatively engaged, thus falling into a pattern of promiscuous and frantic object-seeking. He will also tend to test his objects repeatedly for their fidelity to him, and seek to extort promises from them, angrily turning against them when they do not deliver.

Aside from very strong fixations, the majority of object relations that clinicians must assess fall into a large gray zone where depth and constancy are of very diverse magnitudes, resulting in a variety of patterns that range from striking to commonplace. To organize one's perceptions of these patterns so as to gain diagnostic clarity, attention should be paid not only to the predominance of either libidinal or aggressive drives and affects in the patient's attachments, but to assessing which is under conscious control and thus fairly well modulated, and which is so unconscious that its control is difficult and its expression symptomatic of an unresolved conflict. *Prevailingly libidinal attachments* may be warm, tender, and close, but they may also be demanding or even whining when they are characterized by great dependency. In active people, and with a touch of aggressiveness, they may become somewhat intrusive; in passive people "taking" may so noticeably outweigh "giving" that there is an implied disrespect for the integrity of the object. Beset by inhibitions owing to fear of losing the object or from anticipations of rejection, the person may shyly nurture libidinal longings but not express them, leading to lack of spontaneity.

Predominantly aggressive patterns of attachment also show great variety. Overt sadism is only an extreme form, which, moreover, requires a perverse admixture of libidinal drive components to produce the *pleasure* in cruelty that is its earmark. More often, aggressively toned attachments are bullyish, commandeering, argumentative, or intrusive, lacking respect for the object's right to self-determination, privacy, and integrity. They may be saturated by teasing, subtly denigrating, or nagging attitudes. With social ineptness added, they may consist of a pervasive brusqueness or abruptness. If controlled, aggressive relations may have the character of a habitual aloofness, distance, coldness, or boredom. And, with striking passivity and intense libidinization, aggressive attachments turn into masochistic relationships.

Clinically important are those relations that show sharp momentary contrasts between love and hate, approach and avoidance, acceptance and rejection—the condition of *marked ambivalence*. In a sudden flipflop, the patient's smile turns into a frown, his handshake becomes a painful squeeze, a word of trust is overtaken by an angry remark. Or, if the pattern does not show abrupt alternations, one behavioral act may contain expressions of opposite intentions and affects. For instance, while conveying a sad message to someone the speaker is unable to suppress a (sadistic) smile. A gift or a bit of flattery contains a barb. For such behavioral situations to be truly ambivalent, one impulse or affect is conscious, the other unconscious. Ambivalence is not "mixed feelings"—the latter imply a conscious registration of two sets of feelings, two proclivities, and some kind of weighing of both tendencies.

A rather common example of ambivalent relations is found in marriages in which one partner is an alcoholic. When

drunk, the husband becomes a terror and sadistically as-
saults his wife in words or deeds, only to find her in such
episodes all too willing to put up with his vilification. In
fact, her masochism may stimulate his sadism. But when he
is sober, the wife demands a price for her masochistic
compliance by exerting the utmost control over him—
until the next episode reverses their roles again. Typically,
these intrapsychic and interpersonal alternations occur
without awareness by either party that a dual set of feelings is involved.

Selectiveness of Relations

From the dawn of civilization, human relations have been
guided by principles of selection: incest taboos, totemism, class
and caste, religious affiliations, gender roles, etc., in which
biological, psychological, and social criteria are combined in
various ways. Within the patterns of culture all relations between people are guided in some measure: Choices are limited
and some rules distinguish normality from deviance. In a
given culture, the clinical question is how the individual han-
dles the prescriptions and proscriptions that guide, structure,
and evaluate object relationships.

Perhaps the most obvious and psychodynamically most important selectiveness pertains to *sex*. In past and current object
relations, to which sex is the person most attracted? Which sex
does he or she trust? Which sex has the person's confidence,
attention, or interest? With which sex does the person feel at
home and at ease, without undue inhibitions or watchfulness,
and with spontaneity? With which sex is he or she most relaxed? Each of these questions has its converse: Which sex is
distrusted, which is avoided, with which are the person's relations riddled with conflict, suspiciousness, guardedness, denigration, viciousness, or any form of great unease?

Age is another important principle of selection. In a normal life span, we all experience age-determined relationship
patterns: upward from child to parent, downward from parent to child, laterally with age mates or peers, and our place

in the smaller age-hierarchy among siblings, which makes us an older, middle, or younger child. While none of these relations is unchanging over a lifetime, people tend to assume marked preferences for certain age-determined object relations. Some like the filial mode, even when they are no longer children.

They seek attachments to older people outside their own family: a much older spouse with whom an oedipal relation is enjoyed; an older teacher who becomes a close friend; an older supervisor or boss at work who is variously seen as protective, demanding, or a model to be emulated; an older friend who becomes a parental confidant, etc. Some adolescents and young adults feel ill at ease with their peers and seek the company of middle-aged persons. Others avoid contact with older persons and immerse themselves completely in peer groups, and as they themselves become older they seek membership in fraternal organizations and clubs that expose them over and over to persons of their own age. Some middle-aged and old people feel strongly drawn to youth, with whom they are on the best of terms because they genuinely enjoy the grandparental mode of object relations. Phenomena of the so-called generation gap can in principle occur anywhere along the age axis, and are clinically important not in terms of their sociological actuality but in terms of the feelings with which any particular person experiences and approaches them.

Socioeconomic selectiveness is not only of sociological interest, but has psychological importance also, particularly when one's reality situation or station in life offers diversity. It is one thing to be confined perforce to a class or income group; it is another thing to seek to avoid contacts with one or the other so as to satisfy one's own particular needs. Ambitious persons strive for relations in "higher circles," often disowning their origins in "lower" ones, callously or with inner conflict. Loyalty is thus brought to a test. Others seek to confine themselves to relations within their class or stratum, finding those "above" and "below" them equally untouchable, perhaps even feared. Who, being neither rich nor poor, dares befriend members of these groups? Indeed, how comfortable or anxious does one feel when one is thrown together—e.g., by being drafted into the military—with people from all walks of life? How does a proud middle-class patient feel when he finds himself in a public hospital populated by lower-class people? Conversely, how much training in reality contact and reality testing can be fostered in an exclusive, private sanitarium populated by a well-situated clientele? Given these questions, which are raised from time to time, what is the diagnostic significance of anyone's determination to break conventional class and caste segregations by deliberately seeking object relations outside his own circle? No pat answer is possible. Rising or sinking in the social scale is not always a matter of choice; one often has to make do with the objects at hand. But some sinking is a correlate of an intensification of mental illness, the person ending up on Skid Row, and some rising presents problems of its own, leading to estrangement from one's origins and the proverbial loneliness of the rich, or to a test of marital relations when the spouses are unequally endowed with adaptational skills.

The kind of selectiveness that deliberately breaks class segregation is frequently driven by protest, moral indignation, or compensatory urges. Some young people from sheltered homes actively plunge into "raw life" to test their strength, or to express disdain for parental ambitions. Some seek friends among the poor or shiftless to live up to commands or ideals of their conscience, to discharge an ethical obligation, or to seek atonement for unmerited luck. Noble-sounding rescue fantasies can be enacted, sometimes from marked megalomanic motives. Not to be overlooked is sheer curiosity, particularly of gifted persons, which drives them to widen their horizons and to find out "what people are like," "how the other half lives," or "alternative life styles," all of which entail some "breaking out" of class and caste confines.

For instance, a very intelligent middle-aged man, who had been born and reared in a remote agricultural settlement of a religious denomination with marked tribal organization, broke out of his confining milieu every ten years or so into an ever wider world, quite successfully; but each time the price was a depressive reaction with anxiety, for which he needed psychiatric help.

Selection patterns for *ethnic, ethnoreligious, or racial* distinctions in object relations are beset by the same multiplicity of motives. Given some degree of social pressure to seek one's enduring friendships and especially one's marital choices within one's group of origin, does one conform to it or defy it? And in either case, in what way—anxiously, with equanimity, as a matter of course, in anger, or militantly? Do libidinal or aggressive dynamics prevail in one's actions? To the extent that spoken or unspoken taboos exist against mixing, to cross ethnic or racial boundaries in significant object relations always incurs somebody's wrath, accusations of disloyalty, betrayal, or apprehensions about some unfathomable danger—with all of which one has to cope if one dares to go against the reigning *prejudices.* And if objections are not voiced from the outside, or are only muted apprehensions, they are likely to arise from the inside, by virtue of the self-concept, the ego ideal, and the superego. There is a diagnostic difference between entering into a biracial marriage in the spirit of genuine liberation from prejudice, and doing so out of defiance of one's parents or so as to seek a subtle dominance over one's spouse in the marriage. There is also a difference between sticking to one's kin, people, or race because of the comfort and ease such relations provide, and doing so from great suspicion of or hostility to other families, national groups, or races. The latter choice involves some paranoid bent, with accentuated hostility toward outgroups and the need to define one's own identity against the foil of some assumed enemy.

We shall return to the subject of prejudice as a form of ideology in a subsequent chapter; at this point we have singled out its various effects on the choice of object relations.

Varieties of Satisfaction in Object Relations

Sociologists look at human interactions as role behavior, as products of social differentiation, as status phenomena, or as normative versus deviant patterns. Ethicists regard human relations from a moral point of view, distinguishing right from wrong acts, considering motives, means, and ends. In dynamic psychiatry and psychology, human relations are consistently seen as object relations, i.e., as processes involved in *personal strivings for satisfaction*, originally of congenital drives (however conceived) and eventually of all kinds of acquired needs, wishes, and values that evolve from the processes of maturation and acculturation. In diagnostic work, one wants to know the kinds and degrees of satisfaction a person seeks or obtains by means of the objects with which he or she engages. If a dual drive theory is espoused, two broad groups of needs can in principle be envisaged: the libidinal and the aggressive, whose satisfactions and frustrations will color the particular object relation in question.

Keeping in mind the dimensions of objects set forth earlier in this chapter, we should start with the most overt object relation, namely the person's engagement with *external objects*, i.e., other actual persons. In line with the theory of psychosexual development, in which object relations are a dynamic variable, it is convenient to group the need satisfactions at which a person aims in terms of the major stages: oral, anal, phallic, and genital.

For instance, if a person expects to be met with warmth and given nurturance and protection, and if these satisfactions are demanded with great insistence and without fair reciprocity, *oral* need constellations obviously predominate in his attachments to objects. This is all the more so when the demands are coupled with low frustration tolerance, leading to conspicuous disorganization (anger, depression, anxiety, suspiciousness, etc.) that can only be overcome by rather direct provision of the satisfactions that the person originally hoped for. Warmth, nurturance, and protection as such are of course not specifically oral—it is their preponderance and the style in which they are demanded and given that determine their regressive genetic quality.

Quite different are the prevailing needs to be met in object relations that bear an *anal* stamp. In these relations, the per-

son seeks opportunities for self-assertion so as to test his autonomy, possibly engaging in acts of defiance that bring to a
head the question, Who obeys whom? Closely linked with the
issue of obedience versus disobedience is the tendency to
assume a moralizing attitude: to evaluate the relationship
partners (self and the other) as well as the relationship itself in
terms of their goodness or badness, their rightness or wrong-
ness. The satisfaction of anal needs colors the meaning of the
word "satisfaction" itself by connoting it as "setting straight,"
making or demanding retribution, extorting promises from
one's partner to which one holds him or her legalistically or
with great rigor, and dwelling on various atonement mechanisms to make up for trespasses. Here again we should stress
the preponderance of these needs and the style in which their
satisfaction is sought—it should be obvious that morality, judgments of good and bad, etc., permeate all of life from the cradle
to the grave and enter into all object relations.

Phallic needs load relations to external objects with strivings for dominance and intrusive meddlesomeness. A degree
of prying, maybe spying, besets the relationship, and the object's privacy or integrity is disregarded, or at least frequently
offended. The game is to dominate the object and transform
it to suit one's own goal of pleasure seeking, or use it as a foil
against which to test one's own strength. The object of phallic
strivings is often threatened with wrath or punishment, and
the phallic subject tends to keep track of his partner with
morbid curiosity and in commandeering fashion.

Because of their one-sidedness, these pregenital object relations are easier to describe than the *genital* relation, which
combines diverse strivings in subtle ways and seeks a multitude of satisfactions, each one perhaps modestly small, but
adding up to a substantial amount with a good deal of stability
over time. Outstanding are the capacity for give and take between partners, the ability to make workable compromises in
which neither party is left deprived, and—last but not
least—the enjoyment of precisely those settlements as a satisfaction in its own right. Mutuality is the key word: Each person respects the uniqueness and integrity of the other, finding

the other enjoyable on a reality basis. Genitality does not mean complete freedom from pregenital stirrings, nor does it spell Harmony and Bliss. The genital pattern means that the concept and the experience of self and others have been sufficiently differentiated to allow for the vision of two whole persons (subject and object) with a measure of objectivity; the relationship is regarded as a twosome. It means some liberation from earlier urges to merge with the object, to cling to it passively or dominate it actively, to engage in tight symbiotic bonds, to dread any form of separation, to exploit the object, or—to mention the most primitive condition—to recognize no boundaries between the object and one's self.

At this point we should turn our attention to the *internal objects*, the imagos, introjects, or intrapsychic representations of objects with which a relationship of sorts is also pursued. By definition, internal objects are imperfectly correlated with external objects, and are sometimes greatly at variance with them. They consist essentially of affect-laden reminiscences that propel the person toward the repetitive exercise of certain relationship models, or else become deeply cherished fantasy substitutes for insufficiently satisfying external object relations. With pronounced introversion, as in schizoid personalities, the gaze is turned inward on interior scenes populated with bits and pieces of people, more often fragmented than entire, with whom subvocal conversations are held, with whom one acts according to one's wishes, from whom one receives praise or blame, succor or threats, and whose voices carry some weight and must be heeded.

A young, married woman slowly developed a pattern of alleged neck pains and neck twitchings, greatly exacerbated after she became a mother and found herself preoccupied with the care of her baby, now one year old. She sought various devices to conceal her awkward neck and head motions, wearing long hair, high coat collars, or hats with large brims in the back. In talking about these devices, she also said that they shielded her from the stares of people in back of her. With fear and suspicion she increasingly had the feeling that people were "breathing down her neck." In later interviews she stated that in many of her reveries she had the sensation of an intrusive figure, whom she recognized as being "like my father," standing close behind her and watching her doings, sometimes speaking to her in commanding and hortatory phrases.

As products of the primary process, internal objects lead their own life, so to speak, within a person's emotional household, *but carry force!* They make one feel good or bad, quite apart from the specific emotions engendered by external object engagements, and in that sense determine much of a person's *basic mood,* which has of course a subsequent effect on the nature of his external object relations. In this sense, the notion of internal objects is meant to have explanatory power: These objects codetermine mood, action, perception, and thought, and form nuclei of associations that have a bearing on the attitudes and expectations with which one meets the external world. They also codetermine character and personality structure in the sense that their dynamic traces are the psychic "stuff' or nutrients from which parts of the superego, ego ideal, and ego are built up, and from which the latter derive some of their thematic content.

In regard to internal objects one might say that the kind of relation a person maintains with them varies with their formal status. As stated in the section *What Is an Object?,* internal objects show considerable cognitive and experiential variation. Some are as nebulous as an inexplicable mood, others have rather sharp contours and specificity. Some are experienced as a vague irritant or goad, others are as distinct as an encapsulated foreign body within the organism, like a sore or special pain spot. The body metaphors in these descriptions are no accident, for the body itself is a primary frame of reference for the kind of cognition that prevails in pregenital stages and is central to the nascent conception of the self, as the dynamics of narcissism show. In primary narcissism body and self (we should actually speak here of proto-self) are merged; in secondary narcissism they have become distinguished—the body is partly objectified as a means by which one presents oneself to the world. In that case, it can be consciously adorned or altered to achieve the "best impression."

The body enters into the discussion of internal objects from another side also: the actual object with whom the person has had contact since birth. Not only the proto-self, but also the mother, is first experienced as a bodily substance through sensory channels. The mother offers bodily stimuli of touch, taste, smell, pressure, and temperature; she offers her physical surfaces and contours—all long before she can be apprehended as a whole or as a separate entity. She is, in a multitude of contact fragments, the exterior world presented to the infant, at a time when his mind cannot yet clearly distinguish between inside and outside in reference to the self. The earliest affective reminiscences of pleasure and pain therefore involve somatic fragments that only gradually, with improved cognition, are overtaken by larger somatic units, until in the long run a new distinction between body and person can be made, both for the subject and the object. In this developmental sequence, the *object representations assume a progressively different formal status:* from parts to wholes; from bodies to persons; from good-versus-bad to good-and-bad entities; from fixed, encapsulated introjects that "feel" somewhat foreign to imagos that can be assimilated as identification models or against which counteridentifications can be made.

The diagnostic point to be made is that a full assessment of object relationships should contain some evaluation of the person's relations to his internal objects. The material for such an assessment is largely to be derived from primary-process productions such as dreams, reveries, projective test responses, free associations and, of course, symptoms, including hallucinatory experiences. One special life situation that brings internal object relations into the foreground is the process of mourning. Bereavement throws a person back on his imagos, with which a covert relation is maintained when the overt relation has ended. A noteworthy developmental situation is the stage in which the toddler shows the capacity to be alone, peacefully, which according to Winnicott is a test of his trust in a satisfying interior object whose felt presence tides him over the periods when the mother is unavailable. Special syndromes, such as the depressive reactions, bring the person's relations to interior objects into focus: These objects nag, haunt, oppress, or beset him with a vigor unmatched by the external objects with which he is engaged. Their capacity to find him exclusively "bad" or significantly wanting shows the regressive pull of these internal object relations, for they revert to judgments and affect constellations that precede the phase of ambivalence.

Primitive internal object relations prior to ambivalence are also recaptured in regressive states of euphoria, bliss, or triumph, particularly when these states have an episodic or paroxysmal character. Manic and hypomanic states and certain epileptic aurae appear to be experienced as retreats to a narcissistic proto-self, with boundless inflation of its scope and power. The world and other people fade away as distinct entities; they are reduced to something vaguely benevolent, registered affectively in the oral mode of frantic gulping or eager slaking of one's thirst. The internal part-object of the good, nurturing breast predominates, at least momentarily. But the precariousness of this regressive state is manifest in the person's affective lability. The slightest mishap or some felt decline in the rate or volume of the eagerly sought satisfaction turns the experienced internal object from benevolent into malevolent, and the person then gives way to bursts of rage, diffusely expressed in tantrums, and random smashing of things immediately at hand.

Techniques for Obtaining Satisfactions in Object Relations

By definition, the *mature (or ideal) object relation* is characterized by mutuality and reciprocity, with about equal give and take between the partners, governed by the recognition that the object is a whole person whose needs are as important and urgent to him or her as are one's own needs to oneself. I am not saying that the satisfactions one strives for in such partnerships are obtained without the exertion of some influence on the object. But the techniques of influencing the other embody the mature quality of the relation. With trust, respect, and reliability, in an atmosphere of mutual building up, the means for finding satisfactions will be flexible, to the point, and of agreeable style. Needs and wants can be discussed, plans for meeting them can be made and revised in the light of experience, signals can be clear, and one can use civil and playful means to secure reasonable gratifications. With tact, humor, or charm, by friendly asking or straightforward discussion, one can convey one's wants, being sure at least of a willing ear.

Not so for immature relations beset by immature wants, in which something distorting is bound to happen to either the subject or the object—and, as a consequence of the interaction, to both. Balint[58] has described three basic object-relations models short of the mature one: (1) the anaclitic relation; (2) idealization of the object; (3) humiliation of the object. It is evident that these three models will have a bearing on the interpersonal techniques used to secure satisfactions. The *anaclitic relation* is earmarked by the subject's dependency on his object, a position of juvenile helplessness that places the object in the role of provider, caretaker, and security giver, and imposes on him or her the role of the "strong one" in maintaining the relationship. While the dependent person in an anaclitic relation is likely to use such childish techniques as demanding, whining, griping, and other forms of pressureful asking, he may also have recourse to excessive meekness and perfect obedience, to induce the object to fulfill his wishes. He may be defiant and provocative, tantalizing the object and putting him or her through a test of endurance. He may use deceit and extortion if he has learned that these techniques give him what he wants from an indulgent parental figure.

A middle-aged, single hospital worker who depended very strongly on the continual support of his coworkers and had always felt drawn to working in hospitals on account of what he called their "helpful" atmosphere, had for several years been in psychotherapy for feelings of depression.

With each change of therapist the patient's complaints about gloomy feelings became greatly exacerbated, but without noticeable effect on his work or energy level. He said he could not survive without the particular therapist with whom he had been recently allied. Yet he became easily engaged with the next therapist(s), making a prompt improvement.

Idealization of the object puts the object on a pedestal, to be admired, to be paid homage to, and also to be put at a distance from oneself. This pattern calls for attitudes of deference and a degree of self-abnegation; the subject resorts to such techniques as flattery, excessive or unwarranted praise, and a penchant for playing the role of the humble soul who dares not demand anything for himself, thereby precisely banking on the object's benevolence to provide him with (unmerited) satisfactions. And since it is patently unrealistic to idealize everybody, the idealizing attitude often leads to a division of important classes of objects into good ones and bad, some to be worshiped, others to be despised. So have many men regarded women as either saints or whores, actually making separate packages of their ambivalent feelings and allowing separate channeling of sacred and sinful acts. In strong idealization the discrepancy between the object's elevation and the subject's low status (in his own eyes) facilitates the rationalization of one's own failures to live up to any ideal: "Who would not fall short in comparison to such an exalted model?" Or, "If he (or she) is so good, wise, understanding, forgiving, etc., how dare I ask for anything but through the most subtle indirection?" In the latter case, elaborate obeisances are called for in the hope that they will bring forth gratifications.

Humiliation of the object runs the gamut from subtle denigration and criticism to the crassest defilement. A clinical truism suggests that for every object idealized there is another object humiliated, particularly when the affects are intense. Sometimes the object extolled and the one humiliated are the same, at different moments or in different situations. But if object humiliation is preponderant, the techniques for humiliating will sooner or later become quite overt in any relationship. The literature on sadism and manipulation describes these techniques, which range from teasing, seducing, cajoling, blaming, and assuming a position of conspicuous timidity, via intruding and extorting, all the way to the most brutal infliction of pain, physical or mental. In characterological manipulation and fraudulent attitudes the relational techniques include a conscious or unconscious moment of triumph over having "done in" the object and thereby having made him or her despicable—which in turn may momentarily enhance one's own self-regard for being more clever, powerful, or admirable, or for having effectively avenged oneself for some wrong received.

Humiliation of the object often proceeds from projecting aspects of the "bad self" onto others, and in that case is part of a paranoid system of role reversals and disordered thought. Having this insight, the clinician can extrapolate from extreme guardedness or suspiciousness the likelihood that the patient will be inclined to expose his therapist, at the right opportunity, in a humiliating way, e.g., by exposing his ignorance, accusing him of lying, or insinuating that he is unfaithful.

Capacity for Empathy and Identification

The dramatis personae in anyone's life function not only as direct satisfiers, but also as objects on whom to bestow care, to empathize with, and to value as examples for identification in one respect or another. Engaging with others presupposes a capacity for doing so, based on the overcoming of excessive narcissism. It requires some freedom from self-preoccupation, some recognition that the world and its objects exist and merit attention and involvement, some available energy to invest in these objects.

Thus the fundamental question is whether the patient has any capacity for empathy and identification at all, at least enough to make possible a therapeutic alliance. Sadly, that capacity is not always present: Some patients are so self-absorbed that nothing outside seems to exist for them; others are so engrossed in seeking their own satisfactions that no other person is granted any rights of his own. If *primary narcissism* is unmitigated, no relation has any viability; at best there are only incidental or occasional transactions.

Fortunately, most clinical situations are less extreme. One will want to know how responsive the patient is to other people's needs, other people's predicaments or frustrations, and to what lengths he goes in meeting them or keeping them out of awareness. Whom is he willing to help? Whom does he pity, envy, protect, admire, or emulate? What human situation or predicament enlists his attention, his good will, his care or intervention? Can he place himself in someone else's situation, sad or joyful? In his reading, in what way and to what extent can he vicariously live the life and have the experience of the story's hero?

It is fair to assume that in anyone's turning to others to give help, express sympathy, show compassion, or share joy, *promptness* is a telling point, in that it suggests spontaneity as well as the capacity to move quickly from intention to action. Many sympathies never see the light of day for lack of mobilizing the person to words or deeds.

To foresee aspects of the clinical helping process, the diagnostic interviewer should ask questions about the patient's *typical help-seeking behaviors.* To whom did he turn in the past when problems loomed? If he needs to unburden himself, in whom does he confide? What persons does he trust or see as trustworthy, and for what kinds of confidences or help does he seek them out? Are they typically members of the same sex, the other sex, of parental age, people in leadership roles, or are they nearly always the patient's peers in age or status?

Clues for therapy paradigms can also be derived from inquiring how the patient goes about *settling quarrels* with important people in his social orbit, such as his or her spouse, parents, children, friends, supervisors, teachers, subordinates, or the merchants he patronizes. Does he really settle quarrels and bring problems to a conclusion or resolution, or does he merely argue, bicker, sound off, or get his anger off his chest, perhaps with further deterioration of the relationship? Is "winning an argument" of overriding importance, or is the real substance of differences tackled? Was he able to change his attitude or opinion in the course of an argument? Could he empathize in any way with the other person or did he cling to his own righteousness?

For children, and for many adults too, *empathy for and identification with animals* represent a significant form of object investment. Attitudes toward pets, the length and intensity of attachment to them, their handling, training, and disciplining, should provide some clues to the person's channeling of affection and aggression, including the possibility of their displacement from human beings because of distrust of people.

Sexual Relations and Activities

We began this chapter by reflecting on the origin of the word "object," which we found to lie in drive theory. An object is in the first place a drive satisfier, whatever else it may be. Thus the most directly drive-determined relations involve sexual acts, which therefore merit special attention when the diagnostic task is to evaluate those integrative processes that require intimate relations with other people. But it is well to remember that "other people" are, developmentally, latecomers in anyone's sexual activity. The first sexual activity is autoerotic, and the first sexual object is the body-self. A similar developmental distinction is to be made between the fantasized sexual object in masturbation and the real object with whom one is sexually engaged. The first diagnostic point to be ascertained in an adult, then, is whether he engages in any *sexual activity with real other people* at all, or whether he is stuck with, or thrown back on, *autoerotic* acts or fantasies.

The same drive theory from which the term "object" originated holds that libidinal development entails a choice within the category of "others" as sexual objects: a choice between members of the other sex and members of one's own sex. The heterosexual choice is socially favored and biologically fitting and productive; inasmuch as the homosexual choice forgoes these features, it is dysfunctional and may thus be seen as indicative of incomplete development, no matter how gratifying it may be on other grounds. The distinction between *hetero-* and *homosexual activity* is thus the second diagnostic point to be made.

The four categories thus formed, important as they are for gauging aspects of the patient's reality contact and object preferences, are only a provisional framework, setting the stage for further questions that may have much greater diagnostic importance. For instance, from the psychodynamic point of view it is important to know whether the *prevailing affect* in any sexual act (in any of the four categories) is libidinal and suffused with tenderness, warmth, and nurturance, or is permeated with aggressive impulses, cruelty, or dominance, yielding the perverted pleasure of sadistic or masochistic exploitation. From the energetic point of view one would like to know *which partner typically takes the initiative* in seeking sexual contact, who leads whom, and what distribution of *activity and passivity* prevails in each. From the holistic point of view it is important to consider whether sexual activities are a more or less separate, *encapsulated* part of the person's action repertoire, or whether erotic feelings give rise to other activities as well, in modulated ways, so that life is lived on a *continuum* of eroticism ranging from sublimation to uninhibited sexual acts.

From a developmental point of view the way stations of libidinal growth and the vicissitudes of sexual learning provide a diagnostic ordering system. In adults, what is the balance in time and investment between *foreplay and consummatory act?* What modes of foreplay prevail, and, in the case of some perversions, what part of foreplay represents the ultimate satisfaction, so that it is in fact the consummatory act? How much pleasure-seeking investment is made in *oral* modalities, such as using the mouth (kissing, biting, sucking, etc.) or the eyes (looking and being looked at); in *anal* modalities (smelling, soiling, smearing, etc.); in *phallic* behaviors (triumphant masculine showing off, dominant manipulation, exhibitionism, intrusiveness, etc.)? What are the admixtures of erotic and aggressive elements in any of these behaviors, and what are the proportions of activity and passivity, i.e., "doing" versus "undergoing"?

Apart from sexual acts per se, every person tends to evaluate himself or herself as a *sexual being*, making judgments about adequacy, potency, competence, attractiveness, normality or abnormality, perversity or healthiness. In many cases these judgments are based on untested fantasies or stem from once justified apprehensions that are no longer commensurate with the present life situation. Their psychological effect on performance is so great, however, that many sexual dysfunctions, including temporary ones, set up the spiral effects of self-fulfilling prophecies, in which object relations, emotions, and self-esteem become equally conflict-ridden. For this reason, a person's self-evaluation as a sexual being merits careful exploration. With which sex does the person *identify* himself or herself in innermost fantasy? What aspects of sexual thought or activity tend to be charged with guilt feelings, or shame, or loathing? What is the *primary sexual fantasy* that gives the ultimate and most intimate pleasure, irrespective of the actual sexual partnership in which one is engaged, and on which the fantasy may indeed be mentally superimposed?

Since sexual acts are an intricate combination of motion and emotion ("doing" and "feeling") they tend to be subject to *ritualization*. They may become stylized in such a way that going through certain motions holds the promise of experiencing certain emotions (and subsequent orgastic effects). How much attention is paid to technique? How preoccupying is ritual? Can the person act sexually in a relaxed way, trusting both self and partner? Can sexual activities share in the person's general spontaneity, if any, or are they chained to fixed calendars, places, or occasions?

Finally, for some persons sexual partnerships stand in a tenuous or paradoxical relation to their major object bonds, by virtue of distinctions made between "love" and "carnality." The sexual experience is not always holistic or commensurate with the primary object investments. Therefore, one diagnostic question about sexual relations is, "Who is the preferred sexual partner?" Is it wife or husband; is it the casual friend who happens to come along, unforeseen; is it a "pickup" routinely engaged in; is it an unknown, mysterious stranger or exotic type; is it a young boy or girl, some motherly or fatherly figure, etc.? And does the person seek the preferred persons under an inner compulsion, almost against his or her will, or are the searches fully ego-syntonic and the satisfactions obtained, if any, commensurate with the more abiding emotional tones of the rest of life?

Chapter 12

Assessing Integrative Processes: Relations to the Self

Just as it is unimaginable that a person be without any relations to other people, so is it unimaginable that he or she is
without some concept of, feeling for, and relation to the self,
defined as an entity that is at once the subject and an object of
experience, forming a point of reference that has some constancy from the cradle to the grave. Note the cautious word
usage in the preceding sentence: concept of, feeling for, relation to, point of reference. For what the self is, and how its
essence can be described and defined, is a major philosophical
question that allows diverse answers, and the metaphysical or
ontological status of the self is not our concern here. Our approach to the self is geared to how it is experienced; how it is
perceived, conceived, and evaluated; how it operates, develops, and is articulated, and what its clinical vicissitudes turn
out to be. We shall thus use the term "self" most of the time
as a circumscriptive designation for "person as a whole,"
"human being," "human organism," and for "I" and "me"—
with my particular blinders—rather than in the essentialist
sense of "core of personality" or "innermost being" or "personalistic essence," let alone "soul." At times we will need special words such as "identity," which press close to the
philosophical issues involved in personhood without definitely
shifting from a psychological to a metaphysical perspective.

Consciousness of Self as Subject

Some clinically salient approaches to the self have been formulated by Jaspers,[59] all of them in terms of consciousness. An intact self has the following attributes: (1) a consciousness of *self as contrasted to the "other"* and the "beyond"; (2) a consciousness of *activity* of any kind—"I do..., I feel..., I wish..., I decide...," etc.; (3) a consciousness of *identity*—"I am the same one that I ever was and shall be" despite my obvious changes from infancy to senescence; (4) a consciousness of *singularity*—"I am only one at each moment, for I have (or I am) a unity." Experientially, these four aspects of consciousness of self are clearly relevant to most normal adults; clinically, their usefulness lies in their power to define specific pathological conditions.

For instance, if *consciousness of self as contrasted to others* is disturbed, symptoms of dedifferentiation appear: Judge Schreber began to think he was God's wife; an aggrandized Mr. Nobody assumes a famous name (Hitler, Jesus, Satan) and begins to act accordingly; an autistic youngster runs his fingers in puzzlement over the examiner's body in an apparent experience of merger and loss of personal boundaries (but with a faint trace of "skin" as a natural limit): or, in more attenuated forms, we begin to see involuntary imitation or mimicking of other people's facial expressions, tones of voice, or movements. These symptoms betray a loss or diminution of experienced selfhood, or a breakdown of personal identity, reminiscent of an infantile state in which self and others were presumably not delineated.

A *diminished consciousness of activity* leads to the automaton experience: The patient feels he is at the mercy of extraneous forces that goad him, steer him, or erode his liveliness, or he may think he has turned into a machine. What little action he performs will have a robotlike character, stultified and mechanical. Typically, affect is at its lowest ebb and a feeling of emptiness prevails; time loses its normal flow and seems to stand still. There may be a feeling of utter boredom. In the epilepsies, the "hole in time" cut by the seizure is quickly filled by the patient, on regaining consciousness, by the searching question, "What have I done?"—a very healthy concern that testifies to the power of the activity dimension in normal personality integration.

In *disturbances of consciousness of identity* (in Jaspers's sense) symptoms of depersonalization arise, often centering on experiences of radical transformation, described as "death and rebirth," or as changes in sex. The former self is disowned, rejected, or repressed, sometimes with a virtual amnesia for all that one once was; or it is denigrated as a sham, something one only pretended to be. The sense of continuity is surrendered to a disjointed "before" and "after" scheme. Amnesic for his name, address, and status, the patient may wander about, eventually turning to the police for help in finding out who he is and where he belongs. Long-hospitalized, chronic patients may not recognize themselves in their own earlier photographs; visually confronted with their own images in a mirror, they feel estranged, puzzled, or horrified.

A *disturbed sense of singularity* is manifest in the symptoms of dual or multiple personality, and in experiences of a divided self. Though most of us would acknowledge that we have "many sides" and are not in perfect harmony with ourselves at all times, the sense of singularity convinces us that we are, all told, one and only one person. But some persons feel so deeply divided (e.g., between being good and bad, sinful and saintly, male and female) that they no longer experience such oneness; they may seek a radical transformation to achieve oneness again (e.g., by a conversion), or lapse into chronic ambiguity and ambivalence (leading to bizarreness, abulia, or obsessional stalling). Some begin to alternate between two or more stylized partial enactments of their divided selves, assuming distinct pseudo personalities, which, like Dr. Jekyll and Mr. Hyde, flipflop periodically and appear to be oblivious of one another. But even in such cases of multiple personality where a dividing line has been clearly drawn, the amnesia which blankets Jekyll's awareness of Hyde and Hyde's of Jekyll can be seen as a sign of normalization, as an attempt to preserve some sense of singularity at any given moment!

Consciousness of Self as Special Object

Jaspers's dimensions of awareness focus on the self as subject and action center. Psychoanalysis sees the self also in a different light, namely as an *object that is reflexively perceived and conceived by the subject,* that is esteemed or denigrated, loved or hated, built up or taken down by the very action center it contains. There are two cardinal reasons for this psychoanalytic viewpoint: (1) the empirical fact that a person has (in some sense *is*) a body; (2) the reflexive nature of human consciousness. Both are venerated themes in the history of thought about human nature and are anchored in language: the word "somebody" retains the natural embodiment of persons in its etymology, and the distinction between "I" and "me" in personal pronouns shapes the two points of view that consciousness can have: outward and inward, from the self and toward the self. The expression "I myself" rolls subject and object into one; a phrase such as "I regard myself as . . ." separates the subject and object dimensions of the speaker. In the toddler phase, children refer to themselves in the third person, often by their given name and the corresponding pronoun "he" or "she," before they settle on a clear-cut "I," and in severe psychopathology the adult may revert to such indirect self-reference.

In perception, *the body is given twice:* The kinesthetic sense presents it as an *interior reality,* the distance receptors (especially vision) present it in part as an *exterior datum.* The front of the body and the limbs are frequently a part of any visual scene, "out there" where other things are; my own backside is more mysterious to me and cannot even be seen in a single mirror. The body is thus an ambiguous object, at once outside and inside, subject and object. My own body is the most direct and concrete reference point for practical space dimensions (left-right, front-back, high-low); my body processes (tissue needs and their satisfaction, sleeping and waking, zest and fatigue) give rise to my sense of the flow of time, which memory organizes into time schemes; my voluntary muscle movements give me a sense of agency from which cause and effect sequences are elaborated. All three categories of experience—space, time, and causality—undergo drastic qualitative changes in the diurnal cycle: in dreams and sleep their objective coordinates lose their logical coherence, so that any imagery or thought content is both foreign and peculiarly "mine," with an equivocal sense of activity and passivity.

The ambiguous status of the body cannot fail to affect both the form and the content of consciousness of self. Consciousness is intentional: It is always directed to something outside itself (its content at any given moment), while at the same time its functioning (irrespective of any particular content) and its arousal (irrespective of level of clarity) are the conditions for regarding myself as subject. Like a lighthouse in whose beam of light things appear and "come to light," *consciousness presents subject and object in combination,* and makes it possible to "intend" as its object everything that I consider *mine*—my body, my mind, my character, my memories, my feelings, my fears, my views of the world, my views of myself, and my investment in and dedication to myself. Put philosophically, there is a point at which "being" and "having" coalesce, despite the very different references of these two cardinal verbs.

Since so much of the self (one's body as well as one's mind) is or can be apprehended as object, it is small wonder that personality theories tend to seek a conceptual domain within the personality as a whole to which such functions as consciousness, agency, intending, attending, arousal, together with their waxing and waning, can be referred. No personality theory has held that persons are formed of a homogeneous substance, like sponges; in one way or another they acknowledge that persons are composites of heterogeneous structures and functions, organized in some way to form a more or less viable unit. Psychodynamic theory took the clues for its personality divisions from psychiatric symptoms, whose detailed study allowed groupings of prevailing intrapsychic conflict situations. The structural and functional distinctions that it finds within the self (here clearly standing for the person as a whole) are conceptualized as ego, id, superego, and ego ideal, with constant reference to the ambiguous status of the body and to the external world in its multiple dimensions (all too severely condensed in the term "reality"). And clinically these distinct intrapsychic structures are regarded in their genesis and their historical interaction, as well as in their cross-sectional coordination at the time of the examination.

Relations to the self, then, are approached by describing processes and interactions that go on between two or more intrapsychic structures and between any of these and the world. This format will be our guide throughout the rest of this chapter.

The Ego and the Person It Serves

As I have already indicated in Chapters 2 and 10, to the ego are attributed high-level, cardinal functions in organismic maintenance: attention, perceptual screening, thought organization, registration and organization of affects, guiding the motor system, operating the memory bank, goal setting, and various coordinating functions that enhance adaptation, foster growth, prolong life, and promote resilience under stress. The ego functions like an executive whose company (the person as a whole) is to thrive, or like a head of state whose nation is to achieve well-being. Or, like a ship's captain, the ego's task is to steer a course while keeping the ship in optimal shape; this metaphor makes clear that the captain's vision and awareness (the ego's vigilance) must always be doubly attuned, both to the ship's complex interior and to the exterior world, including distant horizons.

As the organizational executive of the person, the ego is to harmonize diverse parties that present their special claims and pressures, and, much like a company's president, it is engaged in routine tasks as well as in making special or novel determinations. The ego's routines comprise the bodily regulations mediated by the autonomic nervous system that proceed quite automatically, such as breathing and digesting; and many functions mediated by the central nervous system, such as perceptual scanning, attentional gating, muscle tone maintenance, and the almost constant production of mental representations through images, ideas, and words. Many acquired habits and learned reaction patterns belong to the ego's functional repertoire as routines, requiring no explicit thought, especially those coping devices through which it comes to terms with the outer world, and the defense mechanisms by which it deals with intrapsychic demands.

A very large part of the ego's special task is *to provide the organism with the satisfactions it needs to stay alive and grow, and to ward off the noxious influences that come its way.* The needs and noxae that impinge on human organisms are not only biological but psychological, social, and cultural as well, and thus the words "pleasure" (for satisfaction) and "pain" (for harm) must be understood in their broadest meanings. A scowl from somebody may cause a person great pain; working himself to near exhaustion for a cause he believes in may give the person exquisite pleasure.

With all these tasks to be done (tasks that have been described in detail in the previous chapters on "part processes"), the clinical examination of "relations to the self" is addressed to several questions about ego and person. Does the person think that by and large his ego functions or "works" in *adequate* ways? If so, does he think of himself as a *competent* person, able to manage himself as a "good householder" of his internal environment, and able to make a realistic and gratifying adaptation to the outer world? In his or her personal history thus far, can the person recognize, and accept with appropriate pride, some tangible achievement or progress? Is there a sense of zest or buoyancy, or a feeling that he or she is growing and moving forward?

In clinical practice, these formal questions often need not be asked specifically, for the patients may volunteer the answers in their first self-presentation on admission to clinic or hospital. Here is an almost random assortment of initial statements:

"I can't stop myself from crying."

"My back hurts, my legs hurt, my neck hurts, my arms

ache. I feel tired, I am nervous, I do not know what is wrong with me."

"I cannot understand why I always have to act on thoughts without evaluating them first."

"I cannot control my thoughts."

"I am the greatest sinner for whom there is no forgiveness."

"I am unable to get along with people and I am depressed."

"I have trouble controlling my emotions. I lose my temper."

"I believe people are laughing at me and this makes me feel terrible."

"I tried to kill myself."

"Everything just came to a head. I was waiting on a job from the Post Office and had difficulty finding a job because of a poor work record. I have been depressed, crying, and talking about suicide."

"I have a problem, Doc. I've been sniffing glue and gas for the past three years and I cannot seem to stop it."

"I am afraid I am going to hurt someone."

And from an 11-year-old boy:

"I was brought here for testing, maybe because I did the opposite of what my mom said. I don't know why I had to do that."

Obviously, when a person seeks psychiatric help, his *self-regard* is likely to be diminished in some respect. The person may feel grossly inadequate, rather weak, or not quite up to the demands of organismic efficacy and reality adaptation. In asking for help, he may indeed want somebody to lean on, to shore up his faltering functions, to resort at least temporarily to an "auxiliary ego" in the form of the helper, who may take over some decisions for him or simplify his environment. Or the patient may say, when he is at long last participating in a

psychological examination, that he has felt weak and inadequate all his life and that his journey until now has been
an excruciating feat of hiding his shame and covering up for
his failures. But self-regard may also be *inflated:* The patient
may speak about his capacities in glowing terms, overestimat-
ing them in blatant contrast to his proven inadequacies. Then
again, such verbal, sometimes even cocky, overesteem may
have a pathetic quality, barely hiding feelings of weakness and
incompetence that cannot be verbalized.

The feelings of self-regard here assessed should focus on
competence; They are *self-evaluations of the ego's functional
capacities.* They are not moral judgments that the person is in
some sense good or bad, right or wrong, blameless or guilty.
Moral self-evaluations hinge on relations between the ego and
the superego or ego ideal. In addition to judgments about
capacity and competence, however, the self-regard that judges
the ego's functioning may well be affected by aesthetic criteria,
body-image variables, and aspects of skill and aptitudes. One
may consider oneself to be ugly, too large or too small, un-
derdeveloped, mousy, deformed, poorly coordinated, muscu-
larly weak, motorically awkward, singularly ungifted, physically blemished, socially tactless and uncouth, incapable of
such skills as dancing, playing the piano, singing, or any sports
activity. Adolescents in crisis especially tend to be full of self-
judgments of this sort, often swinging widely between moments of too low and too high self-esteem. Many schizoid patients have long felt awkward in one or more aspects of
capacity, physique, or skill, harboring in private a low self-
regard occasionally punctuated by compensatory feelings of
grandiosity, and eventually withdrawing from situations
(mostly social) that would further damage their low self-
esteem.

The schizoid person's withdrawal and compensation in
fantasy reveal the two yardsticks employed in most estimates
of the self's adequacy and competence. There is a *public
yardstick* that comprises judgments about oneself made by
others, gleaned from myriad social messages that come one's
way: frank and head-on verbal appraisals, school grades,

smiles and frowns, social invitations and ostracisms, and the endless ratings and rankings that occur among siblings and between parents and children. There is also a *private yardstick* that comprises little competitions with oneself, views in the mirror, knowledge of one's own goals, and estimates of one's distance from or proximity to them.

There are valid reasons for conceiving of the superego and the ego ideal as separate intrapsychic structures: They originate in processes of introjection and identification, and, once formed, they generate the specific affects of guilt and shame when the ego appears to be in conflict with their demands. But this does not mean that all self-evaluations proceed from these agencies alone. *Within the ego itself there is a kind of ongoing assessment, on the hither side of guilt and shame,* that comes through in feelings of buoyancy or lassitude, activity or passivity, helmsmanship or drifting, potency or weakness, moving or stagnating. The common factor in these paired comparisons has much to do with energy: Does the person feel engaged in coping and having the wherewithal to do so, or does he feel disengaged because of fatigue, depletion, or exhaustion, about ready to give up and say "What's the use?"

One patient, struggling with an acquired handicap, says: "I am slow in everything; I get easily confused; I lose track of time because I am often in a daze; I have to work twice as hard as before on anything; my mind is moving in slow motion." In taking stock of himself, he finds that he lives within an inflationary psychic economy: His satisfactions are meager in proportion to the high cost of his actions. Yet he is far from giving up. He struggles valiantly, but is not content with himself and notes his own gloomy mood, untainted by feelings of shame or guilt. Another patient, in much the same circumstances, has taken to drinking and has allowed himself to regress; alternating between denying his problem and feigning joviality, he settles into a downward spiral until he loses all sense of agency and becomes a wreck. A third patient, restless and flighty, has bungled all his affairs and human relationships, but seems to meet each new day as a new adventure, rushing headlong into new opportunities, full of pep, free from regret or remorse over his past failures. All three patients evaluate themselves, among other things, in terms of *the economies of their energy* and the basic moods these engender. Typical mood-words, such as depression and elation, with their connotation of the "sinking heart" and "triumph," convey the primordial quality of such ego feelings, which may stand quite apart from the complications introduced by the superego and ego ideal. Basic mood and specific affects are different things, produced by different kinds of self-evaluation.

In singling out the energy components of basic mood, self-esteem, and feelings of competence, we see once more the intimate relation between ego and body. Clinical observation makes plain that enormous variations and fluctuations exist in the degree to which the body or any of its parts are cathected. Increases and decreases of body cathexis are telltale signs of psychological and psychosomatic disorders. Whatever a "normal" interest in one's body may be, deviations from customary interest should be noted for their clinical relevance.

Increased body cathexis is manifested in marked curiosity about one's body's functions or organs; in concern over the body's volume or weight, leading to dieting or bust-building attempts; in concern over the body's beauty, revealed in the time spent looking in mirrors, squeezing skin pores, pimples, and rimples. The body's strength may become a vast preoccupation, as muscle-building parlors and magazines show. Pain and itch can siphon off attention from vital activities; trigeminal neuralgia can become almost a way of life, so that its removal by surgery or alcohol block precipitates a major personality disorganization. Polysurgery and repeated plastic surgery prove the never-good-enough quality of a hypercathected body or organ. All hypochondriacal states and preoccupations with sexual potency drain energies from worthier projects. Paranoid hypervigilance about the protection of exposed body parts (e.g., one's back) demonstrates that the body can be experienced largely as a danger zone or focus of attack, requiring constant defense. The somatic delusions of grossly deranged patients (head swelling, stomach bursting, changes in genitals) testify to the same principle: Markedly increased cathexis of the body signifies a change in ego feeling that can be a harbinger of the greatest disorganization.

A similar range of phenomena is produced by *decreased body cathexis.* A noble stoicism in the face of discomfort or pain may become a Spartan endurance test, leading to excessive or dangerous renunciation of needed sustenance. In states of preoccupation or absorption the body may be neglected, meals skipped, sleep given up, and hygiene suspended. Religious ecstasies may be accompanied by not only body neglect but body punishment. Hysterical paralyses and anesthesias imply selective decathexis and hypercathexis of body parts, with displacement and symbolization. Straight denial of illness and pain, as in anosognosia, presupposes a withdrawal of libido from the affected organs, perhaps with a hypercathexis of the intact body zones so as to preserve the body's (and the ego's) partial efficacy. Somatic delusions are often negative: "My head feels dead"; "I have no belly any more." Small wonder, then, that patients with such delusions can engage in self-mutilations without apparent pain. A completely decathected penis or scrotum can be tinkered with, as in attempts at self-castration. Throughout the range of these phenomena the decreased body cathexes bespeak alterations in ego feeling, in basic mood, and in the view of the ego as the agent of organismic maintenance. And with the changes in libidinal cathexis one can expect to find changes in aggressive cathexis also: with withdrawal of libido from the body, the body is likely to become a target for self-directed aggression.

The body is not only the ego's organic substrate, it is also its *symbol,* and an emblem of its social presentation. That is why the changes in body cathexis described in the preceding paragraphs rarely feel ego-alien. Changes in body feeling are a kind of language by means of which the ego signals to the person and to others that something is happening to its adequacy as manager of organismic equilibrium. Although in an interview the bodily changes may at first be described by the patient as a complaint, seemingly requiring medical attention, on closer inspection they turn out to be signals of an ego in distress—true personalistic actions rather than unforeseen biological events that have befallen a helpless victim.

The Ego as a Developmental Acquisition

Thus far our focus has been on adults, who have acquired the functions attributed to the ego and whose bodies have grown more or less according to timetables commensurate with age. What about the ego in children? How does functional expertise in managing the organism's needs and tasks develop?

Undoubtedly, many of the ego's management devices and operational tools are genetically programmed, especially those that hinge on anatomical and physiological givens. Several of them—e.g., perceptual focusing and processing, locomotion, speech and language functions—develop in an average expectable environment according to maturational timetables. But such functions as impulse control, reality testing, affect organization, object constancy, the acquisition of adequate coping devices, and skill in social relations, hinge to a much larger extent on emotional events and qualities experienced in the intrafamilial relationships unique to each infant and child. It is in personal history, charged with meanings, that an idiosyncratic ego develops that in the long run gives the person a distinct character. What typical highlights or way stations of such a personal history of the ego are most relevant to clinical phenomena?

In Chapter 11, we asked how the awareness of others as affective objects comes about, and found that it is linked with a nascent awareness of the self. Now our emphasis is on the *development* of the self, especially the *growth of the ego*. Several points of view compete for recognition: All are derived from clinical observations, and they form an eclectic assembly of clinical truths.

According to one point of view, the ego as a recognizable structure gradually evolves from the rest of personality through the organism's need to protect itself from excessive

stimulation. Overstimulation arouses primordial anxiety, and
is thus a danger signal. A pattern of *barriers and channels* must
therefore be interposed between the sensory and the motor
systems—naturally, from the means offered by the nervous
system and its psychological correlates. This interposed system
is the rudimentary ego: It is a very complex elaboration of the
reflex arc, emerging from the need for organismic self-
defense and adaptation. Its building blocks come from the os-
cillating confrontations between the id (instinctual needs) and
the external world (gratifying or frustrating objects). Always
doubly attuned, with increasing mastery, to an inside and an
outside world, much of the basic ego function is quasi-
perceptual, involving representations and memory images of
inner promptings, needs, and wishes, and outer reality fragments such as people, things, food, shelter, ministrations, and
pain-evoking threats. But the ego is also motoric: As the reg-
ulator and modifier of the motor system it is a priori intertwined with *action* of all kinds, even though one of its great
developmental achievements is the delay or withholding of
motor discharge and the capacity to tolerate tension.

Another point of view stresses the *contemplative* and *valuing*
nature of the ego, linked with the reflexive nature of consciousness: this characteristic allows the child to learn to distinguish between the world of other people, things, environment, etc., which always lie outside consciousness, as its objects, and the self as agent and "bearer" of consciousness, its
subject—and to prize the latter in a unique, fundamental,
proprietary way. Without the primary narcissism of consciousness appreciating itself and distinguishing the self from the
world there can be no object attachment.

A third point of view is that, important as objects are (as
we saw in Chapter 11), the ego is in a sense even more important, for it is on its competence that object selection hinges.
Contact with objects is sought, found, maintained, and distri-
buted by the structure that is interposed between sensation
and motor activity, i.e., the ego. And just as the ego can hold
and make permanent, by means of representations, the fleeting sensations of external objects (turning them into internal

objects), it develops representations of a host of experiential fragments (sensory, motor, ideational, etc.) revolving around the self as the seat of consciousness and action center. The representations are, of course, not the self as such (for that term is a metaphysical construct), but the *image or concept of the self*—which subsequently can be exteriorized in dreams, projected onto external objects, and privately nurtured as a precious possession in need of protection. The image of the self is a real acquisition, without which the relations between the person and his world would remain at the level of reflexes, tropisms, and other very simple forms of adaptation.

The clinical point of convergence of all these views is that the image of the self, once it has taken shape, contains an *evaluative estimate of the ego,* that is, of the person as coper, actor, adaptor—as having skills and as moving forward, engaged in a growth process. Many events, memories, and observations are factored into this evaluation, including praise or blame, encouragements and disparagements received from others, and especially the feelings of joy or sadness these judgments engender. To account for the evolution of the child as a person from his prenatal dyadic beginnings, much has been written about separation and attachment, symbiosis, self-objects, rapprochement, and the capacity to be alone. The common theme in these diverse accounts is to be found in the emergence of a self-representation of increasing complexity, forever to be refined in the crucible of life. Mediated by the ego processes of perception and action, identification, idealization, and reality testing, the self-image is gradually constructed and becomes invested with libido or aggression: It is loved and hated in certain proportions, and it is defended against onslaughts. It needs narcissistic supplies, which it ordinarily gets from engagements with objects.

But conversely, *the self-image is a reference point from which the person appraises the ego's adequacy,* i.e., the sheer competence, strength, weakness, or blunderings and foibles that he can notice in his regulatory processes. The successfully developing child takes pride in his alertness, adroitness, skills, and other adaptive achievements (i.e., ego functions): Their success enhances his self-image, which in turn makes him lovable in his own (and others') eyes. The faltering child, noting his poor coping devices and maladaptations, finds a shadow cast on his self-image that can usually be cleared only by outside encouragement and by being "abundantly loved," that is, by external objects who care and give narcissistic nurture.

Though it seems that self-image and ego appraisal greatly influence each other, they nevertheless appear to function at times quite independently. Many a child, finding himself awkward, unskilled, or rather hapless in his adaptive efforts, will seek to *protect his threatened self-image by altering the scope and setting of his ego activities.* He may partially withdraw from social encounters and activities in which he feels he is being tested, in favor of immersing himself in his inner world of fantasies, dreams, and secret (i.e., nonpublic) imaginative exploits. He may bury himself in reading, create an imaginary playmate, and come to look at his own inner life (indeed, quasi-visually) as a stage behind which he is the puppeteer. In this schizoid development the image of the self is protected and often inflated by a kind of artful dodging, in which unfavorable feedback of the ego's public failures is curtailed. Yet it is obvious that many of the ego's weaknesses are registered by the person himself (and by others, of course), for it is precisely on account of this sad awareness that he seeks the new introversive world, with its greater manageability. The boomerang effect of this schizoid maneuver is, however, a further deskilling of the ego: Its adaptive functions in relation to the outer world are insufficiently practiced, and the rewards for successes in these functions are not experienced.

In other cases, with the *self-image poorly defined* or shattered by trauma, the ego and all its capabilities may be put squarely in the service of *shoring it up,* by hook or crook. Some children, especially those with narcissistic disorders, approach the world with great demandingness, and sometimes manipulatively, to extract from it all manner of dearly desired satisfactions. To gratify impulses instantaneously or to obtain narcissistic supplies, the ego becomes practiced in bullying, deception, and the use of ploys, and in seeking out objects that are weak or masochistic enough to allow an exploitative attachment. Callousness or a smart-aleck wit may come to prevail, to shore up the person's fragile self-image with tokens of its worth obtained by a kind of thievery. In the meantime, pride over his own skillful maneuvering and jubilation over having done in an unsuspecting victim (both of which are ego successes) round off to a triumphant feeling that fills his self-image with primary narcissism.

In children with impulse disorders, the ego's regulatory and control functions are weak in proportion to drive strength. Tolerance of tension is minimal, delay of action is hard to come by, and foresight—by means of which postponed, but more enduring satisfactions gain the upper hand over smaller, instantaneous gratifications—has little chance to be practiced. Since the environment sends these children constant reminders of its demand for self-control, in which it finds them wanting, the self-image becomes buffeted by external rejections (by such words as "bad," "childish," "disobedient," "ungovernable," "impetuous") and short-lived, repeated self-indulgences (in food, attention, toys, and other tokens of pleasure) suffused with chronic anxiety. Habituated to quick tension release, and always ready for motor activity, these children tend to develop an incoherent, inconstant self-image, suspended between elation and depression, often with the oral connotation of feeling "full" or "empty" respectively.

Enough has now been said to indicate that ego development is a long-term project and that the various ego functions can develop in highly idiosyncratic patterns and at strikingly different rates.

The Superego and Ego Ideal

Even more than the ego, the superego and ego ideal are products of development. According to a celebrated psychoanalytic phrase, they are *precipitates of abandoned object relations.* Their Anlagen are less clear than those of the ego;

their foundation is more sociocultural than biological. In an important sense, the formation of superego and ego ideal make acculturation of the individual possible: They furnish him with internal criteria for judgments of good and bad, and make his behavior—and even his thoughts—constant, reliable, and steady, attuned to values viable for long periods, if not a lifetime.

Functionally, the superego and ego ideal are *aides to the ego,* much as the parents and other caretakers during the early period of education are aides to the child's incipient capacities for self-regulation. They are in effect auxiliary egos, lending a hand in guiding the child's conduct, at first by external precepts that have a high chance of becoming internal norms, and thus structural parts of the personality. As the parents are loved, so their values are loved, in the long run becoming friends carried around in one's own bosom where they are permanently available for encouragement and moral guidance. Broadly speaking, superego and ego ideal are the psychological correlates of what both the ethicist and the man in the street call conscience.

First held to be the heir to the Oedipus complex, which meant a rather late origin, the *superego* was gradually seen to have determinants in the anal and oral phases as well. After years of clinical exploration and theorizing, it may now be said that *good-bad judgments and the internal production of guilt feelings occur from infancy on, but acquire along the way some salient, stage-specific qualities.* The first, proto-moral reactions are of an *oral* kind: Good is what satisfies, tastes right, and will eagerly be taken in; bad is what frustrates, tastes nasty, and will be avoided or spat out. The good external object gives; the bad object fails to give; the good internal object or part object is felt as aliment; the bad internal object or part object feels like a foreign body, indigestible or like a toxin, to be eliminated if possible. The proto-self, also divided into a good and bad aspect, is placidly or excitedly libidinous, and angrily aggressive or self-destructive.

In the subsequent stage, *anal* qualities are added. The acquisition of sphincter control and the ritualization of cleanliness impose a forceful pedagogical mandate: Shall the child's own biological rhythms or the culture's temporal and spatial demands prevail? Biology has to be transformed into cultural habits. Behind it all lie these imposing questions conveyed to the child: Who obeys whom or what, in such private matters as elimination? How much autonomy is the child to exercise? Whose will is to be "broken" ("housebroken")? Whose power is to win out? Obviously, this period is one of testing, in which "being good" means being clean and obedient, and "being bad" means being dirty, defiled, obstreperous, and rebellious. In the anal mode, good and bad come to be defined in legalistic fashion, with sanctions for misbehavior, and the child acquires rehabilitation procedures or atonement mechanisms to restore a sense of goodness after having been bad. Lapses from the imposed rules produce guilt feelings, a special form of anxiety that can be eliminated only by making reparations. In fact, in this period of development the child *not only acquires rules to guide his behavior* (incorporates cultural values), *but also learns certain expiation patterns* to regain good standing in his parents' (and his own) eyes. Some parents demand tit-for-tat atonement, others insist on a verbal promise for improvement, still others are content with a confession of sin, and a few retaliate fiercely by making cruel demands that the child can hardly fulfill. In the last case, the superego may cease to be an auxiliary ego or internal friend and become a harsh taskmaster, much to be feared and always to be placated.

In the *oedipal* phase, the erotic sentiments directed toward one parent elicit aggressive sentiments toward, and threats from, the other parent. The child is asked to wait with his erotic advances, to give up his first love-object because she belongs to someone else who has priority and exerts power over her. The threat of castration in boys, and the fantasy in girls of having been castrated or of lacking an external anatomical endowment, act in the direction of repressing the libidinal stirrings and accelerating the desire to grow up to be "like father or mother" and eventually to copy their status in having one's own mate.

Throughout these stages some formal determinants are at work, which eventually put their stamp on the superego and make it a rather stable, firm core of the conscience.

Identifications with parents in the early stages of superego formation tend to be massive and indiscriminate: "I want to be like Daddy, or Mommy." Parental messages that eventually form the superego's content are often nonverbal, conveyed by facial expressions, body postures, and motor acts. Parental reactions to the child's intentions and acts are often involuntary, unconscious expressions of such feelings as loathing, fright, or anger. Much of the learning by identification of norms and values is therefore quite emotional, if not irrational. The specific norms and values taught, and the emotions tied to them, moreover, stem to a large extent from the parents' own superegos and are thus rather more archaic than these same parents' ego perceptions of reality, which are closer to the secondary process.

These formal characteristics of superego formation allow us to envisage another set of learning experiences, experiences that lead to the formation of the *ego ideal*. From school age on, with greater cognitive ability, exposure to wider social circles, and a larger range of experiences, the child continues to acquire norms and values, but by somewhat different processes. The massive identifications of the past give way to discriminated identifications, not necessarily with whole persons, but with particular aspects of persons that elicit emulation. These selective identifications are often transient, in time giving way to new ones. They can be fairly easily verbalized and discussed with peers, tried out, and consciously played with. Idealization, hero worship, and affiliation with like-minded peers combine to lay down a pattern of ideals and values to which the young person vows his *loyalty*. Standards are shaped and interiorized. The person brings them his devotion, and therefore, if he lapses from them he experiences a form of anxiety, namely *shame*, which is a painful interior confrontation between the ego ideal and the ego in which the latter is found wanting.

Tension between superego and ego is experienced as guilt feelings;

tension between ego ideal and ego is experienced as shame. In guilt feelings, there is a sense that rules have been transgressed, that a boundary has been trespassed. Since in the earliest years of life thoughts and acts are psychologically experienced as nearly equivalent, a trespass in thought alone can be as potent as a bad act in eliciting guilt feelings. The painfulness of guilt feelings presses for atonement to restore the psychic balance: Some punishment is to be shouldered or some retribution made in order to get back into good standing vis-à-vis one's own conscience (quite apart from the actual persons against whom one might have transgressed). In shame, there is an experience of failure, a fear of contempt and exposure, and a realization that one might be abandoned by the very "company" that one chose as heroes worthy of one's loyalty. The theme in guilt feelings is: "I am no good—I will be harmed." The theme in shame is: "I am inferior or inadequate—I will be abandoned." In shame, one finds oneself incongruous and exposed: One becomes red in the face, covers the expressive parts of the body, and leaves the company before whom one is now exposed. The metaphor that one can "die of shame" has a firm underpinning in reports of actual death brought on by shame-inducing confrontations.

The foregoing paragraphs are a schematization intended to convey the different phenomenological features of superego and ego-ideal development and functioning. The ego ideal and the affect of shame it produces are likely to have preoedipal roots in loathing; conversely, the superego may well continue to develop beyond the end of the oedipal phase. According to some theorists the superego is the archaic part of conscience, and the ego ideal a more recent acquisition. At any rate, the sketch supports the clinical truism that the superego is by and large more refractory to therapeutic modification in the later years than is the ego ideal, and that it is the more stringent part of conscience, likely to produce pathological features.

To assess the superego and ego ideal it is not enough to focus on their "strength" or "weakness," although these qualities can certainly be important indicators in the depressive syndromes and the impulse disorders respectively. Both may be roughly estimated as hyperactive or hypoactive. Diagnostic discernment demands an answer to specific questions: What aspects of parental models, what aspects of the predominant early objects, were incorporated to form the superego? Which thoughts and deeds were prohibited, which were condoned, and which received moral encouragement? What sanctions were imposed, and how did the person learn to deal with them? What modes of placation were taught, if any? Did the child have to submit passively to punishment, corporal or verbal? Did he typically only have to forgo pleasures, or did he have to submit to pain or cruelty? Was he forced to make confessions or promise to improve? Was he allowed to sulk? Was he granted initiative in making restitutions of his own accord, by his own inventiveness, perhaps even creatively and with spontaneity, or was he held to a strict tit-for-tat principle in which "merit" was carefully measured so as to be equal to "demerit"?

Another set of diagnostic leads is found in the *life styles and enduring mood dispositions engendered by the superego and ego ideal.* Clues are provided by the governing values that have been incorporated and by the ego's felt competence in measuring up to them. For instance, austerity can be extolled as a virtue to the point of casting a pall on all fun and excitement, leaving only the quiet pleasure of conforming to the austerity regime. Suffering and pain may be seen not only as the inevitable lot of man, but as a positive task to be "joyously" shouldered, with masochistic compliance.

Achievement, perfection, correctness, cleanliness, unceasing work, and other precepts may have been ingrained with such stringency that the ego can never quite measure up to them, so that the person feels chronically below par, disposed to a constant, vaguely depressed mood or enduring feelings of inadequacy or defect. The exhortation "never to hurt anybody" may come to produce a habitual forced niceness in all circumstances, a radical denial of feelings of anger or frustration.

Diagnostic curiosity should also extend to the *structural*

status of superego and ego ideal, namely, the degree to which these psychic agencies have become a reliable and permanent internal presence. The ideal of conscience is to guide the person from within, to aid in his decision making and automatize a large part of his behavior, even in the absence of external pressures and enticements—sometimes even to fly in the face of popular currents or cultural drifts. The "man of conscience" can "stand up" against external immorality, i.e., his internal guidelines can prevail over external dictates. Alas, there are persons—and clinical cases of this order seem to be increasing—with structurally inadequate superegos and ego ideals who depend largely on external controls to set limits to their impulse indulgence and hold up ideals they should follow. They need constant reinforcements, reminders, or supervised practice of behavior controls by persons in a position to impose strictures. Since the superego and ego ideal are by definition intrapsychic agencies, it is fallacious to describe these persons as having "external superegos"; their trouble lies precisely in *not* having internal moral guidelines, so that they are thrown back on external regulations by enforced obedience, as very young children are. A finer, technical point in this situation is that the superego, once acquired, can in serious regressions be projected back on representatives of the class of objects from which it was taken, at least in some of its aspects. But in such cases again the person in effect surrenders to external authority (or seeks to manipulate external objects in authority) in the pursuit of the gratification of his (now grossly primitivized) impulses.

Finally, the superego is not automatically and in all persons a reliable and consistent internal guide. It may be *corruptible,* open to bribery and manipulation, strict in some moral matters and surprisingly lenient, if not indulgent, in matters of grave ethical import. By a psychic sleight of hand, the relation between "transgression" and "expiation" may be turned around into a claim, on the basis of some past atonement, to an infinite forgiveness for oneself that amounts to license. To prove that one is "in grace" one may rather lightheartedly engage in "sinning," with a benign, self-excusing smile.

Congruity of Being, Having, and Doing

Though the essence of the self, of personhood, or of personality is a problem to be left to philosophers, clinicians cannot dodge the fact that people who seek their help make some kind of self-presentation, hold certain beliefs about who and what they are, seem to strive for some consistency between their being, having, and doing, and collect themselves according to some definable identity. With certainty or in puzzlement, they are or seek to be "somebody." Their certainty may be fact or fiction, true or false according to certain criteria; their puzzlement may be superficial or profound, a hapless floundering or a purposive quest. But all along they hold *beliefs about themselves* on which they act, and they have some concern about being taken by others as a characteristic this-and-that or as a definable thus-and-so.

Several concepts seem necessary to approach clinical observations about the self with a discerning diagnostic eye. Jung's[60] concept of the *persona* describes a half-adaptive, half-defensive maneuver by which a more or less public image or set of roles is assumed that is at once socially delineated (e.g., loving housewife, successful businessman, savant, artistic connoisseur, Don Juan) and provides a protective screen behind which the intimate self finds a hiding place. The mask, which is the literal meaning of the word *persona*, serves many purposes: It allows one to play a role or present oneself in some distinct fashion to the world; it alleviates fear of being discovered in one's subjective identity; it provides for idealizations that stylize a part of one's character. The clinical importance of this concept thus lies in what it *reveals* as well as in what it *conceals*. For instance, the persona of a patient who always presents himself as meek and mild-mannered is bound to hide some deeper rage or an impulse toward dominance; the persona of being only a cog in the machine and of no account may hide grandiosity; the persona of a sick, helpless, eversuffering hypochondriac may hide efforts at manipulation and an aggressive demandingness. Behind the mask of a Don Juan may lie chronic erotic deficiency or a profound fear of impotence.

The very concept of the persona implies that the mask or role and the manner of self-presentation are at variance with the person's deeper strata. The persona is a compromise formation of a defensive kind, indicating a lack of congruence between what the person is (or feels he is), what he does (or feels he must do), and what he has (i.e., his name, title, tokens of social recognition, etc.).

Erikson's[61] concept of *identity* is a more complex idea, one that emphasizes the developmental struggle to become or be "someone distinct," and is precisely designed to describe a state of approximate congruence between being, having, and doing. It is in this sense the opposite of Jung's persona concept; its analogue is to be found, rather, in Jung's notion of *individuation*, with the qualification that Jung stressed individuation as a task in the second half of life, whereas Erikson has emphasized the acquisition of identity in adolescence and early adulthood, albeit the identity concept is intended to be relevant to the whole life cycle.

Though identity includes role assumption and self-presentation (having and doing), it also involves knowing, believing, and being convinced about *who* and *what* one *is*, and acting on one's *felt* and *experienced* essence. Identity is neither a superficial adaptation nor a defense, but a reflection of the "deep structure" of personality in its interaction with the world. Having identity, feeling that one is someone, imply being relatively at ease with oneself and engaging with spontaneity and skill in well-chosen types of object relations. Identity involves idealizations, and in this sense overlaps the concept of the ego ideal, with emphasis on workable, harmonious relations between ego ideal and ego. Though in his earlier work Erikson demonstrated the social, ethnic, and religious-affiliation dimensions of identity (e.g., being a Sioux, an American, a Jew, etc.), in his later work the ethical and personal spiritual dimensions came into the foreground (e.g., in Luther and Gandhi). With this shift of focus the idea of identity correspondingly changed somewhat, from a conflict-resolving to a task-shouldering principle of personality organization. At any rate, identity gives a person an orientation by which he can achieve a respectable and valued consistency in his life. Small wonder, then, that in a great many clinical cases identity tends to be in some way dysfunctional or inadequate or lacking. In the clinical setting identity is to be achieved or nurtured, forming an aspect of the treatment goal.

Diagnostically, the distinction between *positive* and *negative* identity fragments or strivings is probably of the greatest use. Who or what does the patient. strive *not* to be? What known or fantasied identities does he reject for himself? Or, on the basis of his object relations, what actual persons or kinds of persons does he despise, mistrust, put down, or dismiss—and why? What irked him in his experiencing of them; what were the frustrations he experienced at their hands; what in his pictures of them (realistic or in fantasy) elicits the ire he is now trying to express through his "otherness" from them? And conversely, what real or fantasized others does he not only emulate but have a realistic chance to be like, or at least approximate? In precisely what human traits or character does he seek congruity in being, having, and doing?

In sorting out negative and positive fragments along these lines of questioning, ample room should be left, of course, for *ambivalence and ambiguity.* In fact, too pat a distinction between negative and positive identity models is itself suspect because it is based on an unrealistic polarization. The task involved in identity formation consists precisely of coming to terms with one's own ambivalent feelings on the one hand, and the inevitable ambiguities of objects and object representations on the other hand, and in resolving these into a viable character style that allows for benign and mutually rewarding object relations.

Chapter 13

Assessing Integrative Processes: Relations to Things and Ideas

The principle that provides the rationale for the previous two chapters is that engagement in object relations satisfies (or, if beset by problems, frustrates) a person's needs. These needs range all the way from biological necessities to social mandates and cultural norms—all translated in experiential psychological terms as drives, wishes, demands, longings, strivings, yearnings, goals, aspirations, etc. The psychological role of "objects" is to be "satisfiers"; the meaning of any object to the person rests on its relevance to his well-being and its significance in his emotional household. Personality integration comes from engagements with objects; conversely, the kind of object relations engaged in, and the selection of objects cathected, constitute a picture, pattern, or measure of anyone's personality integration.

The same principle will guide us through the present chapter, whose title suggests an enormously broad span of *nonhuman objects* in which important, and often quite durable, emotional investments are known to be made. The various groups of objects we will consider in this chapter entail love and hate relations, elicit emotional intensities, provide satisfactions or impose frustrations, and, for all their thingish concreteness or ideational abstractness, are often experienced as if they were quasi-human entities: friendly or unfriendly, entic-

ing or forbidding, quiescing or fearsome, soothing or upsetting, embracing or aloof. Dream processes indicate that in the
unconscious, people and things and ideas can substitute for
one another. Common sense gives convincing evidence that
things and ideas, and even the most ephemeral abstractions,
are richly laden with symbolic meanings through which they
satisfy or frustrate a person's needs. One clings to possessions,
is wedded to a cause, embraces an ethic, divorces oneself from
an ideology, hankers after a faith, loves one's collections, hates
certain life styles, yearns for the wide open spaces, or detests
certain art forms—all with affect, often of great intensity. The
material and ideational worlds are full of entities (allowing
certain groupings) on which we thrive, over and above the
groups of "other people" and "self."

Natural Entities

Physically and psychologically nearest to people are, of
course, *animals*. With some animals, namely *pets*, a very close
relation can be maintained, allowing, especially for children, a
great deal of identification. Pets can be thoroughly an-
thropomorphized, and treated as extensions of the self, as
quasi-human children, or as siblings. Pets can function as to-
tems, around which group behavior is organized. Horse and
rider can form a very close bond; sexual intercourse with
domestic animals is a real, albeit perverse, possibility. The de-
mise of a beloved animal elicits a mourning reaction. Children
and adults entertain fantasies about the kind of animal they
would like to be; how they would soar, pounce, crouch, roam,
or roar if given a chance. All these and many more instances
of bonding between man and animal point to the clinical value
of exploring relations to animals for diagnostic leads.

The phrase "kinship with *nature*" suggests the possibility of
an emotional bond between man and the whole chain of
being. The patient who finds solace in the woods, who tends
plants, or feels quickened by a walk on the beach seems to
find nature nurturant, inviting, or friendly, experiencing a

tender oneness with it, and this feeling may compensate for a dearth of or conflict in human relations. Any part of nature can easily be eroticized, as mythology so amply shows. Another patient may savagely want to destroy parts of nature, torture an animal, or wantonly befoul a natural resource or landscape, going way beyond a utilitarian attitude to an arrogant placing of himself outside or above the chain of being. Indeed, why do some persons feel offended by the Darwinian vision of the descent of man, while others can easily, and perhaps with some affection, place their species within the animal series? One person proudly or defensively emphasizes nature's distinctions; the other humbly or warmly stresses the similarities. Whole philosophies, religious belief systems, and ethical edifices can be built on these contrasting attitudes toward nature, a fact that testifies to the diagnostic importance of exploring these attitudes with some care.

Biological and Cultural Necessities

From the virtually endless list of clinically relevant "things," relations to *food* are of obvious importance. Eating disturbances are very frequent in psychiatric and psychosomatic disorders, and attitudes toward food are often pervaded by fantasies and defense mechanisms. The depressed patient neglects his food intake, perhaps finding himself unworthy of nourishment. Great suspiciousness may lead patients with paranoid tendencies to entertain fantasies of being poisoned. Food faddism abounds, ranging from special dietary avoidances to specific preferences, often based on magical thought, as in the selection of foods to enhance sexual potency. In anorexia nervosa the multiple meanings of food are compounded by cathexis of the body image and hence of the self, and the frequent swings in this syndrome between starving and gorging prove the marked ambivalence about the self and the nurturant object that is one of its dynamisms. In normal persons, too, food habits tend to be rather rigid, a fact that becomes apparent when necessity dictates a change. And as culinary experts know, food selection is also linked with social-status awareness.

The embeddedness of food in the mother-infant relation endows it with oral symbolism and other surplus meanings that are also involved in the use of *medicines, tobacco, alcohol,* and *drugs.* Toxins all, the pleasures they enhance and the pains they reduce, in whatever form and with whatever side effects, make them precious to their abusers beyond the dictates of reason and reality testing. In fact, a person's relation to any of these substances tends to have telltale signs of high emotionality and tenuous morality, for the addict or overuser as much as, say, the physically ill patient who refuses to take a safe medicine of known efficacy. The word "indulgence," so often used in connection with various drugs, suggests that their ingestion is at some physical and symbolic level tied to narcissistic needs, whatever other meanings they may acquire. They soothe or provide quiescence when life is tense; they stimulate or provide "kicks" when life is dull; they disinhibit when control is felt to be too tight; they simulate a "companion" when life is empty; they regulate what the person is unable to regulate for himself. In addition, the solitary use that can be made of any drug (as distinct from a social or convivial use) suggests that drugs stand in lieu of an unavailable, over-idealized "good mother" whose ministrations would magically restore some well-being in her disturbed infant, helping the child to overcome a narcissistic disturbance.

The need for *shelter* is as basic as the need for food, and thus a person's relation to his *home and property* is likely to be charged with characteristic feelings of some diagnostic importance. Some homes are invitingly open; others are closed and walled off. Some beckon to guests and visitors; others ward off intruders. Some are uselessly but prestigiously large; others are cozily, and perhaps stingily, small. Some look formal; others are practical and casual. Some homeowners insist on a fence around their acre; others leave their grounds defenselessly open. Such diverse attitudes toward home and property, if strongly held, do bespeak deeper tendencies toward inclusiveness or exclusiveness, fear of or trust of the world, ease or unease in human relations, pride or humility, and even such ideological positions as a safety-seeking conservatism or a venturesome liberalism. They have much to do with life style and the philosophical or ethical rationales marshaled for the style one feels bound to.

The word *possessions* covers, of course, an enormous range, which is to a large extent determined by one's class, luck of inheritance or upbringing, or good fortune in making personal acquisitions. *Money* is an emblematic representation of all possessions. Despite its social pre-eminence, money as an object is rarely explored for the diagnostic information it offers about character, superego, and interpersonal relations. In fact, except for purposes of fee setting in the psychiatric relationship, money seems to be a taboo subject. But if the strength of a taboo is proportionate to the intensity of the wish it curbs, attitudes toward money should be explored in any thorough psychological examination for the glimpses they give of a person's "private life." Both the possession and the acquisition of money may be charged with guilt feelings, which in turn may lead to finding ways of sharing it, liberally, graciously, or demonstratively; freely or with strings attached; impulsively or with great caution lest the gifts end up in the "wrong hands." Conversely, having or acquiring money is for some persons singularly free from ethical considerations and may even be coupled with great callousness, exploitativeness, or extortionist methods.

As anthropologists have shown, money (as a shorthand term for possessions) and what one may or should do with it are highly regulated by social customs and mores, ritualized in the giving and receiving of gifts and their occasions. Therefore, both the giving of something when it is not expected and the withholding of something when it is expected are powerful ways of demonstrating one's feelings toward other persons, involving moments of triumph, retaliation, good will or ill will. Giving gifts also allows the most perfunctory and tokenist politeness that conceals deeper feelings of coldness, contempt, spite, or rancor.

Possessions are not merely to be regarded in terms of their monetary or market value; the psychological ties one has to lifeless possessions may derive their strength from interpersonal bonds. This fact is clear in some persons' attachments to heirlooms, family knickknacks, old homesteads, collections begun by forebears, parental furniture—as well as in the often abrupt and radical detachments from such things sought when an estate is divided. Attachments to books, records, and other collectible items that tend to cause clutter are frequently unrealistic—until one discovers how much keeping these tokens at hand may help a person maintain continuity with his own past.

Few things are as close to a person's ego and his body as his *clothes,* and few objects are at once so personal and so social. Used for self-presentation as well as concealment, for the most personal adornment as well as the tritest role identity, clothes and their choice and upkeep convey a gamut of meanings and messages. Erotic motifs, decency, sex roles, narcissistic needs, class consciousness, wealth, ethnic loyalty, vocational identity, and a host of other factors enter into clothing, all carefully calibrated to combine personal wishes with social norms, governed by public tastes whose momentary prescriptions border on the sacred and whose proscriptions have the strength of taboos. The fact that clothing functions in several perversions, such as fetishism and transvestism, underscores the multiplicity of associations to articles of dress. Clerical garb and monk's robes curb individuality; the regulation of dress by religious groups curbs ostentation and worldliness; the donning of a uniform fosters group identification or designates a social role. Dress codes are highly age-specific, the more so in an era of accentuated intergenerational conflicts. For all these reasons, and because of their unique visibility, dress preferences convey potent clues about personality factors such as self-esteem, narcissism, social awareness, inhibitions, moods, conformity strivings, and even ethical precepts.

Space and Time

Not all inanimate objects are things; the class also contains abstract entities that have organizing power over human life and the ideas man lives by. Among these entities are space, time, work, and play, which are at once philosophical ideas and down-to-earth realities that harness energies and determine specific living arrangements.

Whatever philosophers may say about *space*, the psychological fact is that each person marks out or creates a space of his own so as to enhance his well-being and minimize frustrations. We adapt ourselves to available space, but also structure space to be adaptive to our needs, by making *personal space arrangements* that can be quite idiosyncratic. As agoraphobia, acrophobia, and claustrophobia show, certain spaces elicit specific feelings: dread, horror, coziness, or comfort. One person feels at home in close quarters; another wants wide vistas; a third wants heights from which to look down. On a smaller scale, some persons write a characteristically cramped hand, cramming the maximum on a sheet of paper, whereas others spread their handwriting lavishly, "wasting" paper space. One person gesticulates widely, surrounding himself as it were with a large proprietary nimbus over which he feels he has command; another allows himself only the slightest motions, as if to imply that he must not intrude on the outside space.

The infant's liberation from the amniotic sac into the world initiates a series of ventures into space in which certain spatial arrangements become selectively cathected. Beyond the womb is the arms-and-breast space of the mother; beyond that the lap of a trusted adult; then the play pen, after which the toddler finds snugness under tables, until he gradually ventures into more open and ever wider orbits. At each developmental stage there is an emotional evaluation: Is the universe a friendly abode or is it a frightening, horrible expanse? Fixation and regression determine the answers to this question, with clinical consequences: Some sleepwalkers invariably seek their mothers; some children dare not leave home; some adolescents yearn to remove themselves far from home; some inhibited adults are afraid to venture beyond their home towns. I remember a miner who, after years of working underground and in the dark, became acutely paranoid when the mine closed and he was forced to seek employment above ground in plain daylight. Fear of flying is not uncommon. Some homes are arranged to resemble wombs; others stress openness to the world. Feelings of security tend to be enhanced by idiosyncratic spatial arrangements: tight clothes, enclosures within and around homes, door locks and fences, closeness to neighbors, living in crowded areas. Some drivers are afraid to cross bridges, or to progress beyond the town limits into the countryside, their unease having a phobic intensity.

The other coordinate of experience, *time*, is also perceived in markedly personal ways, some of which are tied to psychological syndromes. Time's major practical distinctions are: past, present, future; progression and regression; flow or stagnation. How does a person experience these dimensions and how does he value them? It takes very little clinical acumen to note that severely depressed patients dwell on the past, seem fixated to memories, and have too little energy to pay attention to the future, or even to act in the present. It is also evident that obsessional patients cannot finish a thought but are doomed to ruminating. Severely compulsive patients waste time on endless preparatory acts, rarely reaching a consummation. In either case, nothing seems to be left behind to distinguish the past from the present—everything remains unfinished. In addition, time is brought to a standstill, or is fragmented into bits which altogether lack flow. These pathologies are deviations from an optimal time experience, which has a clear forward thrust and allows some freedom for selectively attending to past, present, and future in accordance with one's goals. As phenomenologists often point out, time experience and a subjective sense of freedom are related: Only when one has adequate freedom *from* one's past does one have freedom *for* or *toward* the future. Unresolved neurotic conflicts doom one to repeat the same old absurdities. Nostalgia, insatiable longing for a lost paradise, and the pressure of unresolved guilt feelings for past wrongs exert a regressive pull that prevents heartfelt involvement in the present and makes for a fear of the future. On the other hand, some people seem unable to come to terms with their past at all and, unable to learn from it, rashly thrust themselves into action without forethought: These are the impulse-ridden characters and various psychopathic personalities.

Benjamin Franklin's phrase "Time is money" highlights in baldly capitalistic fashion the diverse values we place on time. Apart from a person's situation on the age scale (youngsters having lots of time ahead and oldsters running out of it), there are strikingly different patterns of *husbanding time*. Some persons are characteristically stingy with it; others spend their time lavishly and make it freely available for all kinds of pursuits. Some persons schedule their activities by the clock; others proceed by intuition or biological rhythms, or heedlessly. Cultural differences aside, some persons are always late for any occasion, whereas others are typically always early, or exactly on the dot. Punctuality appears to be a trait that needs cultivation: The noblest intentions can go awry for lack of promptness. Apart from the buoyancy produced by ample energy, such character traits as tardiness, procrastination, and stalling suggest that the will also encroaches on the husbanding of time. For all his health and good intentions, Oblomov was abulic and therefore could not (would not) engage in action. The ambivalent person stalls because he cannot (dare not) decide; the doubter sees obstacles everywhere; the anxious mind seeks safety in nonaction or defensive retreats.

It fits the needs of narcissistic personalities and persons with a strong achievement motivation to do a great deal of anticipating, to look longingly toward the future, dreaming of glory or conquests. The hypervigilance and guardedness of very suspicious or paranoid persons gear them to an anxious apprehension about the immediate future ("Something is going to happen, I must watch out!"), making their present absorbed by defensiveness and blocking their view of the larger future. A part of the agitation often seen in aged persons can be ascribed to ambiguities in their experience of time: Being no longer part of the work force, they may have ample time, often too much, to reminisce and ruminate, while they know they have too little actual time left for the realization of ideals, let alone for correcting whatever they may have come to deplore in their pasts. In postencephalitic children one can observe, together with their restlessness and distractibility, profound disturbances of diurnal rhythms (e.g., sleep disturbances) on account of which their sense of time (and hence their management of time) is grossly awry.

Work and Play

In all these clinical instances, something has happened to time experience that disrupts the good fit between the various dimensions of time, undermining the satisfactions inherent in an ordered time experience. This observation leads us to the next "object" we cathect, namely *work*, which has a large bearing on our dealings with time. The first thing to emphasize is that work structures time: The work schedule (and school hours for children) organizes the available waking hours into manageable periods allocated to distinct pursuits. Apart from other considerations, the importance of structure is reason enough to set up definite schedules, commensurate with individual needs, for patients in a psychiatric hospital. If the day is not structured by scheduled activities (work, recreation, meals, rest periods, etc.), it becomes a tedious, amorphous stretch of time that heightens confusion and dangerously stimulates primary-process activity.

Freud is alleged to have considered working (and loving) a pillar of mental health. Why? Work harnesses and channels energies, allowing the sublimation of erotic and the neutralization of aggressive forces into activities that are ideally constructive, if not creative; generally useful, or at least innocuous. Most people intuitively like work, knowing that they need it for their own mental benefit—witness the psychological calamities that accompany prolonged layoffs, joblessness, or forced retirement. Even though much industrial work is sheer drudgery, it still acts as a stabilizer for personality. Most people endow their work, even the most menial or tedious tasks, with social or even quasi-sacred values that make them feel important in the scheme of things.

Inasmuch as work is a relational term, standing in opposition to play, leisure, or recreation, it incorporates superego values having to do with merit, duty, and responsibility. It may carry a religious connotation: In working, the person may feel that by his sense of vocation he assists the deity in sustaining the work and order of creation. Thus for most persons in Western lands, leisure is to be limited and earned. And sadly, because so much work is drudgery, leisure is to stand in contrast to work as a form of playing. I think it is clinically important to ask what tensions, if any, a person experiences in relation to work and play. Do the two sharply contrast with each other? Or do they show few differences, as when work is done zestfully and leisure is used productively? Does a person look forward to retirement from his work because he loathes his job, or does he approach retirement anxiously, not knowing what to do with so much time on his hands? Does a person have ethical compunctions about the work he does, e. g., when it involves the making of weapons, poisons, or is in some sense exploitative? Or does he callously consider a job a job—no questions asked about its implications for society?

Work also helps, as Freud indicated and all therapists know, to force a person to make and maintain contact with reality. It curbs the primary-process tendency; it forces us to come to grips with matter, substances, facts, workable ideas and procedures, and with a host of social processes, such as rules, that are communally necessary. It enhances the important function of reality testing and harnesses energies, providing them with objects. It creates an orderly division of life, making it manageable: One can talk about home while at work, and discuss the events of the work day while at home. In structuring time in this way, work sets up distinct spheres of experiences, and encourages reflection on experience by providing topics for conversation.

Leisure, recreation, and *play,* however these are differentiated from work, are to be assessed for the clues they offer about temperament, cardinal traits, and life styles. Does the person have a strong penchant for sports and games that entail obedience to rules and fair play, or would he rather hike or camp or tinker in his workshop? In spending his leisure

time, does the person feel drawn to a group, or does he prefer solitary activity or the intimacy of spouse, children, a few
friends? Does he select sports that require maximum competition within the group, or those that demand maximum cooperation? Are the person's leisure-time pursuits mostly aggressive or mostly libidinal in their motivation? Is the person's engagement mostly at the spectator level, or does he actively
participate? Some prefer motor activities, by direct involvement or vicariously, by watching the motions of performers.
Others find pleasure in sensory experiences—viewing art or
listening to music. Still others are avid readers, or spend their
free hours working for social or humane causes. All these dimensions of leisure-time spending throw light on character
and life style, as well as on the impact of the patient's current
symptoms or syndromes. Radical changes in habitual patterns
may also suggest an insidious or abrupt turnabout, for instance, from activity to passivity; from a normal husbanding of
energy to lethargy or hypomanic flurries; from habitual shyness to a frantic search for objects; from sociability to withdrawal.

Authority

In view of the current prominence of behavior deviance
among actual or prospective psychiatric patients, any patient's
conception of and relation to authority should be given careful
psychological scrutiny. How does the person relate to power,
and what power does he assume or would he like to appropriate? Who and what are power symbols with which he con-
tends? If he is critical of social institutions, which one arouses
his greatest ire? If he feels alienated from mores, life patterns,
or institutions, what grounds does he have for feeling he is an
"outsider," and in what way might he stylize his "otherness?"
If he flouts established authority, what other authorities—
not part of the establishment—does he conjure up or acknowledge? For what power, if any, would he bow down?
Obviously, such inquiries not only address such factors

as self-esteem, sense of autonomy, belongingness to certain groups and ideals, and embeddedness in object relations and values, but also allow a glimpse of what the person finds a permissible or congenial form for his protest. Does he mostly sulk, in moody passivity, or does he take action? If the latter, is it overt or covert, on target or diffuse, reasoned or explosive, zestful or tired, verbal or behavioral, as leader or as follower, constructive or destructive? How impulsive or reality-tested are the person's actions? For instance, if the person expresses quite revolutionary ideas, is he at all interested in the differences between successful and unsuccessful revolutions or protests and in taking these differences into account in his plans? Or is he merely afire, unconcerned with the effects of his feelings, words, or deeds?

Relations to authority may also provide clues to the sense of well-being or frustration a person may experience in various types of organization. Some men thrive on the hierarchical ordering of military life, enjoying clear-cut positions of subordination to superiors. Others feel trapped by such arrangements, and seek a less structured and strict milieu in which they can try their wings and exercise freedom. Since religious denominations vary in organizational structure and in the rigidity of their demands, one finds in some cases of insidious or gradually increasing psychopathology the phenomenon of "church hopping": As the fear of "falling apart" increases, the patient may move from a mainstream denomination, seen by him as rather lenient, to a more strict, demanding, and actively morally supporting group, often a sect, which does not hesitate to lay out clear do's and don't's, thereby reinforcing his superego and ego controls.

But authority is not only vested in persons and institutions; it is also attached to ideas and symbols, e.g., science, learning, brotherhood, deity, peace, sacred books, service to mankind, a faith or noble cause and its emblems. Loyalty to such chosen authorities may conflict with demands for obedience, conformity, adaptation, or reality testing. Such tensions are manifested in the phenomenon of civil disobedience, a selective opposition to or claim of exemption from imposed patterns of conformity, for which the person takes some risks: He is labeled "deviant," is fined, imprisoned, or otherwise penalized. Usually, much group support is needed to maintain a position of civil (selective) disobedience, and the tendency may wax and wane, especially in late adolescence and early adulthood when major patterns of ego identity are tried and sorted out. Lifton has coined the term "Protean personality" for people who alternate very rapidly, frequently, and abruptly from one ideological identity to another, in rather hapless tryouts, sooner or later developing clinical symptoms that express a fundamental instability.

Aesthetic, Religious, and Ethical Ideas

Among the more abstract and ethereal but operationally powerful ideas with which people maintain an object relation are *aesthetic, religious,* and *ethical notions* that are held (and often externally imposed) as *values.* For various reasons, psychiatric and psychological examiners tend to be somewhat shy about assessing the impact of these values on a patient's life, possibly feeling that in so doing they would approach a taboo region of privacy. Or they may be afraid of getting trapped in countertransference reactions from which they prefer to stay clear. They may have a (justifiable) apprehension of being caught in propensities toward intellectualization, spurious abstractions, peculiar language use (e.g., God-talk, moralisms, art idioms), which they do not want to stimulate in their patients or in which they feel themselves inept or un-trained. But in leaving these special object relations un-examined, or in only making untested conjectures about them that are little more than clichés, they forgo opportunities for diagnostic differentiation.

For instance, a young Jewish man was admitted to the hospital. After years of being shy and socially awkward he had more recently proclaimed his belief that he was the Messiah, destined to set the world straight from its crooked path. From careful interrogation about this belief, and how it came to have a hold over him, it appeared that it emerged largely as a response to his observation (or fantasy) that people were rejecting him. The megalomanic core of his fantasy was clear enough to a trained ear, but further inquiry revealed the importance of a thought disorder: The patient "reasoned" that he must be the Messiah *because* people rejected him, as they did all other pretenders to that title. It was also brought out that he could not and dared not express his sense of alienation from his family, and his aggression toward them, in other than religious terms, which gave him a margin of safety by allowing him to act out his opposition *under a pious cloak,* i.e., under pseudodivine auspices. The latter also placed him beyond retaliation by mortal man, and gave him the added satisfaction of appearing more sincere and courageous than his (allegedly) hypocritical parents. Moreover, his oddity was now hallowed, and if he should take revenge through a destructive act such as murdering someone, he would not be in his own eyes a "common criminal" but a divine agent, steered by the noblest motives.

Short of such religious delusions, clinicians encounter patients or prospective patients full of apprehension that what they consider their highest values will be undermined or tinkered with during diagnostic or therapeutic work. They enter the first interview determined to forge a special contract, stipulating that their ethical or religious values are beyond legitimate clinical exploration, or that they should be assessed only by a person with an identical ethical or religious worldview who will allegedly understand (and spare) them. From a diagnostic point of view such wishes or claims should not be granted or laid to rest unexplored, for they will give important clues to the patient's fears or demands. The insistence on being matched with like-minded and like-believing examiners may on exploration turn out to be motivated by grandiosity ("I am a very special person deserving a very special, circumspect approach"), by a particular form of narcissism ("I am entitled to persons I can look up to and idealize"), by simple resistance ("I will only settle for a kind of cozy *entre-nous* with someone I can regard as a friend"), or by a more or less dim anticipation that the attested religious or moral values are quite shaky, or their profession phony, with the fear that their phoniness will be disclosed. Many motives may hide under the patient's search for a well-matched examiner or helper, and the patient's insistence on a "special contract" may itself be seen as the *first presenting symptom*, warranting serious, immediate inquiry.

I have already referred to the phenomenon of "church hopping" and its diagnostic implications. If one explores precisely what the patient prizes in his religious or ethical tradition or affiliation, typological differences often come to the fore. *Legalists* emphasize the rules, taboos, or folkways that assist the person to do the "right thing." The legalistic codes are seized on as guides for conduct and as a defense against the experience of terror. There are also *supralegalists* who share with the legalists a preoccupation with right conduct, but do not take the stated rules of their tradition for granted. They search for deeper or more ultimate and ideal codes, well knowing that these are not always in line with the popular rules. Nevertheless, they stress the regulatory function of these more refined guides to conduct. Persons given to *orthodoxy* put a premium on correct knowledge; having the right beliefs or values not only aids them in feeling aligned with the proper authorities, but makes them participate in their power. This position too can undergo a refinement: The *supraorthodox* person digs beneath popular truth for a more ultimate truth that he hopes to discover personally or existentially, so as to have the unarguably "right" belief. Others value in religion an *aesthetic* component: They seek beauty in its forms and practices, which they enact with absolute perfection or watch with intense pleasure. Still others have a special appreciation of religion's *symbolic or sacramental features*, through which they participate in the transcendent, divine power that symbols and rites conjure up. For all we know, these typological proclivities may be quite durable parts of the person's character, correlating with attitudes, styles, and preferences that predominate in other spheres of his life.

From a clinical point of view it is useful to regard religious ideation, fantasy formation, and behavior as coping devices. They do not have to be invented by an individual; typically, they are adopted, frequently under the pressure of instruction and parental modeling, from an already available, communal reservoir of strategies for allaying anxiety, guilt feelings, or some other important unease in life. Confessing is a clear case in point, however the act is stylized. The mechanism of denial is built into some metaphysical and religious positions that give no formal ontological status to death, illness, or other forms of evil (e.g., Christian Science). Withdrawal may take the form of mystical musings or monastic living arrangements. Phobic reactions are not infrequently attached to praying, with prominent fears of blaspheming, committing the "unpardonable sin," or spoiling a sacramental act by sloppy performance. Religious ideas and practices, particularly the do's and don't's inherent in them, provide guidelines for "right thinking" and "right conduct," but are also an arena for obsessive-compulsive character defenses. Austerity may become intensified into asceticism or self-mortification to expunge a felt sinfulness. And it is a clinical commonplace that any form of autism or thought disorder, any pathological narcissism, and any deep crisis may assume religious content, composed of building blocks taken from various religious traditions.

Ethical ideas and positions may also create a symptomatic backlash. In some persons, ideas of right and wrong or good and bad never lose the rigidity with which the anal phase tends to endow them. In others, they may be saturated with oral connotations, which lock goodness into feeding and being fed, and badness into scarcity, depletion, or hunger, both with a narcissistic self-reference: Good and bad are what are good and bad *for me*. The pursuit of ethical values may become distorted into a prevailing attitude of faultfinding—with others or with one's self—lacking any grace or forgiveness. A furious righteousness may lead to hypervigilance, suspiciousness, or even paranoid ideation, and not infrequently to the adoption of devious or outright immoral means to accomplish the lofty-sounding ethical goals. Systems of good and bad are pushed to an extreme in the phenomena of prejudice—the unblushing adoption of a double standard, one for insiders and another for outsiders, however these are socially defined.

If ethical considerations are indeed the powerful values they are considered to be, it is clinically important to ascertain something about the *scope and rigor* with which a person applies them to his life. Does the patient make striking exemptions to their applicability, e.g., excluding them from his business operations, profession, or trade? If a parent, does the patient try to instill morals in his children to which he is personally conspicuously unfaithful? If a man, does the patient claim for himself certain exemptions from moral precepts that he would not grant to a woman? Is money, which according to an ancient adage "does not smell," excluded from the ethical precepts the person otherwise seeks to abide by? The scope of ethics has recently been greatly enlarged by conservationists and others who decry the backlash of technology and the despoliation of nature. This expansion gives clinicians an opportunity to assess the reach and consequences of any person's alleged morals: Does he allow himself a callous attitude toward nature, claiming the "right" to waste scarce or endangered resources, or seek to hoard or consume a disproportionate share of diminishing material goods?

Attunement to *beauty* and *aesthetic values* can take many forms and can be pursued in various spheres: the arts, nature, the presentation of the self, the quality of life and of human relations. Likes and dislikes abound, and tastes are immensely varied; they are apparently held to be so personal that the saying exhorts us not to dispute them. Granted this cautionary note, are aesthetic values of any clinical relevance?

I have known a patient plagued (and nearly exhausted) by phobias and given to periods of profound depression, who regarded her symptoms, her fantasies, and even her conflicts with the utmost aesthetic appreciation, turning them, as it were, into a fascinating piece of literature. She did not dramatize her behavior or act histrionically; rather, she found her misery in some curious way intriguing and beautiful to behold, as if she were watching a drama. It gave her an existential thrill to be so wonderfully plagued, so intricately composed, so picturesque in her complaints. To look at one's predicaments in this way obviously requires taking some distance from one's self, and indeed the schizoid mechanism of projecting one's experiences on an inner screen was present in this patient. But instead of emphasizing the strangeness of her experiences, she accentuated what she felt was their exquisite beauty, and was moved by it. What was from one angle seen as illness to be alleviated, appeared to her from another angle as a thing of beauty to be valued.

Like moral values, aesthetic values can become hypertrophied. A frantic flight from ugliness and "bad taste" may impoverish one's contact with reality and drive one to withdraw into a spuriously beautified milieu—not only of nice things and pleasant color schemes, but also of nice, well-modulated speech in all circumstances; of genteel word choice and manners that conceal nastier intentions or feelings; of soft, nonprovocative music; or of a perfectionistic maintenance of unruffled composure. A strict adherence to such attitudes, with a fear of sanctions when one lapses from them, shows that the superego and ego ideal contain schemes not only for moral judgments but for aesthetic judgments as well. And in fact the two schemes appear linked: The moralist sees fittingness, harmony, and beauty in the right thought and the good act, and the aesthete finds righteous pleasure in the beauty of a thought or deed. Ugliness can make him indignant: Vulgar tastes offend his aesthetic as well as his moral sense.

Lack of aesthetic development may come through as a callous disregard for order, propriety, balance, harmony, or proper fit: passively by "living in a mess"; actively by disdaining certain cultural goods and being averse to museums, libraries, flower shows, or contemplative walks in nature; aggressively by dumping beer cans in the countryside or disfiguring monuments.

Finally, there is the pursuit of primitive aesthetic pleasures, unrefined and uncreative and unbalanced by moral considerations, known as *sensuality*. With varying admixtures of refinement or coarseness, the range of sensuality covers certain points of fixation: The gourmand puts his faith in food and

drink, the "sharp dresser" seeks narcissistic supplies from his
body adornments, the sexual adventurer can operate on oral,
anal, phallic, or polymorphously perverse levels and, if predominantly genital, sacrifice intimacy or fidelity to an un-
restrained indulgence in momentary lust. The epicure may
combine all of these emphases into a whole lifestyle, carefully
buttressed by the trappings of prestige, usually with great disdain for the allegedly vulgar masses and narrow-minded
moralists.

Prejudice

Years ago, Allport[62] raised the question whether *prejudice* is
a societal or a personal quirk. He answered that it is both.
Dedicated as they are to assessing any person's object relations, clinicians cannot and should not take it lightly when a
patient harbors a strong hatred, suspicion, or fear of certain
persons on the basis of stereotypes, approaching them with
denigration or worse—no matter how widely such a rejection
may be shared in his community. What may sociologically appear as conformism is psychologically a bit of pathology that
should be studied diagnostically.

Though everybody has preferences in seeking and maintaining his object relations, and approaches his human world
with selective closeness and distance patterns, prejudice goes
beyond preference in being a response to unreasonable fear:
fear of chaos, of loss of certainty, of parental disapproval, or
of punishment for "wrong" thinking and doing. Reservoirs of
unverbalized anxieties lie behind prejudice: primitive apprehensions about sexual seduction, both desired and forbidden; intimations of revenge and retaliation; or sadistic
promptings barely held in check. Reservoirs of narcissism,
too—i.e., participation in the group narcissism of small or
large differences—lie behind prejudice: the need to be on the
winning side, to display power, or to have a flattering self-
image that is superior to that of others.

So the clinical diagnostic question is basically: "What kind of people do you hate or despise?" followed by "Why?" In raising such questions, reworded so as not to arouse the patient's defensiveness, one catches at least a glimpse of a person's negative identity and perhaps a good deal more of his callousness toward those he discriminates against. When these questions were asked of a patient who was a successful self-made businessman with very little formal education, it turned out that he was profoundly biased against "eggheads" and professionals (including the examiner) whom he believed were rather inept—or so he said at first. Moments later he proved to be intensely jealous of persons with learning, and with support from his cronies he belittled them at every opportunity. With a brazen air, he obstructed the diagnostic process at every step until it was made clear to him that the procedures were meant to enable him to arrive at a self-diagnosis with the examiner's help.

Chapter 14

The Patient's Relations to
His Predicament

Now that the details of the psychological examination and the ordering principles guiding it have been given (Chapters 4-13), the task I undertook in this book may seem to have been completed. But not quite. For something remains to be ascertained that, in a sense, transcends the psychological examination as well as the history of the patient. If, as I said in Chapter 2, psychiatric evaluation requires both longitudinal and cross-sectional views of the patient, which are to be combined or integrated for a comprehensive diagnostic understanding, the ultimate justification for that comprehensive understanding lies in its use as an aid in planning therapy. Diagnosis must make a difference—to the patient as well as to the diagnostician-healer. And its making that difference or enhancing that promise should be sensed from the start of the diagnostic process. Precisely in this sense, diagnosis and therapy overlap and intertwine, even when orderly procedure and logical thinking require that a distinctly diagnostic phase precede a distinctly therapeutic phase in the total helping process.

Granted, then, that history taking and psychological examining are distinguished more by their specific ordering principles and manner of being recorded than by the time at which they are done. Granted, too, that diagnosis and therapy are distinguished more by time-bound emphasis and procedure than by intention. The turning point from a diagnostic to a therapeutic preoccupation occurs when, in the course of the assessment, the patient begins to give hints about his future, no matter how greatly these hints may be affected by his current bewilderment. Clearly or in a bungled way, the questions "What is going to happen?" and "What is to be done?" are raised. It can be assumed that the patient is in some predicament, or else there would be no occasion for clinical evaluation. But how does he see this predicament, what does he make of it, how does it affect his fears or hopes for his future?

With these kinds of questions, global and provisional as they are, any clinician's mind will almost automatically turn to concepts that have *both diagnostic and prognostic* import. The clinician will think of *acute* and *chronic* disorders and will make a tentative differentiation along these lines, a differentiation that cannot be made by cross-sectional observation alone. He will think of *episodic* and *static* disorders, which also requires a long and retrospective view. He will think in some quasi-quantitative way about how *mild, moderate,* or *severe* the current clinical picture is, and what hopeful or ominous implications it has for any possibility of melioration. If he is psychodynamically oriented, the clinician will muse about *secondary gains,* about the patient's *motivation for change,* and about the *adaptive* or *defensive function* of the patient's disorder and symptom choice in the pattern and course of his life. If he is alert to suggestibility and social conditioning, he may even ponder the *possible iatrogenic impact of the diagnostic process* itself on the patient's condition. And if the clinician is also an experienced psychotherapist, he will pay much attention to *the patient's attitudes toward the examiner(s)* and, conversely, to his own attitude toward the patient, registering the particular transference and countertransference relations that have developed in the diagnostic interaction. All such thoughts will affect the diagnostic formulation and the prognostic estimate. They lead to specific questions that press for answers in which psychiatric *judgment* is exercised.

The Patient's (and Others') View of the Present Situation

To facilitate and buttress the psychiatric judgment that is to be made as an integral part of the diagnostic formulation, orderly thinking suggests a few specific considerations, all of which are suitable interview topics.

For many patients, the *discomfort experienced* will surely be a weighty consideration in seeking help in the first place, in actively participating in the diagnostic process, and in a sustained involvement in therapy. Their *symptoms* are felt as painful, costly, or demanding; they tax the person's energy, open him up to unexpected boomerang effects, and often produce too much wear and tear in proportion to the slim satisfactions they provide. The more acute the symptoms, the more likely is the patient to perceive them with some consternation. The more ego-alien the complaints, the more likely is the patient to feel hampered or obstructed by them.

But *not all symptoms are ego-alien or acute.* Compulsions often come on slowly, at first appearing merely as "funny habits." Alcohol addiction often proceeds by steady increments over years. It may take years for shyness to become a pronounced and active withdrawal. With an insidious onset of mental disorder, the chance for some degree of habituation to otherwise upsetting symptoms increases. As a result, in some forms of severe psychopathology the patient does not as a rule express severe discomfort *directly.* With increased withdrawal, decreased reality testing, and the onset of regression, the patient may indeed have settled for a position of relative comfort, albeit a primitive one, that he experiences as benign in comparison to earlier turmoil or panic. In such cases, then, the discomfort experienced will have to be judged empathically by the examiner, and against the patient's history. In addition, some of the patient's current symptoms should then be seen as restitution attempts that mask an existential condition more painful than the symptoms, such as profound loneliness or continuous, nagging self-accusations.

In other cases, the symptoms are neither acute nor insidious in their onset, and certainly not felt as ego-alien. They are *symptoms that have become character traits or peculiarities of personality* and that, despite their untoward or unpleasant social effects or backlash on the patients themselves, remain outside the patients' critical awareness. Often, patients even prize them as wonderful talents or assets. The painful effects of the symptoms are felt by others, who are duped, deceived, or manipulated by the patient's nasty character traits; therefore the psychiatric referral is often made by second parties, such as relatives, employers, or legal authorities.

Discomfort Experienced or Inflicted

In conditions that produce marked lethargy, such as severe depressions, the *discomfort experienced by the patient may be very great, but lacks the quality or power for motivating the patient to seek help.* In deep gloom, with psychomotor retardation and possibly suicidal ruminations, the patient seems to an outsider to be almost hell-bent on worsening his condition rather than desiring its alleviation. By and large, the same impression is given by patients with marked or prolonged hypochondriacal complaints: while the symptoms are cause for complaining, they do not seem to stimulate a wish for deliverance from aches and pains beyond the momentary lament.

As this quick overview suggests, it is not always easy for the clinician to ascertain with confidence the kind and degree of discomfort any patient experiences in his presenting condition. The nature and course of psychological disorders create widely differing states of discomfort, accommodation, denial, habituation, blunting, or even perverse forms of pride. Each disorder seems to have its own phenomenological accent of hope or despair, affective sharpening or dulling, motivating or disorganizing anxiety, experiential strangeness or naturalness.

In the foregoing paragraphs some allusion has already been made to *discomfort inflicted*—commonly understood to mean *by* the patient *on* others. Mainly through the advent of family therapy it has been learned that this common-sense observation needs to be corrected by some analysis of the process whereby families come to *designate* one of their members as the patient. This process may involve scapegoating and displacement, unilateral blaming, and a host of subtle interpersonal maneuvers that exempt some family members from criticism while heaping scorn on one (or more) who is held to be disorganized, ill, a thorn in the side, and the "cause" of family troubles. This correction will lead to a multilateral or *interactional assessment of discomfort inflicted,* and will take spiral effects of interpersonal conflicts into account. In some cases, the designated patient who is alleged to have inflicted much discomfort may have to be delivered from the "sick role" into which he has been pushed. When the diagnostic focus shifts from him to others, or to the family as a whole, spectacular changes may occur in the balance and distribution of family discomfort experienced and discomfort inflicted.

Nevertheless, the *effects of anyone's symptoms on others vary with the nature of the diagnosed disorder,* and the kind of discomfort inflicted on others is sometimes itself a pathognomonic sign. For instance, phobias and hysterical conversion reactions typically demand from the patient's relatives not only sympathy, but actual extra work, e.g., in guiding the patient around dangerous places, in screening him from upsetting stimuli, or in performing tasks that he cannot do for himself on account of, say, a paralysis. It was in these conditions that the so-called secondary gain from neurotic symptoms was first noted: The special attention these patients' symptoms demanded from those living with them, and the conspicuous outbursts of anger that were inflicted on their surroundings became additional pointers to the diagnosis of these conditions.

But *some degree of secondary gain attaches to almost all disorders,* purely mental as well as neurological. There is nearly always some narcissistic withdrawal, some claim to special attention and consideration, some increased dependence, some proneness to emotional lability, with quicker tears, angry attacks, or snappish verbalizations. In some disorders, the patient's keen suspiciousness or accusatory apprehension puts the family under special duress, requiring much tact and restraint from those who have to live with him. Depressed states put the family under a pall of gloom. Manic and hypomanic conditions disrupt family routines and make life unpredictable.

While these discomforts are very real, some discomforts amount to veritable *injuries inflicted on other persons.* Patients with certain types of character disorder may steal, embezzle, extort, lie, cheat, secretly or openly spend the family's money, or in some other way sully the family's name and reputation in the community. These acts are not secondary gains to the patient, but primary hurts to others. In addition, they may shade from personal vice into actual crime, and involve the patient (and his family) in lawsuits.

In a word, then, the diagnostician's judgment about the severity of any disorder can rarely proceed from the complaints expressed by the patient alone; it must *take other people into account.* These other persons can range from spouse, parents, or family to a neighborhood or whole community, whose expressed sentiments are to be given some weight.

The Patient's Concept of His Illness and Recovery

A third variable of the patient's relations to his predicament is to be assessed: It is *the patient's own intuitive concept of his illness or affliction and capacity to recover.* The diagnostician's concept of mental disorder is of course a rather formalized one, stemming from his profession's conceptual system and technical knowledge base. The patient's concept (or notion) may be a very different one, not only in the sense of being that of a layman, but also in the sense that it tends to be laden with existential, idiosyncratic meanings.

Though frankly demonological interpretations of mental illness may be rare today, or confined to religious fringe groups, the vaguer notion of the illness as a "visitation" and the more definite notion of its being some form of *punishment* are by no means rare. Even when the patient feels his condition or symptoms are ego-alien, he is likely to cast about for reasons for and meanings of his affliction that derive from his past and present life view, his philosophical, religious, or ethical convictions, and his sense of agency.

If the patient's sense of personal agency never was strong and has been even further diminished (or destroyed) by his symptom choice, a *passive attitude* can be expected. He may feel overcome, put out, victimized, his means and ends so effectively cut off that he considers himself beyond help. Or he may believe that the help he needs is simply not available, because it requires superhuman ingenuity. He may have no confidence in the stamina and skill of any prospective therapist. Short of such a bleak outlook, the patient may see his present state as the result of years of doomful preparation: He has long seen his eventual collapse coming, and the inexorable downhill course of events in his life now proves to him that he has not much ground for hope. Yet he may see a glimmer of light at the end of the tunnel to which, through some magic, the enormous good will of others, or a turn of fortune, he may be brought closer. With a low sense of agency, however, he may accept many ministrations from others without actively cooperating in the efforts that are made for him.

When the *sense of agency* is *preserved,* or has been characteristically strong, the patient will probably attribute some personal or cosmic meaning, even purpose, to his current predicament. Such *meanings and purposes* may widely vary in content. If a large reservoir of guilt feelings is present, the affliction is likely to attain at some level of awareness the meaning of punishment (whether deserved or undeserved), or of an atonement process. If so, the symptoms will not be quite ego-alien or, if they were at first, they will shift slightly in a more ego-syntonic direction. Or the affliction and the arduous process of its melioration (its "working through") will assume a task character for the patient—a task that can and must be shouldered even when the eventual outcome is unclear. Cosmic associations about the assumed purpose of illness can be predominantly benevolent or malevolent, and are of course very often ambivalent. There is a large gray area between assuming utter damnation and feeling that one is now stricken for one's own ulterior good or eventual improvement. There may even be a narcissistic fantasy of having been singled out for a Messianic task, which proves one's superiority in the midst of one's affliction.

Motivation for treatment and hope for improvement do not require that the patient see his presenting disorder as an irksome, noxious thing from which he seeks deliverance with the greatest possible dispatch. In fact, if such an attitude prevails the patient may make a quick symptomatic improvement when treatment starts, or even during the process of diagnosis, but be unable to sustain it. In a way, this position implies a *denial* that the illness has any meaning, a denial that may expand into a denial of the symptoms also—which apparently can be done for some short time. It is a clinical truism that the outlook is much better when the patient thoughtfully and soberly attributes some meaning to his condition—for instance, that he played some part in bringing it about, that he has some *responsibility* for its coming and eventual going, that his current state cannot be ascribed to chance but is to be understood as an orderly process that has its "reasons," and that these reasons might be grasped. The patient may even sense that his "illness" is not without constructive or creative aspects from which he may emerge enriched or with desirable wisdom or insight.

In acute conditions one often observes that the patient is in a state of *puzzlement*. Groping for reasons, he may ask in perplexity: What does it all mean? Such states can be ominous, especially when coupled with behavioral regression; Emily Dickinson describes their essence in an autobiographical poem:

And then a plank in reason broke,
and I dropped down and down—
and hit a world at every plunge,
and finished knowing then.[63]

Without regression, a patient's state of puzzlement can be a sign that he is beginning to search for some order or design in his illness. If so, he may see the diagnostic process as most apropos and as holding a promise of clarification. This attitude is the ideal basis for diagnosis to become essentially a process of self-diagnosis, with the assistance of an expert.

At this point it is appropriate to note, however, that the *patient's ideas about his illness and his outlook on recovery will be affected by the symptoms and coping mechanisms he has resorted to* in his attempts to alleviate his felt distress. Any present or threatened disintegration elicits coping behaviors whose styles have psychoeconomic implications. Distress is felt as or accompanied by pain, high tension, anxiety, guilty feelings, shame, or perplexity, which are by definition (or else there would be no need for a diagnostic study) beyond the patient's current tolerance, endurance, or mastery. In this tense state, the patient may not be able to verbalize his feelings or formulate anything like specific complaints. Instead, his body may produce a host of involuntary psychophysiological signs that are not only beyond his control but outside his awareness. In such cases it is not enough for the diagnostician to be a good and sensitive listener. He must also be a keen and shrewd observer, and have a gift for empathic registration of feelings as well, if he is to discern, however tentatively, the patient's notions of illness and recovery.

Three groups of observations are recommended: some study of *interference phenomena,* alertness to *excess behavior,* and an appreciation of *restitution* phenomena as distinct from primary symptoms.

Interference phenomena are by and large the boomerang effects or unforeseen or unintended consequences of defenses, coping mechanisms, or major symptoms. Depending on their quality, scope, and intensity, something else follows in their wake—e.g., a marked reduction of spontaneity, or a general shrinking of the patient's action radius. The patient's speech may be impaired not only by blocking, which interrupts its normal flow, but also by difficulties in remembering produced by hyperrepression. The patient's work capacity may show a significant impairment, not necessarily admitted by him, but noted by others. Such impairment can be the result of obsessive ruminations, of a depressed mood, of time- and energy-demanding compulsive rituals, or of lethargy. He may be unable to engage in recreational activities because of uncontrollable preoccupations or somatic complaints. Whether such interference phenomena are admitted by the patient or not, for the diagnostician they are telltale signs of the severity of the patient's disorder. Above all, some clinical judgment must be made about the amount and quality of pleasure the patient is now able to experience. As a rule, pleasure is diminished in all mental disorders, and this diminution is the most general and common interference phenomenon.

Excess behavior is easy to notice when it occurs in the motor sphere: jitteriness, trembling, frequent sighing or hand wringing, pacing the floor, springing up from the chair in agitation, do not escape the eye of even a casual observer. In the *perceptual* sphere, excess behavior may take the form of hyperalert visual scanning or tense attempts to hear everything in one's milieu, to observe danger signals. But there are subtler forms of excess behavior that are more or less *attitudinal*, or built into certain defense mechanisms. Bravado is one of those excesses, becoming symptomatic precisely when it fails convincingly to mask fear or a sense of weakness and helplessness. Much in the hypomanic display of motor restlessness, flight of fancy, fast speech, wandering attention, and jocular utterances and postures is an attempt to conceal or counteract a depressive substratum. Counterphobic defenses are notable for their driven, excessive quality of bravery. Reaction formations that turn aggressive impulses into acts of forced niceness and seemingly loving deeds are symptomatic bits of excess behavior precisely to the extent that the substitute acts appear overdone. Without these symptomatic features they would be successful sublimations or neutralizations.

Finally, in the more serious disorders in which flagrant breaks with reality have occurred, we encounter certain acts and attitudes that are *restitution phenomena*, or *restitution symptoms*. By and large, these are attempts to recapture reality after the patient has severed himself from it, but now at a lower level commensurate with the depth of his regression. For instance, when a patient, after much scolding and naggings, finds himself saddled with a "bad self" image, withdraws from social engagements, and loses his hold on reality, he may project onto others, e.g., his clinical helpers, some of his old introjections. He may come to see his helpers as persecutors, and precisely on that account he needs to be alert to their doings and in self-defense seek a new contact with the world, for his former withdrawal from it would greatly endanger him. While his perceptions may be delusional or hallucinatory, he may also seek a partial resocialization to shield himself against dangers or gain some minimal satisfactions to keep himself going. Moreover, the object losses he has sustained by his withdrawal (augmented by his relatives' rejection of or hopelessness about him) now open him up to previously discarded fantasies, often accompanied by narcissistic ideas of power and grandiose attitudes to compensate for the losses.

Relations to Reality

It is obvious from the foregoing that in all these vicissitudes the patient's *relations to reality* need to be assessed if the diagnosis is to make a prognostic difference and lead to the best possible therapy. All too often, the patient's relations to reality are approached only categorically—reality contact is assessed as "present" or "absent," in the latter case with the verdict of "psychosis." Some differences need to be envisaged between reality testing, adherence or loyalty to reality, and various views of reality that any patient may hold, as well as the particular environments or situations that are adaptationally relevant for him.

Reality testing hinges largely on perceptual and cognitive skills and the capacity to communicate in consensually validated terms. It entails making discerning observations, sorting out useful and harmful things, taking things "as they are" in their substance and with their resistances, keeping perceptual and cognitive errors to a tolerable minimum, and exercising judgments that foster survival and provide vital satisfactions for growth and well-being, while staving off threats of harm, disorganization, and imbalance that would hasten the person's eventual dissolution in death. Implied in this concept of reality testing is *a common-sense view of the world* as dictated by elementary biological, physical, and social necessities. In this common-sense view, hallucinatory deviations from ordinary sense perception and delusional aberrations of thought can be identified, contradicted, or corrected. If a wall is patently blank, someone who sees pink elephants on it is out of touch.

Inadequate tools can make reality testing difficult. Sensory defects, very low intelligence, or inability to form elementary concepts make coming to terms with reality difficult, and a person thus handicapped may need other people or special instruments in order to survive. Yet impressive jobs of reality testing can be done with poor tools, and inadequate equipment does not necessarily undermine the person's desire to test reality or weaken his loyalty to it. In the clinical concept of reality testing there is, then, an implied recognition that *the person's intentions* count. Poor reality testing caused by perceptual, cognitive, or motor handicaps differs from poor reality testing caused by an avoidance of the world on emotional grounds, e.g., because reality is seen as overwhelming, too demanding, dangerous, or oppressive. The latter kind is an intended withdrawal from reality in favor of an autistic fantasy world that is felt to be less demanding (although it may turn out to be a haunted one).

But reality testing is also a matter of practice. The environment must be enticing and diversified enough to provide opportunities for the person to perfect his tools for testing and his skill in using them. Deprived of a favorable environment, the skills of formerly good reality testers may wither, as police agents know from their methods of forced indoctrination by imposed isolation. The ego's competence is undermined, fantasy takes over, and a more primitive personality organization emerges, one that is highly suggestible and malleable. Clinical observations show that schizoid personalities accustomed to looking inward run the risk of not looking outward often and keenly enough, and the resulting atrophy of their reality-testing skills eventually brings them to the verge of complete withdrawal.

Adherence or loyalty to reality can be maintained in the face of grave difficulties in reality testing. This effort is clinically visible in the initial stages of various syndromes of dementia. With failing cognitive capacities and linguistic functions, such patients may nevertheless strive—sometimes with great effort—to remain in contact with the world and its cultural opportunities and demands. I have seen too many aphasic patients take up crossword puzzles not to be impressed by their *desire for contact* and for sharpening their poor linguistic tools. Much of the emotional lability of dementing patients is attributable to an accurate perception of their losses and dysfunctions; their frequent spells of tearfulness express their justified chagrin. Similar *feelings of regret* (and remorse) in patients with poor impulse control suggest that the desire for reality adaptation and reality testing can be present in lives that are punctuated by gross disturbances in reality contact. Such clinical findings are to be counted as assets that can be put to therapeutic use and lead to a more hopeful prognosis.

Views of reality may turn out to be so idiosyncratic or particular that they fly in the face of common sense. Certain psychiatric patients hold noncommonsensical world views that they allege are superior to ordinary notions of reality—more spiritual or more ethical—in ways that justify or condone their symptoms. Certain philosophical or religious positions may be marshaled to substantiate the patients' *special world views.*

> For instance, an excessively shy and socially inept boy in his late adolescent years gave up his studies, drifted into a small religious sect, began to disdain working for a living, started to pilfer, had a brush with the law, and was sent by the judge to a state hospital for observation. He turned out to be obsessional and full of phobic reactions, but he attempted to justify his life style and actions by a utopian vision of a world in which property is shared and no tasks are assigned. He regarded himself as quite normal, even ethically advanced over the mass of his fellow men, and he thought that even his phobias were morally justified—all because he held a certain view of reality, allegedly "higher" than common sense.

Indeed, at times only a fine line separates a paranoid system from the world view of creative reformers, prophets, or agents of change who have realizable dreams of a better world. The differential diagnosis can be difficult, not only to make, but to defend. For *idealism* is, after all, a legitimate and healthy part of adequate reality testing. And if this point sounds paradoxical, it is only because in such cases we approach the borderland between clinical psychiatry and philosophy. In clinical practice, the examiner is well-advised to stick to a pragmatic, common-sense view of reality, no matter what his private world view may be—and no matter whether philosophers would describe this professional outlook as a case of "naïve realism."

Lastly, examiners should be aware that nobody ever deals with all of reality. Each person lives in only a small segment of it, a particular *Umwelt* that is his locus. *Adaptational demands are situationally determined,* and each person's adaptive skills are gained and practiced in a specific milieu. Someone who has maintained a workable equilibrium in a small town may lose it when he moves to a busy city. A young person may do poorly at college but thrive in the Army. Another may do well as a single person but fail in marriage. The "average expectable environment" is a rather loose notion, statistically important but not always clinically useful. Clinicians, too, live in a particular environment, on account of which their views of other environments or their fantasies about an "average expectable environment" may be quite skewed.

And so the patient will have to be seen in the light of his particular segment of reality, and his reality contact, his reality-testing skills, and his views of reality will have to be assessed in terms of his particular *Umwelt*. Stress reactions produced by dislocation from one's customary habitat, by rapid change in any environment, by culture shock, by changes in employment, etc., may say much about the rigidity of certain personalities, but they also require the clinician to approach the notions of "reality" and "the environment" with considerable specificity.

Notes

1. K. A. Menninger, M. Mayman, & P. W. Pruyser, *A Manual for Psychiatric Case Study*, 2nd ed. New York: Grune & Stratton, 1962.
2. K. A. Menninger, M. Mayman, & P. W. Pruyser, *The Vital Balance: The Life Process in Mental Health and Illness*. New York: Viking, 1963.
3. W. James, *Psychology: Briefer Course*. New York: Holt, 1892, p. 29.
4. E. Kraepelin, *Clinical Psychiatry: A Textbook for Students and Physicians*, abstr. & adapt. from the 7th German edition of *Lehrbuch der Psychiatrie* by R. Diefendorf. New York: Macmillan, 1907.
5. A. Meyer, *Psychobiology: A Science of Man*, comp. & ed. E. E. Winters & A. M. Bowers. Springfield, Ill.: Thomas, 1957.
6. S. Freud (1905), Three Essays on the Theory of Sexuality. *Standard Edition*, 7:125-245. London: Hogarth Press, 1953.
7. C. E. Osgood, *Method and Theory in Experimental Psychology*. New York: Oxford University Press, 1943, pp. 193-228.
8. C. M. Solley & G. Murphy, *Development of the Perceptual World*. New York: Basic Books, 1960.
9. J. S. Bruner & C. C. Goodman, Value and Need as Organizing Factors in Perception. *J. Abnorm. Soc. Psychol.*, 42:33-44, 1947.
10. S. Freud (1912), Recommendations to Physicians Practising Psycho-Analysis. *Standard Edition*, 12:109-120. London: Hogarth Press, 1958.
11. E. Jaensch, *Eidetic Imagery and Typological Methods of Investigation*, trans. O. Oeser. New York: Harcourt, Brace, 1930.
12. V. K. Kandinski, *Kritische und klinische Betrachtungen im Gebiete der Sinnestaeuschungen*. Berlin: Friedlaender, 1885.
13. L. Staudenmaier, *Die Magie als experimentelle Naturwissenschaft*. Leipzig: 1912. (A self-description of hallucinatory states, quoted in K. Jaspers, *General Psychopathology*, and W. Mayer-Gross, E. Slater, & M. Roth, *Clinical Psychiatry*.)
14. B. A. Morel, *Études cliniques: traité théorique et pratique des maladies mentales*. Paris: Masson, 1852-1853.
15. G. D. Stoddard, *The Meaning of Intelligence*. New York: Macmillan, 1943.

16. J. Gerstmann, Syndrome of Finger Agnosia, Disorientation for Left and Right, Agraphia and Acalculia. *Arch. Neurol. Psychiat.*, 44:398-408, 1940.

17. J. Gerstmann, Psychological and Phenomenological Aspects of Disorders of the Body Image. *J. Nerv. Ment. Dis.*, 126: 499-512, 1958.

18. O. Pötzl, R. Allers, & J. Teler, Preconscious Stimulation in Dreams, Associations, and Images. *Psychol. Issues*, Monogr. 7. New York: International Universities Press, 1960.

19. T. A. Ribot, *Diseases of Memory*, trans. W. H. Smith. New York: Appleton, 1882.

20. T. H. Johnson, ed., *The Complete Poems of Emily Dickinson*, Boston: Little, Brown, 1960, No. 701, p. 345.

21. S. Freud (1901), The Psychopathology of Everyday Life. *Standard Edition*, 6. London: Hogarth Press, 1960.

22. Johnson, *op. cit.*, No. 744, p. 365.

23. B. Zeigarnik, Über das Behalten von erledigten und unerledigten Handlungen. *Psychol. Forsch.*, 9:1-85, 1927.

24. C. G. Jung, *Experimental Researches*, trans. L. Stein & D. Riviere. *Collected Works*, 2. (Bollingen Series XX.) Princeton: Princeton University Press, 1973.

25. W. Köhler, *The Mentality of Apes*, trans. E. Winter. New York: Harcourt, Brace, 1926.

26. A. Bain, *Mind and Body*. New York: Appleton, 1873.

27. J. B. Watson, Psychology as the Behaviorist Sees It. *Psychol. Rev.*, 20:158-177, 1913.

28. S. Freud (1911), Formulations on the Two Principles of Mental Functioning. *Standard Edition*, 12:215-226. London: Hogarth Press, 1958.

29. S. Freud (1900), The Interpretation of Dreams. *Standard Edition*, 4 & 5. London: Hogarth Press, 1953.

30. E. Bleuler (1911), *Dementia Praecox or the Group of Schizophrenias*, trans. J. Zinkin. New York: International Universities Press, 1950.

31. P. McKellar, *Imagination and Thinking: A Psychological Analysis*. New York: Basic Books, 1957.

32. S. Freud (1911), Psycho-Analytic Notes on an Autobiographical Account of a Case of Paranoia. *Standard Edition* 12:3-82, London: Hogarth Press, 1958.

33. H. Werner, *Comparative Psychology of Mental Development*, rev. ed. New York: International Universities Press, 1957.

34. J. Piaget, *The Origins of Intelligence in Children*, trans. M. Cook. New York: International Universities Press, 1952.

35. C. Lévi-Strauss, *The Raw and the Cooked; Introduction to a Science of Mythology:* I. trans. J. & D. Weightman. New York: Harper & Row, 1969.

36. M. L. Hayward & J. E. Taylor, A Schizophrenic Patient Describes the Action of Intensive Psychotherapy. *Psychiat. Quart.,* 30:211-248, 1956.
37. P. Janet, *The Major Symptoms of Hysteria.* New York: Macmillan, 1907.
38. A. L. Gesell, A Case of Symbolistic Writing with Senile Delusions. *Amer. J. Psychol.,* 16:519-536, 1905.
39. E. Kretschmer, *Der sensitive Beziehungswahn,* 3e Aufl. Berlin: Springer, 1950.
40. K. Goldstein, *Language and Language Disturbances.* New York: Grune & Stratton, 1948.
41. H. S. Sullivan, *Clinical Studies in Psychiatry,* ed. H. S. Perry, M. L. Gawel, & M. Gibbon. New York: Norton, 1956, pp. 185-186.
42. C. L. Rousey & A. E. Moriarty, *Diagnostic Implications of Speech Sounds.* Springfield, Ill.: Thomas, 1965.
43. R. L. Birdwhistell, *Kinesics and Context: Essays on Body Motion Communication.* Philadelphia: University of Pennsylvania Press, 1970.
44. Johnson, *op. cit.,* No. 536, p. 262.
45. Johnson, *op. cit.,* No. 599, p. 294.
46. Johnson, *op. cit.,* No. 341, p. 162.
47. W. James, *The Principles of Psychology,* 2 vols. New York: Holt, 1890, Ch. XXV.
48. C. Darwin (1872), *The Expression of the Emotions in Man and Animals.* Chicago: University of Chicago Press, 1965.
49. W. B. Cannon, *Bodily Changes in Pain, Hunger, Fear and Rage,* 2nd ed. Boston: Branford, 1953.
50. P. Janet, *Psychological Healing, a Historical and Clinical Study,* 2 vols. trans. E. & C. Paul. New York: Macmillan, 1925, pp. 692-693.
51. W. McDougall, *The Energies of Men: A Study of the Fundamentals of Dynamic Psychology.* New York: Scribner, 1933.
52. Johnson, *op. cit.,* No. 252, p. 115.
53. J. Hughlings Jackson, *Selected Writings,* 2 vols. London: Hodder & Stoughton, 1932.
54. J.-P. Sartre, *The Emotions: Outline of a Theory,* trans. B. Frechtman. New York: Philosophical Library, 1948.
55. B. L. Barrington, A List of Words Descriptive of Affective Reactions. *J. Clin. Psychol.,* 19:259-262, 1963.
56. G. E. Coghill, *Anatomy and the Problem of Behavior.* Cambridge: Harvard University Press, 1929.
57. M. Buber, *I and Thou.* New York: Scribner, 1958.
58. M. Balint, *Problems of Human Pleasure and Behavior.* New York: Liveright, 1957.
59. K. Jaspers, *General Psychopathology,* trans. J. Hoenig & M. W. Hamilton. Chicago: University of Chicago Press, 1963.

60. C. G. Jung, *Two Essays on Analytical Psychology*, 2nd ed., trans. R. F. C. Hull. *Collected Works*, 7. (Bollingen Series XX.) New York: Pantheon Books, 1966.
61. E. H. Erikson, Identity and the Life Cycle: Selected Papers. *Psychol. Issues*, Monogr. 1. New York: International Universities Press, 1959.
62. G. W. Allport, *The Nature of Prejudice*. Cambridge: Addison-Wesley, 1954.
63. Johnson, *op. cit.*, No. 280, pp. 128-129.

APPENDIX
Selected Reading Lists

A book such as this one, which aims at summarizing for instructional purposes a large accumulation of clinical knowledge from psychology, psychiatry, and neurology, could have a virtually endless bibliography if everything stated in the text were to be documented. To keep the book practical and the text uncluttered it was decided to furnish, in addition to textual references, a selected listing of major and classical works (many of which have their own extensive bibliographies) that would stand the learner of psychological examining in good stead. This list is subdivided into seven sections that may serve the special interests of various examiners depending on their professional orientation. Special emphasis has been placed on works in English, whenever possible in the most easily available editions. The sections are: (1) biographical, autobiographical, and fictional accounts of mental disturbance; (2) clinical psychiatric works; (3) clinical neurological works; (4) clinical psychological works; (5) psychoanalytic works—clinical and theoretical; (6) works on psychodiagnostic testing; (7) dictionaries and glossaries.

1. Biographical, Autobiographical, and Fictional Accounts
of Mental Disturbance

Barnes, M. & Berke, J., *Mary Barnes: Two Accounts of a Journey through Madness.* New York: Harcourt Brace Jovanovich, 1971.
Beers, C. W., *A Mind That Found Itself.* New York: Longmans, Green, 1908.

Boisen, A. T., *The Exploration of the Inner World*. Chicago: Willet, Clark, 1936.
Boisen, A. T., *Out of the Depths*. New York: Harper, 1960.
Green, H., *I Never Promised You a Rose Garden*. New York: Holt, Rinehart & Winston, 1964.
Kaplan, B., *The Inner World of Mental Illness*. New York: Harper & Row, 1964.
Kiel, N., *The Adolescent through Fiction*. New York: International Universities Press, 1959.
Landis, C., *Varieties of Psychopathological Experience*, ed. F. A. Mettler. New York: Holt, Rinehart & Winston, 1964.
Leon, G. R., *Case Histories of Deviant Behavior: A Social Learning Analysis*. Boston: Holbrook Press, 1975.
Maine, H., *If a Man Be Mad*. Garden City, N.Y.: Doubleday, 1947.
Peters, F., *The World Next Door*. New York: Farrar, Straus, 1949.
Prince, M. (1906), *The Dissociation of a Personality: A Biographical Study in Abnormal Psychology*. Westport, Conn.: Greenwood Press, 1969.
Schreber, D. P. (1903), *Memoirs of My Nervous Illness*. trans. & ed. I. MacAlpine & R. A. Hunter. London: Dawson, 1955.
Sechehaye, M. A., *Symbolic Realization: A New Method of Psychotherapy Applied to a Case of Schizophrenia*. trans. B. Wursten & H. Wursten. New York: International Universities Press, 1951.

2. Clinical Psychiatric Works

Arieti, S., ed., *American Handbook of Psychiatry*, 3 vols. New York: Basic Books, 1959-1966.
Arieti, S., et al., eds., *American Handbook of Psychiatry*, rev. ed., 6 vols. New York: Basic Books, 1974-1975.
Beck, A. T., *Depression: Clinical, Experimental, and Theoretical Aspects*. New York: Hoeber Medical Division, Harper & Row, 1967.
Bellak, L. & Loeb, L., eds., *The Schizophrenic Syndrome*. New York: Grune & Stratton, 1969.
Bleuler, E. (1911), *Dementia Praecox or the Group of Schizophrenias*, trans. J. Zinkin. New York: International Universities Press, 1950.
Cameron, N. A., *Personality Development and Psychopathology: A Dynamic Approach*. Boston: Houghton Mifflin, 1963.
Deutsch, F. & Murphy, W. F., *The Clinical Interview*, Vol. I: *Diagnosis*. New York: International Universities Press, 1954.
Easson, W. M., *The Severely Disturbed Adolescent: Inpatient, Residential and Hospital Treatment*. New York: International Universities Press, 1969.

Freedman, A. M. & Kaplan, H. I., *Comprehensive Textbook of Psychiatry*. Baltimore: Williams & Wilkins, 1967.

Freedman, A. M., Kaplan, H. I., & Sadock, B. J., eds., *Comprehensive Textbook of Psychiatry*, 2nd ed., 2 vols. Baltimore: Williams & Wilkins, 1975.

Freeman, T., with Cameron, J. L., & McGhie, A., *Studies on Psychosis: Descriptive, Psychoanalytic, and Psychological Aspects*. New York: International Universities Press, 1965.

Freeman, T., *Psychopathology of the Psychoses*. New York: International Universities Press, 1972.

Jung, C. G. (1907), *The Psychology of Dementia Praecox*, trans. R. F. C. Hull. (Bollingen Series XX.) Princeton: Princeton University Press, 1974 (paper).

Kanner, L., *Child Psychiatry*, 4th ed. Springfield, Ill.: Thomas, 1972.

Kolb, L. C., *Noyes' Modern Clinical Psychiatry*, 7th ed. Philadelphia: Saunders Co., 1968.

Kraepelin, E., *Lectures on Clinical Psychiatry*, rev. ed. T. Johnstone. New York: Hafner, 1968.

Kretschmer, E., *A Text-book of Medical Psychology*, trans. E. G. Strauss. London: Hogarth Press, 1952.

Lidz, T., Fleck, S., & Cornelison, A. R., *Schizophrenia and the Family*. New York: International Universities Press, 1965.

Lief, H., ed., *The Commonsense Psychiatry of Adolf Meyer*. New York: McGraw-Hill, 1948.

Masserman, J. H., *Principles of Dynamic Psychiatry*, 2nd ed. Philadelphia: Saunders, 1961.

Mayer-Gross, W., Slater, E., & Roth, M., *Clinical Psychiatry*. Baltimore: Williams & Wilkins, 1955.

Menninger, K. A., *Man against Himself*. New York: Harcourt, Brace, 1938.

Menninger, K. A., *The Human Mind*, rev. ed. New York: Knopf, 1945.

Meyer, A., *Collected Papers*, 4 vols., ed. E. E. Winters. Baltimore: Johns Hopkins Press, 1950-1952.

Monroe, R. R., *Episodic Behavioral Disorders: A Psychodynamic and Neurophysiologic Analysis*. Cambridge: Harvard University Press, 1970.

Pruyser, P. W., ed., Diagnosis and the Difference It Makes. *Bull. Menninger Clin.*, 40:409-602, 1976. Reprinted as *Diagnosis and the Difference It Makes*. New York: Aronson, 1977.

Redlich, F. C. & Freedman, D. X., *The Theory and Practice of Psychiatry*. New York: Basic Books, 1966.

Schilder, P. (1935), *The Image and Appearance of the Human Body*. New York: International Universities Press, 1950.

Schilder, P., *Contributions to Developmental Neuropsychiatry*, ed. L. Bender. New York: International Universities Press, 1964.

Stengel, E., On the Aetiology of the Fugue States. *J. Ment. Sci.,* 87:572-599, 1941.
Straus, E., *On Obsession.* New York: Nervous and Mental Disease Publications, 1948.
Sullivan, H. S., *Collected Works,* 2 vols. New York: Norton, 1953.
Thomä, H., *Anorexia Nervosa.* New York: International Universities Press, 1967.
Tomkins, S. S., ed., *Contemporary Psychopathology: A Source Book.* Cambridge: Harvard University Press, 1947.

3. Clinical Neurological Works

Bain's Diseases of the Nervous System, 7th ed., rev. Lord Brain & J. N. Walton. London: Oxford University Press, 1969.
Baker, A. B., ed., *Clinical Neurology,* 2nd ed., 4 vols. New York: Hoeber Medical Division, Harper, 1962.
Critchley, M. (1953), *The Parietal Lobes.* New York: Hafner, 1966.
Critchley, M., *Aphasiology and Other Aspects of Language.* Baltimore: Williams & Wilkins, 1970.
Critchley, M., *The Dyslexic Child.* Springfield, Ill.: Thomas, 1970.
Denny-Brown, D., The Nature of Apraxia. *J. Nerv. Ment. Dis.,* 126:9-32, 1958.
Elliot, F. A., *Clinical Neurology.* Philadelphia: Saunders, 1964.
Goldstein, K., *Human Nature in the Light of Psychopathology.* Cambridge: Harvard University Press, 1947.
Goldstein, K., *Language and Language Disturbances.* New York: Grune & Stratton, 1948.
Head, H., *Aphasia and Kindred Disorders of Speech.* New York: Macmillan, 1926.
Lennox, W. G. & Lennox, M. A., *Epilepsy and Related Disorders,* 2 vols. Boston: Little, Brown, 1960.
Nielsen, J. M., *Agnosia, Apraxia, Aphasia: Their Value in Cerebral Localization.* Los Angeles: Los Angeles Neurological Society, 1936.
Penfield, W. & Jasper, H., *Epilepsy and the Functional Anatomy of the Human Brain.* Boston: Little, Brown, 1954.
Walshe, J. M., *Diseases of the Nervous System,* 10th ed. Baltimore: Williams & Wilkins, 1963.
Wechsler, I. S., *Clinical Neurology,* 9th ed. Philadelphia: Saunders, 1963.

4. Clinical Psychological Works

Barbara, D. G., *Psychological and Psychiatric Aspects of Speech and Hearing.* Springfield, Ill.: Thomas, 1960.

Bartlett, F. C., *Remembering: A Study in Experimental and Social Psychology*. Cambridge, Eng.: Cambridge University Press, 1932.

Bowlby, J., *Attachment and Loss*, 2 vols. New York: Basic Books, 1969-1973.

Brentano, F., *Psychologie vom Empirischen Standpunkte*. Leipzig: Dunker R. Humbolt, 1874.

Bruner, J. S., Goodnow, J. J., & Austin, G. A., *A Study of Thinking*. New York: Wiley, 1956.

Cannon, W. B., *The Wisdom of the Body*. New York: Norton, 1939.

Ekman, P., Friesen, W. V., & Ellsworth, P., *Emotion in the Human Face*. New York: Pergamon Press, 1972.

Goldberg, H. K. & Schiffman, G. B., *Dyslexia: Problems of Reading Disabilities*. New York: Grune & Stratton, 1972.

Hall, C. S. & Lindzey, G., *Theories of Personality*, 2nd ed. New York: Wiley, 1970.

Hanfmann, E. & Kasanin, J., *Conceptual Thinking in Schizophrenia*. New York: Nervous and Mental Disease Monograph, 1942.

Hebb, D. O., *The Organization of Behavior: A Neuropsychological Theory*. New York: Wiley, 1949.

Horowitz, M. J., *Image Formation and Cognition*. New York: Appleton-Century-Crofts, 1970.

Hunt, J. McV., ed., *Personality and the Behavior Disorders*, 2 vols. New York: Ronald Press, 1944.

Inhelder, B. & Piaget, J. (1955), *The Growth of Logical Thinking from Childhood to Adolescence*, trans. A. Parsons & S. Milgram. New York: Basic Books, 1958.

James, W. (1890), *The Principles of Psychology*, 2 vols. New York: Dover, 1950.

Jung, C. G. (1921), *Psychological Types*, trans. H. G. Baynes. *The Collected Works of C. G. Jung*, Vol. 6. (Bollingen Series XX.) Princeton: Princeton University Press, 1971.

Kaplan, B. & Wapner, S., eds., *Perspectives in Psychological Theory: Essays in Honor of Heinz Werner*. New York: International Universities Press, 1960.

Kasanin, J. S., ed., *Language and Thought in Schizophrenia*. Berkeley & Los Angeles: University of California Press, 1944.

Katz, D., *The World of Colour*, trans. R. B. MacLeod & C. W. Fox. London: Kegan Paul, Trench, Trubner, 1935.

Klasen, E., *The Syndrome of Specific Dyslexia*. Baltimore: University Park Press, 1972.

Klein, G. S., *Perception, Motives, and Personality*. New York: Knopf, 1970.

Knapp, P. H., ed., *Expression of the Emotions in Man*. New York: International Universities Press, 1963.

Koffka, K., *Principles of Gestalt Psychology*. New York: Harcourt, Brace, 1935.

Kohlberg, L., The Adolescent as a Philosopher. In *Twelve to Sixteen: Early Adolescence*, ed. J. Kagan & R. Coles. New York: Norton, 1972.

Korchin, S. J., *Modern Clinical Psychology: Principles of Intervention in the Clinic and Community*. New York: Basic Books, 1976.

Lorenz, M. & Cobb, S., Language Patterns in Psychotic and Psychoneurotic Subjects. *Arch. Neurol. Psychiat.*, 72:665-673, 1954.

Lynd, N. M., *On Shame and the Search for Identity*. New York: Harcourt, Brace, 1958.

May, R., Angel, E., & Ellenberger, H. F., eds., *Existence: A New Dimension in Psychiatry and Psychology*. New York: Basic Books, 1958.

Merleau-Ponty, M., *Phenomenology of Perception*, trans. C. Smith. London: Routledge & Kegan Paul, 1962.

Merleau-Ponty, M., *The Structure of Behavior*, trans. by A. L. Fisher. Boston: Beacon Press, 1963.

Murphy, G., *Personality: A Biosocial Approach to Origins and Structure*. New York: Harper, 1947.

Murphy, G. & Spohn, H. E., *Encounter with Reality*. Boston: Houghton Mifflin, 1968.

Murray, H. A., et al., *Explorations in Personality*. New York: Oxford University Press, 1938.

Piaget, J. (1923), *The Language and Thought of the Child*, 3rd ed., trans. M. Gabain. New York: Humanities Press, 1962.

Piaget, J. (1924), *Judgment and Reasoning in the Child*, trans. M. Warden. New York: Humanities Press, 1962.

Piaget, J. (1926), *The Child's Conception of the World*, trans. J. Tomlinson & A. Tomlinson. New York: Humanities Press, 1960.

Piaget, J. (1927), *The Child's Conception of Physical Causality*, trans. M. Gabain. New York: Humanities Press, 1966.

Piaget, J. (1932), *The Moral Judgment of the Child*, trans. M. Gabain. New York: Free Press, 1965.

Piaget, J. (1936), *The Origins of Intelligence in Children*, trans. M. Cook. New York: International Universities Press, 1952.

Rapaport, D., ed., *Organization and Pathology of Thought*. New York: Columbia University Press, 1951.

Rapaport, D., *The Collected Papers of . . .*, ed. M. M. Gill. New York: Basic Books, 1967.

Ribot, T. A., *The Diseases of the Will*, trans. M. M. Snell. Chicago: Open Court, 1894.

Rylander, G., *Personality Changes after Operations of the Frontal Lobe: A Clinical Study of 32 Cases*. London: Milford, 1939.

Sarason, S. B., *Psychological Problems in Mental Deficiency*. New York: Harper, 1949.

Schachtel, E. G., *Metamorphosis: On the Development of Affect, Perception, Attention, and Memory*. New York: Basic Books, 1959.

Schiller, C. H., ed., *Instinctive Behavior: The Development of a Modern Concept.* New York: International Universities Press, 1957.

Stern, W., *General Psychology from the Personalistic Standpoint.* New York: Macmillan, 1938.

Thorne, F. C., *Principles of Psychological Examining.* Brandon, Vt.: Clinical Psychology, 1955.

Vigotsky, L., Thought in Schizophrenia. *Arch. Neurol. Psychiat.,* 31:1063-1077, 1934.

Wallin, J. E. W., *Mental Deficiency in Relation to Problems of Genesis, Social and Occupational Consequences, Utilization, Control and Prevention.* Brandon, Vt.: Clinical Psychology, 1956.

Watzlawick, P., Beavin, J. H., & Jackson, D. D., *Pragmatics of Human Communication: A Study of Interactional Patterns, Pathologies, and Paradoxes.* New York: Norton, 1967.

Weisenburg, T. H. & McBride, K. E., *Aphasia, a Clinical and Psychological Study.* New York: Commonwealth Fund, 1935.

Wepman, J., *Recovery from Aphasia.* New York: Ronald Press, 1951.

Werner, H. *Comparative Psychology of Mental Development,* rev. ed. New York: International Universities Press, 1957.

Werner, H. & Kaplan, B., *Symbol Formation: An Organismic-Developmental Approach to Language and the Expression of Thought.* New York: Wiley, 1963.

White, R. W., *The Abnormal Personality.* New York: Ronald Press, 1948.

Wolman, B. B., *Handbook of Clinical Psychology.* New York: McGraw-Hill, 1965.

5. Psychoanalytic Works—Theoretical and Clinical

Blanck, G. & Blanck, R., *Ego Psychology: Theory and Practice.* New York: Columbia University Press, 1974.

Blos, P., *On Adolescence: A Psychoanalytic Interpretation.* Glencoe, Ill.: Free Press, 1961.

Brenner, C., *An Elementary Textbook of Psychoanalysis,* rev. ed. New York: International Universities Press, 1973.

Brody, S., *Passivity: A Study of Its Development and Expression in Boys.* New York: International Universities Press, 1964.

Deutsch, F., Analytic Posturology and Synesthesiology. *Psychoanal. Rev.,* 50:40-67, 1963.

Ellenberger, H. E., *The Discovery of the Unconscious: The History and Evolution of Dynamic Psychiatry.* New York: Basic Books, 1970.

Erikson, E. H., *Childhood and Society,* 2nd ed. New York: Norton, 1963.

Erikson, E. H., *Identity: Youth and Crisis.* New York: Norton, 1968.

Fairbairn, W. R. D., *An Object-Relations Theory of the Personality*. New York: Basic Books, 1954.

Fenichel, O., *The Psychoanalytic Theory of Neurosis*. New York: Norton, 1945.

Fraiberg, S., *The Magic Years*. New York, Scribner, 1959.

Freud, A. *The Ego and the Mechanisms of Defense*, rev. ed., trans. C. Baines. New York: International Universities Press, 1966.

Freud, S., *The Standard Edition of the Complete Psychological Works of . . .*, 24 vols., trans. J. Strachey. London: Hogarth Press, 1953-1974.

Greenacre, P., ed., *Affective Disorders: Psychoanalytic Contributions to Their Study*. New York: International Universities Press, 1953.

Guntrip, H., *Personality Structure and Human Interaction: The Developing Synthesis of Psychodynamic Theory*. New York: International Universities Press, 1961.

Guntrip, H., *Schizoid Phenomena, Object Relations, and the Self*. New York: International Universities Press, 1968.

Holzman, P. S., *Psychoanalysis and Psychopathology*. New York: McGraw-Hill, 1969.

Jacobson, E., *The Self and the Object World*. New York: International Universities Press, 1964.

Jacobson, E., *Depression: Comparative Studies of Normal, Neurotic, and Psychotic Conditions*. New York: International Universities Press, 1971.

Klein, M., *Contributions to Psycho-Analysis, 1921-1945*. London: Hogarth Press, 1948.

Knight, R. P. & Friedman, C. R., eds., *Psychoanalytic Psychiatry and Psychology*. New York: International Universities Press, 1954.

Kohut, H., *The Analysis of the Self: A Systematic Approach to the Psychoanalytic Treatment of Narcissistic Personality Disorders*. New York: International Universities Press, 1970.

Loewenstein, R., Newman, L. M., Schur, M., & Solnit, A. J., eds., *Psychoanalysis—A General Psychology: Essays in Honor of Heinz Hartmann*. New York: International Universities Press, 1966.

Mahler, M., with M. Furer, *On Human Symbiosis and the Vicissitudes of Individuation*, Vol. 1: *Infantile Psychoses*. New York: International Universities Press, 1968.

Mahler, M. S., Pine, F., & Bergman, A., *The Psychological Birth of the Human Infant: Symbiosis and Individuation*. New York: Basic Books, 1975.

Nunberg, H., *Principles of Psychoanalysis: Their Application to the Neuroses*. New York: International Universities Press, 1955.

Piers, G. & Singer, M. B., *Shame and Guilt: A Psychoanalytic and Cultural Study*. Springfield, Ill.: Thomas, 1953.

Rapaport, D., The Structure of Psychoanalytic Theory: A Systematizing Attempt. *Psychol. Issues,* Monogr. 6. New York: International Universities Press. 1960.

Schafer, R., *Aspects of Internalization.* New York: International Universities Press, 1968.

Schur, M., *The Id and the Regulatory Principles of Mental Functioning.* New York: International Universities Press, 1966.

Searles, H. F., *The Nonhuman Environment in Normal Development and in Schizophrenia.* New York: International Universities Press, 1960.

Searles, H. F., *Collected Papers on Schizophrenia and Related Subjects.* New York: International Universities Press, 1965.

Spitz, R. A., *No and Yes: On the Genesis of Human Communication.* New York: International Universities Press, 1957.

Stoller, R. J., *Perversion: The Erotic Form of Hatred.* New York: Pantheon, 1975.

Volkan, V. D., *Primitive Internalized Object Relations: A Clinical Study of Schizophrenic, Borderline, and Narcissistic Patients.* New York: International Universities Press, 1975.

Winnicott, D. W., *Collected Papers: Through Paediatrics to Psychoanalysis.* New York: Basic Books, 1958.

Winnicott, D. W., *The Maturational Processes and the Facilitating Environment.* New York: International Universities Press, 1965.

Zetzel, E. & Meissner, W. W., *Basic Concepts of Psychoanalytic Psychiatry.* New York: Basic Books, 1973.

6. Works on Psychodiagnostic Testing

Bolles, M., The Basis of Pertinence. *Arch. Psychol.,* 212:1-51, 1937. (This article contains a description of the BRL Sorting Test.)

Eisenson, J., *Examining for Aphasia: A Manual for the Examination of Aphasia and Related Disturbances.* New York: Psychological Corporation, 1954.

Frank, L. K., *Projective Methods.* Springfield, Ill.: Thomas, 1948.

Goldstein, K. & Scheerer, M., Abstract and Concrete Behavior. *Psychol. Monogr.,* 53, No. 2, 1941.

Halstead, W. C., *Brain and Intelligence: A Quantitative Study of the Frontal Lobes.* Chicago: University of Chicago Press, 1947.

Hanfmann, E. & Kasanin, J., A Method for the Study of Concept Formation. *J. Psychol.,* 3:521-540, 1936.

Lezak, M. D., *Neuropsychological Assessment.* New York: Oxford University Press, 1976.

Luria, A. R., *The Working Brain,* trans. B. Haigh. New York: Basic Books, 1974.

Luria, A. R., *The Neuropsychology of Memory.* Washington, D. C.: Winston, a Division of Scripta Technica, 1976.

Matarazzo, J. D. & Wechsler, D., *Wechsler's Measurement and Appraisal of Adult Intelligence*, 5th ed. New York: Oxford University Press, 1972.

Murray, H. A., *Manual for the Thematic Apperception Test*. Cambridge: Harvard University Press, 1953.

Rapaport, D., Gill, M. M., & Schafer, R., *Diagnostic Psychological Testing*, 2 vols. Chicago: Year Book Publishers, 1945-1946.

Rapaport, D., Gill, M. M., & Schafer, R., *Diagnostic Psychological Testing*, rev. ed., ed. R. R. Holt. New York: International Universities Press, 1968.

Reitan, R. M. & Davison, L. A., eds., *Clinical Neuropsychology: Current Status and Applications*. Washington, D. C.: Winston, 1974.

Rorschach, H., *Psychodiagnostics*, 5th ed., trans. B. Krunenberg & P. Lemkau, ed. W. Morgenthaler, New York: Grune & Stratton, 1951.

Russell, E. W., Neuringer, C., & Goldstein, G., *Assessment of Brain Damage: A Neuropsychological Key Approach*. New York: Wiley-Interscience, 1970.

Schafer, R., *The Clinical Application of Psychological Tests: Diagnostic Summaries and Case Studies*. New York: International Universities Press, 1948.

Terman, L. M. & Merrill, M. A., *Measuring Intelligence: A Guide to the Administration of the New Revised Stanford-Binet Tests of Intelligence*. Boston: Houghton Mifflin, 1937.

Wechsler, D., *The Measurement of Adult Intelligence*, 3rd ed. Baltimore: Williams & Wilkins, 1944.

7. Dictionaries and Glossaries

American Psychiatric Association, *A Psychiatric Glossary: The Meaning of Terms Frequently Used in Psychiatry*, 4th ed. New York: Basic Books, 1975.

English, H. B. & English, A. C., *A Comprehensive Dictionary of Psychological and Psychoanalytic Terms*. New York: McKay, 1958.

Eysenck, H. J., Arnold, W. & Meili, R., eds., *Encyclopedia of Psychology*, 3 vols. New York: Seabury, 1972.

Heidenreich, C. A., *A Dictionary of General Psychology: Basic Terminology and Key Concepts*, rev. ed. Fair Oaks, Calif.: Heidenreich, 1970.

Hinsie, L. E. & Campbell, R. J., *Psychiatric Dictionary*, 4th ed. New York: Oxford University Press, 1970.

Laplanche, J. & Pontalis, J.-B., *The Language of Psycho-Analysis*, trans. D. Nicholson-Smith. New York: Norton, 1973.

Menninger, K. A., *A Guide to Psychiatric Books*, 3rd ed. New York: Grune & Stratton, 1972.

Moore, B. E. & Fine, B. D., eds., *A Glossary of Psychoanalytic Terms and Concepts.* New York: American Psychoanalytic Association, 1967.
Wolman, B. B., ed., *Dictionary of Behavioral Science.* New York: Van Nostrand Reinhold, 1973.

Index